THE SCOUTS OF STONEWALL
THE STORY OF THE GREAT VALLEY CAMPAIGN

By

JOSEPH A. ALTSHELER

The Scouts Of Stonewall
The Story Of The Great Valley Campaign
by **Joseph A. Altsheler**

ISBN: 978-93-57486-15-6

Published by

DOUBLE 9 BOOKS

2/13-B, Ansari Road, Daryaganj
New Delhi – 110002
info@double9books.com
www.double9books.com
Tel. 011-40042856

ABOUT THE AUTHOR

Joseph A. Altsheler was born on April 29, 1862, in Three Springs, Hart County, Kentucky, to Joseph and Louise Altsheler. He was a newspaper reporter, editor, and author of popular juvenile historical fiction. He wrote fifty novels and at least fifty-three short stories. Seven of his novels were in sequence. He worked as an editor at the Louisville Courier-Journal in 1885. In 1892, he started to work for New York World and then as the editor of the World's tri-weekly magazine. He wrote children's stories due to a lack of suitable stories. On May 30, 1880, Altsheler married Sarah Boles and had a son named Sidney. In 1914, during World War I Altsheler and his family were in Germany and they were forced to remain there. Altsheler died at the age of 57, on June 5, 1919, in New York. His wife, Sarah Boles died after 30 years. Their bodies are buried at the Cave Hill Cemetery in Louisville, Kentucky. Although each of the thirty-two novels constitutes an independent story, Altsheler suggested reading in sequence for each series (that is, he numbered the volumes). You can read the remaining eighteen novels in any order.

CONTENTS

CHAPTER I.
IN THE VALLEY

A young officer in dingy Confederate gray rode slowly on a powerful bay horse through a forest of oak. It was a noble woodland, clear of undergrowth, the fine trees standing in rows, like those of a park. They were bare of leaves but the winter had been mild so far, and a carpet of short grass, yet green, covered the ground. To the rider's right flowed a small river of clear water, one of the beautiful streams of the great Virginia valleys.

Harry Kenton threw his head back a little and drew deep breaths of the cool, crisp air. The light wind had the touch of life in it. As the cool puffs blew upon him and filled his lungs his chest expanded and his strong pulses beat more strongly. But a boy in years, he had already done a man's work, and he had been through those deeps of passion and despair which war alone brings.

A year spent in the open and with few nights under roof had enlarged Harry Kenton's frame and had colored his face a deep red. His great ancestor, Henry Ware, had been very fair, and Harry, like him, became scarlet of cheek under the beat of wind and rain.

Had anyone with a discerning eye been there, to see, he would have called this youth one of the finest types of the South that rode forth so boldly to war. He sat his saddle with the ease and grace that come only of long practice, and he controlled his horse with the slightest touch of the rein. The open, frank face showed hate of nobody, although the soul behind it was devoted without any reserve to the cause for which he fought.

Harry was on scout duty. Although an officer on the staff of Colonel Talbot, commander of the Invincibles, originally a South Carolina regiment, he had developed so much skill in forest and field, he had such acuteness of eye and ear, that he was sent often to seek the camps of the enemy or to discover his plans. His friends said that these forest powers were inherited, that they came from some far-away ancestor who had spent his life in the wilderness, and Harry knew that what they said was true.

Despite the peaceful aspect of the forest and the lack of human presence save his own, he rode now on an errand that was full of danger. The Union camp must lie on the other side of that little river, not many miles farther on, and he might meet, at any moment, the pickets of the foe. He meant to take the uttermost risk, but he had no notion of being captured. He would suffer anything, any chance, rather than that. He had lately come into contact with a man who had breathed into him the fire and spirit belonging to legendary heroes. To this man, short of words and plain of dress, nothing was impossible, and Harry caught from him not merely the belief, but the conviction also.

Late in the autumn the Invincibles, who had suffered severely at Bull Run and afterward had been cut down greatly in several small actions in the mountains, had been transferred to the command of Stonewall Jackson in the Shenandoah Valley. Disease and the hospital had reduced the regiment to less than three hundred, but their spirits were as high as ever. Their ranks were renewed partly with Virginians. Colonel Talbot and Lieutenant-Colonel St. Hilaire had recovered from small wounds, and St. Clair and Langdon were whole and as hard as iron. After a period of waiting they were now longing for action.

There was some complaint among the Invincibles when they were detached from the main army to the service of Jackson, but Harry did not share in it. When he heard of the order he remembered that dread afternoon at Bull Run, when all seemed lost, and the most vivid of his memories was the calm figure riding back and forth just beyond the pines among which he stood, and gathering for a fresh charge the stern ranks of his men who were to turn almost sure defeat into absolutely sure victory. The picture of the man in the heart of that red glare among the showers of bullets had been burned so deeply into Harry's memory that he could call it up, almost as vivid as life itself at any time. Surely that was a leader to follow, and he, at least, would wish to ride where Stonewall led.

But action did not come as soon as he had expected. Jackson was held by commands from Richmond. The great army of the South waited, because the great army of the North, under McClellan, also waited and temporized while the autumn was passing fast.

But Jackson, while held in the bonds of orders, did not sleep. The most active youth of his command rode day and night toward the northern end of the valley, where the forces of the Union were gathering. The movements of Banks and Kelly and the other Northern commanders were watched continually by keen eyes trained in the southern forests. Slim striplings passed in the night through the little towns, and the people, intensely loyal to the South, gave them the news of everything.

Harry had seen the whole autumn pass and winter come, and the war, save for a fitful skirmish now and then, stood at a pause in the valley. Yet he rode incessantly, both with the others and alone, on scouting duty. He knew every square mile of the country over a wide range, and he had passed whole nights in the forest, when hail or snow was whistling by. But these had been few. Mostly mild winds blew and the hoofs of his horse fell on green turf.

Harry was intensely alert now. He was far from his command, and he knew that he must see and hear everything or he would soon be in the hands of the enemy. He rode on rather slowly, and amid continued silence. He saw on his left a white house with green shutters and a portico. But the shutters were closed tightly and no smoke rose from the chimneys. Although house and grounds showed no touch of harm, they seemed to bear the brand of desolation. The owners had fled, knowing that the sinister march of war would pass here.

Harry's mood changed suddenly from gladness to depression. The desolate house brought home to him the terrible nature of war. It meant destruction, wounds and death, and they were all the worse because it was a nation divided against itself, people of the same blood and the same traditions fighting one another.

But youth cannot stay gloomy long, and his spirits presently flowed back. There was too much tang and life in that crisp wind from the west for his body to droop, and a lad could not be sad long, with brilliant sunshine around him and that shining little river before him.

The thrill of high adventure shot up from his soul. He had ceased to hate the Northern soldiers, if he had ever hated them at all. Now they were merely brave opponents, with whom he contended, and success demanded of either skill, daring and energy to the utmost degree. He was resolved not to fail in any of these qualities.

He left the desolate house a mile behind, and then the river curved a little. The woods on the farther shore came down in dense masses to the edge of the stream, and despite the lack of foliage Harry could not see far into them. The strong, inherited instincts leaped up. His nostrils expanded and a warning note was sounded somewhere in the back of his brain.

He turned his horse to the left and entered the forest on his own side of the river. They were ancient trees that he rode among, with many drooping and twisted boughs, and he was concealed well, although he could yet see from his covert the river and the forest on the other shore.

The song of a trumpet suddenly came from the deep woodland across the shining stream. It was a musical song, mellow and triumphant on every key, and the forest and hills on either shore gave it back, soft and beautiful on its dying echoes. It seemed to Harry that the volume of sound, rounded and full, must come from a trumpet of pure gold. He had read the old romances of the Round Table, and for the moment his head was full of them. Some knight in the thicket was sending forth a challenge to him.

But Harry gave no answering defiance. Now the medieval glow was gone, and he was modern and watchful to the core. He had felt instinctively that it was a trumpet of the foe, and the Northern trumpets were not likely to sing there in Virginia unless many Northern horsemen rode together.

Then he saw their arms glinting among the trees, the brilliant beams of the sun dancing on the polished steel of saber hilt and rifle barrel. A minute more, and three hundred Union horsemen emerged from the forest and rode, in beautiful order, down to the edge of the stream.

Harry regarded them with an admiration which was touched by no hate. They were heavily built, strong young men, riding powerful horses, and it was easy for anyone to see that they had been drilled long and well. Their clothes and arms were in perfect order, every horse had been tended as if it were to be entered in a ring for a prize. It was his thought that they were not really enemies, but worthy foes.

That ancient spirit of the tournament, where men strove for the sake of striving, came to him again.

The Union horsemen rode along the edge of the stream a little space, and then plunged into a ford. The water rose to their saddle skirts, but they preserved their even line and Harry still admired. When all were on his own shore the golden trumpet sang merrily again, and they turned the heads of their horses southward.

Harry rode deeper into the ancient wood. They might throw out scouts or skirmishers and he had no mind to be taken. It was his belief that they came from Romney, where a Northern army had gathered in great force and would eventually march toward Jackson at Winchester. But whatever their errand, here was something for him to watch, and he meant to know what they intended.

The Northern troop, youths also, the average of their age not much more than twenty, rode briskly along the edge of the little river, which was a shining one for them, too, as well as Harry. They knew that no enemy in force was near, and they did not suspect that a single horseman followed, keeping in the edge of the woods, his eyes missing nothing that they did.

As for themselves, they were in the open now and the brilliant sunshine quickened their blood. Some of them had been at Bull Run, but the sting of that day was going with time. They were now in powerful force at the head of the great Virginia valleys, and they would sweep down them with such impact that nothing could stand before them. The trumpet sang its mellow triumphant note again, and from across a far range of hills came its like, a low mellow note, faint, almost an echo, but a certain reply. It was the answer from another troop of their men who rode on a parallel line several miles away.

The lone lad in the edge of the forest heard the distant note also, but he gave it no heed. His eyes were always for the troop before him. He had already learned from Stonewall Jackson that you cannot do two things at once, but the one thing that you do you must do with all your might.

The troop presently left the river and entered the fields from which the crops had been reaped long since. When the horsemen came to a fence twelve men dismounted and threw down enough panels for the others to ride through without breaking their formation.

Everything was done with order and precision. Harry could not keep from admiring. It was not often that he saw so early in the war troops who were drilled so beautifully, and who marched so well together.

Harry always kept on the far side of the fields, and as the fences were of rails with stakes and riders he was able by bending very low in the saddle to keep hidden behind them. Nevertheless it was delicate work. He was sure that if seen he could escape to the forest through the speed of his horse. But he did not want to be driven off. He wished to follow that troop to its ultimate destination.

Another mile or two and the Union force bore away to the right, entering the forest and following a road, where the men rode in files, six abreast. They did not make much noise, beyond the steady beating of the hoofs, but they did not seem to seek concealment. Harry made the obvious deduction that they thought themselves too far beyond the range of the Southern scouts to be noticed. He felt a thrill of satisfaction, because he was there and he had seen them.

He rode in the forest parallel with the troop and at a distance of about four hundred yards. There was scattered undergrowth, enough to hide him, but not enough to conceal those three hundred men who rode in close files along a well-used road.

Harry soon saw the forest thinning ahead of him and then the trumpet sang its mellow, golden note again. From a point perhaps a mile ahead came a reply, also the musical call of the trumpet. Not an echo, but the voice of a second trumpet, and now Harry knew that another force was coming to join the first. All his pulses began to beat hard, not with nervousness, but with intense eagerness to know what was afoot. Evidently it must be something of importance or strong bodies of Union cavalry would not be meeting in the woods in this manner.

After the reply neither trumpet sounded again, and the troop that Harry was following stopped while yet in the woods. He rode his horse behind a tall and dense clump of bushes, where, well hidden, he could yet see all that might happen, and waited.

He heard in a few minutes the beat of many hoofs upon the hard road, advancing with the precision and regularity of trained cavalry. He saw the head of a column emerge upon the road and an officer ride forward to meet the commander of the first troop. They exchanged a few words and then the united force rode southward through the open woods, with the watchful lad always hanging on their rear.

Harry judged that the new troop numbered about five hundred men, and eight hundred cavalry would not march on any mere scouting expedition. His opinion that this was a ride of importance now became a conviction, and he hardened his purpose to follow them to the end, no matter what the risk.

It was now about noon, and the sun became warm despite the December day. The turf softened under the rays and the Union cavalry left an immense wide trail through the forest. It was impossible to miss it, and Harry, careful not to ride into an ambush of rear guard pickets, dropped back a little, and also kept slightly to the left of the great trail. He could not see the soldiers now, but occasionally he heard the deep sound of so many hoofs sinking into the soft turf. Beyond that turfy sigh no sound from the marching men came to him.

The Union troop halted about two o'clock in the afternoon, and the men ate cold food from the knapsacks. They also rested a full hour, and Harry, watching from a distance, felt sure that their lack of hurry indicated a night attack of some kind. They had altered their course slightly, twice, and when they started anew they did so a third time.

Now their purpose occurred suddenly to Harry. It came in a flash of intuition, and he did not again doubt it for a moment. The head of the column was pointed straight toward a tiny village in which food and ammunition for Stonewall Jackson were stored. The place did not have more than a dozen houses, but one of them was a huge tobacco barn stuffed with powder, lead, medicines, which were already worth their weight in gold in the Confederacy, and other invaluable supplies. It had been planned to begin their removal on the morrow to the Southern camp at Winchester, but it would be too late unless he intervened.

If he did not intervene! He, a boy, riding alone through the forest, to defeat the energies of so many men, equipped splendidly! The Confederacy was almost wholly agricultural, and was able to produce few such supplies of its own. Nor could it obtain them in great quantities from Europe as the Northern navy was drawing its belt of steel about the Southern coasts. That huge tobacco barn contained a treasure beyond price, and Harry was resolved to save it.

He did not yet know how he would save it, but he felt that he would. All the courage of those border ancestors who won every new day of life as the prize of skill and courage sprang up in him. It was no vain heritage. Happy chance must aid those who trusted, and, taking a deep curve to the left, he galloped through the woods. His horse comparatively fresh after easy riding, went many miles without showing any signs of weariness.

The boy knew the country well, and it was the object of his circuit to take him ahead of the Union troop and to the village which held a small guard of perhaps two hundred men. If the happy chance in which he trusted should fail him after all, these men could carry off a part of the supplies, and the rest could be destroyed to keep them from falling into Northern hands.

He gave his horse a little breathing space and then galloped harder than ever, reckoning that he would reach the village in another hour. He turned from the woods into one of the narrow roads between farms, just wide enough for wagons, and increased his speed.

The afternoon sun was declining, filling the west with dusky gold, and Harry still rode at a great pace along the rough road, wondering all the while what would be the nature of the lucky chance, in which he was trusting so firmly. Lower sank the sun and the broad band of dusky gold was narrowing before the advance of the twilight. The village was not now more than two miles away, and the road dipped down before him. Sounds like that made by the force behind him, the rattle of arms, the creak of leather and the beat of hoofs, came suddenly to his ears.

Harry halted abruptly and reined his horse into some bushes beside the road. Then he heard the sounds more plainly. They were made by cavalry, riding slowly. The great pulses in his throat leaped in quick alarm. Was it possible that they had sent a portion of their force swiftly by another route, and that it was now between him and the village?

He listened again and with every faculty strained. The cavalrymen were riding toward him and they could not be a part of the Union force. Then they must be of his own South. Surely this was the happy chance of which he had dreamed! Again the great pulses leaped, but with a different emotion.

Scorning every risk, he reined his horse back into the road and rode straight forward. The heads of men were just topping the rise, and a few moments later they and the horses they bestrode came into full view. It was a thankful thrill that shot through him now. The sun, almost sunk, sent a last golden shower across them and disclosed the dingy gray of their uniforms and the lean, tanned faces.

Uttering a shout of joy and holding up a hand to show that he was a friend, Harry galloped forward. A young man at the head of the troop, a captain by his uniform, and evidently the leader, gave the signal to his men to stop, and received the boy who came alone.

"Who are you?" he asked.

"I'm Harry Kenton, a lieutenant in the army of Stonewall Jackson, and an aide on the staff of Colonel Leonidas Talbot, colonel of the regiment known as the Invincibles."

"I've heard of that regiment. South Carolinians at first, but now mostly Virginians."

"The Virginians filled up the gaps that were made on the battlefield."

Harry spoke proudly, and the young captain smiled. The boy regarded him with increasing interest. Somehow he was reminded of Jeb Stuart, although this man was younger, not having passed his boyhood long.

It was evident that he was tall. Thick, yellow curls showed from under the edge of his cap. His face, like Harry's, had turned red before wind and rain. His dress was a marvel, made of the finest gray without a spot or stain. A sash of light blue silk encircled his waist, and the costly gray cloak thrown back a little from his shoulders revealed a silk lining of the same delicate blue tint. His gauntlets were made of the finest buckskin, and a gold-hilted small sword swung from his sash.

"A dandy," thought Harry, "but the bravest of the brave, for all that."

"My name's Sherburne, Captain Philip Sherburne," said the young leader. "I'm from the Valley of Virginia, and so are my men. We belong to Stonewall Jackson's army, too, but we've been away most of the time on scouting duty. That's the reason you don't know us. We're going toward Winchester, after another of our fruitless rides."

"But it won't be fruitless this time!" exclaimed Harry, eagerly. "A Union force of nearly a thousand men is on its way to destroy the stores at the village, the stores that were to be moved to a safer place to-morrow!"

"How do you know?"

"I've seen 'em. I was behind 'em at first and followed 'em for a long time before I guessed their purpose. Then I curved about 'em, galloped through the woods, and rode on here, hoping for the lucky chance that has come with you."

Harry, as he spoke, saw the eyes of the young captain leap and flame, and he knew he was in the presence of one of those knightly souls, thrown up so often in the war, most often by the border States. They were youths who rode forth to battle in the spirit of high romance.

"You ask us to go back to the village and help defend the stores?" said Philip Sherburne.

"That's just what I do ask—and expect."

"Of course. We'd have done it without the asking, and glad of it. What a chance for us, as well as for you!"

He turned and faced his men. The golden glow of the sun was gone now, but a silver tint from the twilight touched his face. Harry saw there the blaze of the knightly spirit that craved adventure.

"Men," he said in clear, happy tones, "we've ridden for days and days in quests that brought nothing. Now the enemy is at hand, nearly a thousand strong, and means to destroy our stores. There are two hundred of you and there are two hundred more guarding the stores. If there's a single one among you who says he must ride on to Winchester, let him hold up his hand."

Not a hand was raised, and the bold young captain laughed.

"I don't need to put the other side of the question," he said to Harry. "They're as eager as I am to scorch the faces of the Yankees."

The order was given to turn and ride. The "men," not one of whom was over twenty-five, obeyed it eagerly, and galloped for the village, every heart throbbing with the desire for action. They were all from the rich farms in the valleys. Splendid horsemen, fine marksmen, and alive with youth and courage, no deed was too great for them. Harry was proud to ride with them, and he told more of the story to Sherburne as they covered the short distance to the village.

"Old Jack would order us to do just what we're doing," said Sherburne. "He wants his officers to obey orders, but he wants them to think, too."

Harry saw his eyes flash again, and something in his own mind answered to the spirit of adventure which burned so brightly in this young man. He looked over the troop, and as far as he could see the faces of all were flushed with the same hope. He knew with sudden certainty that the Union forces would never take that warehouse and its precious contents. These were the very flower of that cavalry of the South destined to become so famous.

"You know the village?" said Sherburne to Harry.

"Yes, I passed there last night."

"What defense has it?"

"About two hundred men. They are strangers to the region, drawn from the Tidewater country, and I don't think they're as good as most of General Jackson's men."

"Lack of discipline, you think?"

"Yes, but the material is fine."

"All right. Then we'll see that they acquire discipline. Nothing like the enemy's fire to teach men what war is."

They were riding at good speed toward the village, while they talked, and Harry had become at once the friend and lieutenant of young Captain Sherburne. His manner was so pleasant, so intimate, so full of charm, that he did not have the power or the will to resist it.

They soon saw Hertford, a village so little that it was not able to put itself on the map. It stood on the crest of a low hill, and the tobacco barn was about as large as all the other buildings combined. The twilight had now merged into night, but there was a bright sky and plenty of stars, and they saw well.

Captain Sherburne stopped his troop at a distance of three or four hundred yards, while they were still under cover of the forest.

"What's the name of the commander there?" he asked.

"McGee," Harry replied. "Means well, but rather obstinate."

"That's the way with most of these untrained men. We mustn't risk being shot up by those whom we've come to help. Lasley, give them a call from the bugle. Make it low and soft though. We don't want those behind us to hear it."

Lasley, a boy no older than Harry, rode forward a dozen yards in front of the troop, put his bugle to his lips and blew a soft, warning call. Harry had been stirred by the first sound of a hostile trumpet hours before, and now this, the note of a friend, thrilled him again. He gazed intently at the village, knowing that the pickets would be on watch, and presently he saw men appear at the edge of the hill just in front of the great warehouse. They were the pickets, beyond a doubt, because the silver starshine glinted along the blades of their bayonets.

The bugler gave one more call. It was a soft and pleasing sound. It said very plainly that the one who blew and those with him were friends. Two men in uniform joined the pickets beside the warehouse, and looked toward the point whence the note of the bugle came.

"Forward!" said Captain Philip Sherburne, himself leading the way, Harry by his side. The troops, wheeling back into the road and marching by fours in perfect order, rode straight toward the village.

"Who comes?" was the stern hail.

"A troop of Stonewall Jackson's cavalry to help you," replied Sherburne. "You are about to be attacked by a Northern division eight hundred strong."

"Who says so?" came the question in a tone tinged with unbelief, and Harry knew that it was the stubborn and dogmatic McGee who spoke.

"Lieutenant Harry Kenton of the Invincibles, one of Stonewall Jackson's best regiments, has seen them. You know him; he was here yesterday."

As he spoke, Captain Sherburne sprang from his horse and pointed to Harry.

"You remember me, Captain McGee," said Harry. "I stopped with you a minute yesterday. I rode on a scouting expedition, and I have seen the Union force myself. It outnumbers us at least two to one, but we'll have the advantage of the defense."

"Yes, I know you," said McGee, his heavy and strong, but not very intelligent face, brightening a little. "But it's a great responsibility I've got here. We ought to have had more troops to defend such valuable stores. I've got two hundred men, captain, and I should say that you've about the same."

It was then that Captain Philip Sherburne showed his knightly character, speaking words that made Harry's admiration of him immense.

"I haven't any men, Captain McGee," he said, "but you have four hundred, and I'll help my commander as much as I can."

McGee's eyes gleamed. Harry saw that while not of alert mind he was nevertheless a gentleman.

"We work together, Captain Sherburne," he said gratefully, "and I thank God you've come. What splendid men you have!"

Captain Sherburne's eyes gleamed also. This troop of his was his pride, and he sought always to keep it bright and sharp like a polished sword blade.

"Whatever you wish, Captain McGee. But it will take us all to repel the enemy. Kenton here, who saw them well, says they have a fine, disciplined force."

The men now dismounted and led their horses to a little grove just in the rear of the warehouse, where they were tethered under the guard of the villagers, all red-hot partisans of the South. Then the four hundred men, armed with rifles and carbines, disposed themselves about the warehouse, the bulk of them watching the road along which the attacking force was almost sure to come.

Harry took his place with Sherburne, and once more he was compelled to admire the young captain's tact and charm of manner. He directed everything by example and suggestion, but all the while he made the heavy Captain McGee think that he himself was doing it.

Sherburne and Harry walked down the road a little distance.

"Aren't you glad to be here, Kenton?" asked the captain in a somewhat whimsical tone.

"I'm glad to help, of course."

"Yes, but there's more. When I came to war I came to fight. And if we save the stores look how we'll stand in Old Jack's mind. Lord, Kenton, but he's a queer man! You'd never take any notice of him, if you didn't know who he was, but I'd rather have one flash of approval from those solemn eyes of his than whole dictionaries of praise from all the other generals I know."

"I saw him at Bull Run, when he saved the day."

"So did I. The regiment that I was with didn't come up until near the close, but our baptism of battle was pretty thorough, all the same. Hark! did you think you heard anything, Kenton?"

Harry listened attentively.

"Yes, I hear something," he replied. "It's very soft, but I should say that it's the distant beat of hoofs."

"And of many hoofs."

"So I think."

"Then it's our friends of the North, coming to take what we want to keep. A few minutes more, Kenton, and they'll be here."

They slipped back toward the warehouse, and Harry's heart began to throb heavily. He knew that Sherburne's words would soon come true.

CHAPTER II.
THE FOOT CAVALRY

Captain Sherburne told Captain McGee that the invaders were coming, and there was a stir in the ranks of the defenders. The cavalrymen, disciplined and eager, said nothing, but merely moved a little in order to see better along the road over which the enemy was advancing. The original defenders, who were infantry, talked in whispers, despite commands, and exchanged doubts and apprehensions.

Harry walked up and down in front of the warehouse with Captain Sherburne, and both watched the road.

"If we only had a little artillery, just a light gun or two," said Sherburne, "we'd give 'em such a surprise that they'd never get over it."

"But we haven't got it."

"No, we haven't, but maybe rifles and carbines will serve."

The hoofbeats were fast growing louder, and Harry knew that the head of the Northern column would appear in a minute or two. Every light in the warehouse or about it and all in the village had been extinguished, but the moonlight was clear and more stars had come into the full sky.

"We can see well enough for a fight," murmured Captain Sherburne.

Everybody could hear the hoofbeats now, and again there was a stir in the ranks of the defenders. The dark line appeared in the road three or four hundred yards away and then, as the horsemen emerged into the open, they deployed rapidly by companies. They, too, were trained men, and keen eyes among their officers caught sight of the armed dark line before the warehouse. The voice of the trumpet suddenly pealed forth again, and now it was loud and menacing.

"It's the charge!" cried Sherburne, "and I can see that they're all you said, Kenton! A magnificent body, truly! Ready, men! Ready! For God's sake don't fire too soon! Wait for the word! Wait for the word!"

He was all the leader now, and in the excitement of the moment McGee did not notice it. The superior mind, the one keen to see and to act, was in control.

"Here, Kenton!" cried Sherburne, "hold back these recruits! My own men will do exactly as I say!"

Harry ran along the infantry line, and here and there he knocked down rifles which were raised already, although the enemy was yet three hundred yards away. But he saw a figure in front of the charging horsemen wave a sword. Then the trumpet blew another call, short but fierce and menacing, and the ground thundered as nearly a thousand horsemen swept forward, uttering a tremendous shout, their sabers flashing in the moonlight.

Harry felt a moment of admiration and then another moment of pity. These men, charging so grandly, did not know that the defenders had been reinforced. Nor did they know that they rode straight to what was swift and sudden death for many of them.

It was hard to stand steady and not pull the trigger, while that line of flashing steel galloped upon them, but the dismounted cavalrymen looked to their leader for commands, and the officer held the infantry. Harry's moment of admiration and pity passed. These were soldiers coming to defeat and destroy, and it was his business to help prevent it. His own pulse of battle began to beat hard.

That front of steel, spread wide across the open, was within two hundred yards now! Then a hundred and fifty! Then a hundred! Then less, and fierce and sharp like the crack of a rifle came Captain Sherburne's command: "Fire!"

Four hundred rifles leaped to the shoulder and four hundred fingers pressed trigger so close together that four hundred rifles sang together as one. The charge halted in its tracks. The entire front rank was shot away. Horses and men went down together, and the horses uttered neighs of pain, far more terrific than the groans of the wounded men. Many of them, riderless, galloped up and down between the lines.

But the splendid horsemen behind came on again, after the momentary stop. Half of them armed with short carbines sent a volley at the defenders, who were shoving in cartridges in frantic haste, and the swordsmen galloped straight upon the Virginians.

Harry saw a great saber flashing directly in his face. It was wielded by a man on a powerful horse that seemed wild with the battle fever. The horse, at the moment, was more terrible than his rider. His mouth was dripping with foam, and his lips were curled back from his cruel, white teeth. His eyes, large and shot with blood, were like those of some huge, carnivorous animal.

The boy recoiled, more in fear of the horse than of the saber, and snatching a heavy pistol from his belt, fired directly at the great foam-flecked head. The horse crashed down, but his rider sprang clear and retreated into the smoke. Almost at the same instant the defenders had fired the second volley, and the charge was beaten back from their very faces.

The Southerners at the war's opening had the advantage of an almost universal familiarity with the rifle, and now they used it well. Sherburne's two hundred men, always cool and steady, fired like trained marksmen, and the others did almost as well. Most of them had new rifles, using cartridges, and no cavalry on earth could stand before such a fire.

Harry again saw the flashing sabers more than once, and there was a vast turmoil of fire and smoke in front of him, but in a few minutes the trumpet sounded again, loud and clear over the crash of battle, and now it was calling to the men to come back.

The two forces broke apart. The horsemen, save for the wounded and dead, retreated to the forest, and the defenders, victorious for the present, fired no more, while the wounded, who could, crawled away to shelter. They reloaded their rifles and at first there was no exultation. They barely had time to think of anything. The impact had been so terrible and there had been such a blaze of firing that they were yet in a daze, and scarcely realized what had happened.

"Down, men! Down!" cried Captain Sherburne, as he ran along the line. "They'll open fire from the wood!"

All the defenders threw themselves upon the ground and lay there, much less exposed and also concealed partly. One edge of the wood ran within two hundred yards of the warehouse, and presently the Northern soldiers, hidden behind the trees at that point, opened a heavy rifle fire. Bullets whistled over the heads of the defenders, and kept up a constant patter upon the walls of the warehouse, but did little damage.

A few of the men in gray had been killed, and all the wounded were taken inside the warehouse, into which the great tobacco barn had been turned. Two competent surgeons attended to them by the light of candles, while the garrison outside lay still and waiting under the heavy fire.

"A waste of lead," said Sherburne to Harry. "They reckon, perhaps, that we're all recruits, and will be frightened into retreat or surrender."

"If we had those guns now we could clear out the woods in short order," said Harry.

"And if they had 'em they could soon blow up this barn, everything in it and a lot of us at the same time. So we are more than even on the matter of the lack of guns."

The fire from the wood died in about fifteen minutes and was succeeded by a long and trying silence. The light of the moon deepened, and silvered the faces of the dead lying in the open. All the survivors of the attack were hidden, but the defenders knew that they were yet in the forest.

"Kenton," said Captain Sherburne, "you know the way to General Jackson's camp at Winchester."

"I've been over it a dozen times."

"Then you must mount and ride. This force is sitting down before us for a siege, and it probably has pickets about the village, but you must get through somehow. Bring help! The Yankees are likely to send back for help, too, but we've got to win here."

"I'm off in five minutes," said Harry, "and I'll come with a brigade by dawn."

"I believe you will," said Sherburne. "But get to Old Jack! Get there! If you can only reach him, we're saved! He may not have any horsemen at hand, but his foot cavalry can march nearly as fast! Lord, how Stonewall Jackson can cover ground!"

Their hands met in the hearty grasp of a friendship which was already old and firm, and Harry, without looking back, slipped into the wood, where the men from the village were watching over the horses. Sherburne had told him to take any horse he needed, but he chose his own, convinced that he had no equal, slipped into the saddle, and rode to the edge of the wood.

"There's a creek just back of us; you can see the water shining through the break in the trees," said a man who kept the village store. "The timber's pretty thick along it, and you'd best keep in its shelter. Here, you Tom, show him the way."

A boy of fourteen stepped up to the horse's head.

"My son," said the storekeeper. "He knows every inch of the ground."

But Harry waved him back.

"No," he said. "I'll be shot at, and the boy on foot can't escape. I'll find my way through. No, I tell you he must not go!"

He almost pushed back the boy who was eager for the task, rode out of the wood which was on the slope of the hill away from the point of attack, and gained the fringe of timber along the creek. It was about fifty yards from cover to cover, but he believed he had not been seen, as neither shout nor shot followed him.

Yet the Union pickets could not be far away. He had seen enough to know that the besiegers were disciplined men led by able officers and they would certainly make a cordon about the whole Southern position.

He rode his horse into a dense clump of trees and paused to listen. He heard nothing but the faint murmur of the creek, and the occasional rustle of dry branches as puffs of wind passed. He dismounted for the sake of caution and silence as far as possible, and led his horse down the fringe of trees, always keeping well under cover.

Another hundred yards and he stopped again to listen. All those old inherited instincts and senses leaped into life. He was, for the moment, the pioneer lad, seeking to detect the ambush of his foe. Now, his acute ears caught the hostile sound. It was low, merely the footsteps of a man, steadily walking back and forth.

Harry peeped from his covert and saw a Union sentinel not far away, pacing his beat, rifle on shoulder, the point of the bayonet tipped with silver flame from the moon. And he saw further on another sentinel, and then another, all silent and watchful. He knew that the circle about the defense was complete.

He could have escaped easily through the line, had he been willing to leave his horse, and for a few moments he was sorely tempted to do so, but he recalled that time was more precious than jewels. If he ever got beyond the line of pickets he must go and go fast.

He was three or four hundred yards from the village and no one had yet observed him, but he did not believe that he could go much farther undetected. Some one was bound to hear the heavy footsteps of the horse.

The creek shallowed presently and the banks became very low. Then Harry decided suddenly upon his course. He would put everything to the touch and win or lose in one wild dash. Springing upon the back of his horse, he raked him with the spur and put him straight at the creek. The startled animal was across in two jumps, and then Harry sent him racing across the fields. He heard two or three shouts and several shots, but fortunately none touched him or his mount, and, not looking back, he continually urged the horse to greater speed.

Bending low he heard the distant sound of hoofbeats behind him, but they soon died away. Then he entered a belt of forest, and when he passed out on the other side no pursuit could be seen. But he did not slacken speed. He knew that all Sherburne had said about Stonewall Jackson was true. He would forgive no dallying by the way. He demanded of every man his uttermost.

He turned from the unfenced field into the road, and rode at a full gallop toward Winchester. The cold wind swept past and his spirits rose high. Every pulse was beating with exultation. It was he who had brought the warning to the defenders of the stores. It was he who had brought Sherburne's troop to help beat off the attack, and now it was he who, bursting through the ring of steel, was riding to Jackson and sure relief.

His horse seemed to share his triumph. He ran on and on without a swerve or jar. Once he stretched out his long head, and uttered a shrill neigh. The sound died in far echoes, and then followed only the rapid beat of his hoofs on the hard road.

Harry knew that there was no longer any danger to him from the enemy, and he resolved now not to go to his own colonel, but to ride straight to the tent of Jackson himself.

The night had never grown dark. Moon and stars still shed an abundant light for the flying horseman, and presently he caught fleeting glimpses through the trees of roofs that belonged to Winchester. Then two men in gray spring into the road, and, leveling their rifles, gave him the command to stop.

"I'm Lieutenant Kenton of the Invincibles," he cried, "and I come for help. A strong force of the Yankees is besieging Hertford, and four hundred of our men are defending it. There is no time to waste! They must have help there before dawn, or everything is lost! Which way is General Jackson's tent?"

"In that field on the hillock!" replied one of the men, pointing two or three hundred yards away.

Harry raced toward the tent, which rose in modest size out of the darkness, and sprang to the ground, when his horse reached it. A single sentinel, rifle across his arms, was standing before it, but the flap was thrown back and a light was burning inside.

"I'm a messenger for General Jackson!" cried Harry. "I've news that can't wait!"

The sentinel hesitated a moment, but a figure within stepped to the door of the tent and Harry for the first time was face to face with Stonewall Jackson. He had seen him often near or far, but now he stood before him, and was to speak with him.

Jackson was dressed fully and the fine wrinkles of thought showed on his brow, as if he had intended to study and plan the night through. He was a tallish man, with good features cut clearly, high brow, short brown beard and ruddy complexion. His uniform was quite plain and his appearance was not imposing, but his eyes of deep blue regarded the boy keenly.

"I'm Lieutenant Kenton, sir, of Colonel Talbot's. Invincibles," replied Harry to the question which was not spoken, but which nevertheless was asked. "Our arsenal at Hertford is besieged by a strong force of the enemy, a force that is likely to be increased heavily by dawn. Luckily Captain Sherburne and his troop of valley Virginians came up in time to help, and I have slipped through the besieging lines to bring more aid."

Harry had touched his cap as he spoke and now he stood in silence while the blue eyes looked him through.

"I know you. I've observed you," said Jackson in calm, even tones, showing not a trace of excitement. "I did not think that the Federal troops would make a movement so soon, but we will meet it. A brigade will march in half an hour."

"Don't I go with it?" exclaimed Harry pleadingly. "You know, I brought the news, sir!"

"You do. Your regiment will form part of the brigade. Rejoin Colonel Talbot at once. The Invincibles, with you as guide, shall lead the way. You have done well, Lieutenant Kenton."

Harry flushed with pride at the brief words of praise, which meant so much coming from Stonewall Jackson, and saluting again hurried to his immediate command. Already the messengers were flying to the different regiments, bidding them to be up and march at once.

The Invincibles were upon their feet in fifteen minutes, fully clothed and armed, and ready for the road. The cavalry were not available that night, and the brigade would march on foot save for the officers. Harry was back on his horse, and St. Clair and Langdon were beside him. The colonels, Talbot and St. Hilaire, sat on their horses at the head of the Invincibles, the first regiment.

"What is it?" said Langdon to Harry. "Have you brought this night march upon us?"

"I have, and we're going to strike the Yankees before dawn at Hertford," replied Harry to both questions.

"I like the nights for rest," said Langdon, "but it could be worse; I've had four hours' sleep anyway."

"You'll have no more this night, that's certain," said St. Clair. "Look, General Jackson, himself, is going with us. See him climbing upon Little Sorrel! Lord pity the foot cavalry!"

General Jackson, mounted upon the sorrel horse destined to become so famous, rode to the head of the brigade, which was now in ranks, and beckoned to Harry.

"I've decided to attend to this affair myself, Lieutenant Kenton," he said. "Keep by my side. You know the way. Be sure that you lead us right."

His voice was not raised, but his words had an edge of steel. The cold blue eyes swept him with a single chilly glance and Harry felt the fear of God in his soul. Lead them right? His faculties could not fail with Stonewall Jackson by his side.

The general himself gave the word, the brigade swung into the broad road and it marched. It did not dawdle along. It marched, and it marched fast. It actually seemed to Harry after the first mile that it was running, running toward the enemy.

Not in vain had the infantry of Stonewall Jackson been called foot cavalry. Harry now for the first time saw men really march. The road spun behind them and the forest swept by. They were nearly all open-air Virginians, long of limb, deep of chest and great of muscle. There was no time for whispering among them, and the exchange of guesses about their destination. They needed every particle of air in their lungs for the terrible man who made them march as men had seldom marched before.

Jackson cast a grim eye on the long files that sank away in the darkness behind him.

"They march very well," he said, "but they will do better with more practice. Ride to the rear, Lieutenant Kenton, and see if there are any stragglers. If you find any order them back into line and if they refuse to obey, shoot."

Again his voice was not raised, but an electric current of fiery energy seemed to leap from this grave, somber man and to infuse itself through the veins of the lad to whom he gave the orders.

Harry saluted and, wheeling his horse, rode swiftly along the edge of the forest toward the rear. Now, the spirit of indomitable youth broke forth. Many in the columns were as young as he and some younger. In the earlier years of the war, and indeed, to the very close, there was little outward respect for rank among the citizen soldiers of either army. Harry was saluted with a running fire of chaff.

"Turn your horse's head, young feller, the enemy ain't that way. He's in front."

"He's forgot his toothbrush, Bill, and he's going back in a hurry to get it."

"If I had a horse like that I'd ride him in the right direction."

"Tell 'em in Winchester that the foot cavalry are marchin' a hundred miles an hour."

Harry did not resent these comments. He merely flung back an occasional comment of his own and hurried on until he reached the rear. Then in the dusk of the road he found four or five men limping along, and ready when convenient to drop away in the darkness. Harry wasted no time. The fire in his blood that had come from Jackson was still burning. He snatched a pistol from his belt and, riding directly at them, cried:

"Forward and into the ranks at once, or I shoot!"

"But we are lame, sir!" cried one of the men. "See my foot is bleeding!"

He held up one foot and red drops were falling from the ragged shoe.

"It makes no difference," cried Harry. "Barefooted men should be glad to march for Stonewall Jackson! One, two, three! Hurry, all of you, or I shoot!"

The men took one look at the flaming face, and broke into a run for the rear guard. Harry saw them in the ranks and then beat up the woods on either side of the road, but saw no more stragglers or deserters. Then he galloped through the edge of the forest and rejoined the general at the head of the command.

"Were they all marching?" asked Jackson.

"All but four, sir."

"And the four?"

"They're marching now, too."

"Good. How far are we from the arsenal?"

"About eight miles, sir."

"Isn't it nearer nine?"

"I should say nearer eight, sir."

"You should know, and at any rate we'll soon see."

Jackson did not speak to him again directly, evidently keeping him at his side now for sure guidance, but he continually sent other aides along the long lines to urge more speed. The men were panting, and, despite the cold of the winter night, beads of perspiration stood on every face. But Jackson was pitiless. He continually spurred them on, and now Harry knew with the certainty of fate that he would get there in time. He would reach Hertford before fresh Union troops could come. He was as infallible as fate.

There was no breath left for whispering in the ranks of Jackson's men. Nothing was heard but the steady beat of marching feet, and now and then, the low command of an officer. But such commands were few. There were no more stragglers, and the chief himself rode at their head. They knew how to follow.

The moon faded and many of the stars went back into infinite space. A dusky film was drawn across the sky, and at a distance the fields and forest blended into one great shadow. Harry looked back at the brigade which wound in a long dark coil among the trees. He could not see faces of the men now, only the sinuous black shape of illimitable length that their solid lines made.

This long black shape moved fast, and occasionally it gave forth a sinister glitter, as stray moonbeams fell upon blade or bayonet. It seemed to Harry that there was something deadly and inevitable about it, and he began to feel sorry for the Union troops who were besieging the village and who did not know that Stonewall Jackson was coming.

He cast a sidelong glance at the leader. He rode, leaning a little further forward in the saddle than usual, and the wintry blue eyes gazed steadily before him. Harry knew that they missed nothing.

"You are sure that we are on the right road, Mr. Kenton?" said Jackson.

"Quite sure of it, sir."

The general did not speak again for some time. Then, when he caught the faint glimmer of water through the dark, he said:

"This is the creek, is it not?"

"Yes, sir, and the Yankees can't be more than a mile away."

"And it's a full hour until dawn. The reinforcements for the enemy cannot have come up. Lieutenant Kenton, I wish you to stay with me. I will have a messenger tell Colonel Talbot that for the present you are detached for my service."

"Thank you, sir," said Harry.

"Why?"

"I wish to see how you crumple up the enemy."

The cold blue eyes gleamed for a moment. Harry more than guessed the depths of passion and resolve that lay behind the impenetrable mask of Jackson's face. He felt again the rays of the white, hot fire that burned in the great Virginian's soul.

A few hundred yards further and the brigade began to spread out in the dusk. Companies filed off to right and left, and in a few minutes came shots from the pickets, sounding wonderfully clear and sharp in the stillness of the night. Red dots from the rifle muzzles appeared here and there in the woods, and then Harry caught the glint of late starshine on the eaves of the warehouse.

Jackson drew his horse a little to one side of the road, and Harry, obedient to orders, followed him. A regiment massed directly behind them drew up close. Harry saw that it was his own Invincibles. There were Colonel Leonidas Talbot and Lieutenant-Colonel Hector St. Hilaire on horseback, looking very proud and eager. Further away were Langdon and St. Clair also mounted, but Harry could not see the expression on their faces.

"Tell Colonel Talbot to have the charge sounded and then to attack with all his might," said Jackson to his young aide.

Harry carried the order eagerly and rejoined the general at once. The drums of the Invincibles beat the charge, and on both sides of them the drums of other regiments played the same tune. Then the drum-beat was lost in that wild and thrilling shout, the rebel yell, more terrible than the war-whoop of the Indians, and the whole brigade rushed forward in a vast half-circle that enclosed the village between the two horns of the curve.

The scattered firing of the pickets was lost in the great shout of the South, and, by the time the Northern sentinels could give the alarm to their main body, the rush of Jackson's men was upon them, clearing out the woods and fields in a few instants and driving the Union horsemen in swift flight northward.

Harry kept close to his general. He saw a spark of fire shoot from the blue eye, and the nostrils expand. Then the mask became as impenetrable as ever. He let the reins fall on the neck of Little Sorrel, and watched his men as they swept into the open, passed the warehouse, and followed the enemy into the forest beyond.

But the bugles quickly sounded the recall. It was not Jackson's purpose to waste his men in frays which could produce little. The pursuing regiments returned reluctantly to the open where the inhabitants of the village were welcoming Jackson with great rejoicings. The encounter had been too swift and short to cause great loss, but all the stores were saved and Captain Sherburne and Captain McGee rode forward to salute their commander.

"You made a good defense," said Stonewall Jackson, crisply and briefly. "We begin the removal of the stores at once. Wagons will come up shortly for that purpose. Take your cavalry, Captain Sherburne, and scout the country. If they need sleep they can get it later when there is nothing else to do."

Captain Sherburne saluted and Harry saw his face flush with pride. The indomitable spirit of Jackson was communicated fast to all his men. The sentence to more work appealed to Sherburne with much greater force than the sentence of rest could have done. In a moment he and his men were off, searching the woods and fields in the direction of the Union camp.

"Ride back on the road, Lieutenant Kenton, and tell the wagons to hurry," said General Jackson to Harry. "Before I left Winchester I gave orders for them to follow, and we must not waste time here."

"Yes, sir," said Harry, as he turned and rode into the forest through which they had come. He, too, felt the same emotion that had made the face of Sherburne flush with pride. What were sleep and rest to a young soldier, following a man who carried victory in the hollow of his hand; not the victory of luck or chance, but the victory of forethought, of minute preparation, and of courage.

He galloped fast, and the hard road gave back the ring of steel shod hoofs. A silver streak showed in the eastern sky. The dawn was breaking. He increased his pace. The woods and fields fled by. Then he heard the cracking of whips, and the sound of voices urging on reluctant animals. Another minute and the long line of wagons was in sight straining along the road.

"Hurry up!" cried Harry to the leader who drove, bareheaded.

"Has Old Jack finished the job?" asked the man.

"Yes."

"How long did it take him?"

"About five minutes."

"I win," called the man to the second driver just behind him. "You 'lowed it would take him ten minutes, but I said not more'n seven at the very furthest."

The train broke into a trot, and Harry, turning his horse, rode by the side of the leader.

"How did you know that it would take General Jackson so little time to scatter the enemy?" the boy asked the man.

"'Cause I know Old Jack."

"But he has not yet done much in independent command."

"No, but I've seen him gettin' ready, an' I've watched him. He sees everything, an' he prays. I tell you he prays. I ain't a prayin' man myself. But when a man kneels down in the bushes an' talks humble an' respectful to his God, an' then rises up an' jumps at the enemy, it's time for that enemy to run. I'd rather be attacked by the worst bully and desperado that ever lived than by a prayin' man. You see, I want to live, an' what chance have I got ag'in a man that's not only not afraid to die, but that's willin' to die, an' rather glad to die, knowin' that he's goin' straight to Heaven an' eternal joy? I tell you, young man, that unbelievers ain't ever got any chance against believers; no, not in nothin'."

"I believe you're right."

"Right! Of course I'm right! Why did Old Jack order these waggins to come along an' get them stores? 'Cause he believed he was goin' to save 'em. An' mebbe he saved 'em, 'cause he believed he was goin' to do it. It works both ways. Git up!"

The shout of "Git up!" was to his horses, which added a little more to their pace, and now Harry saw troops coming back to meet them and form an escort.

In half an hour they were at the village. Already the ammunition and supplies had been brought forth and were stacked, ready to be loaded on the wagons. General Jackson was everywhere, riding back and forth on his sorrel horse, directing the removal just as he had directed the march and the brief combat. His words were brief but always dynamic. He seemed insensible to weariness.

It was now full morning, wintry and clear. The small population of the village and people from the surrounding country, intensely Southern and surcharged with enthusiasm, were bringing hot coffee and hot breakfast for the troops. Jackson permitted them to eat and drink in relays. As many as could get at the task helped to load the wagons. Little compulsion was needed. Officers themselves toiled at boxes and casks. The spirit of Jackson had flowed into them all.

"I've gone into training," said Langdon to Harry.

"Training? What kind of training, Tom?"

"I see that my days of play are over forever, and I'm practicing hard, so I can learn how to do without food, sleep or rest for months at a time."

"It's well you're training," interrupted St. Clair. "I foresee that you're going to need all the practice you can get. Everything's loaded in the wagons now, and I wager you my chances of promotion against one of our new Confederate dollar bills that we start inside of a minute."

The word "minute" was scarcely out of his mouth, when Jackson gave the sharp order to march. Sherburne's troop sprang to saddle and led the way, their bugler blowing a mellow salute to the morning and victory. Many whips cracked, and the wagons bearing the precious stores swung into line. Behind came the brigade, the foot cavalry. The breakfast and the loading of the wagons had not occupied more than half an hour. It was yet early morning when the whole force left the village and marched at a swift pace toward Winchester.

General Jackson beckoned to Harry.

"Ride with me," he said. "I've notified Colonel Talbot that you are detached from his staff and will serve on mine."

Although loath to leave his comrades Harry appreciated the favor and flushed with pleasure.

"Thank you, sir," he said briefly.

Jackson nodded. He seemed to like the lack of effusive words. Harry knew that his general had not tasted food. Neither had he. He had actually forgotten it in his keenness for his work, and now he was proud of the fact. He was proud, too, of the comradeship of abstention that it gave him with Stonewall Jackson. As he rode in silence by the side of the great commander he made for himself an ideal. He would strive in his own youthful way to show the zeal, the courage and the untiring devotion that marked the general.

The sun, wintry but golden, rose higher and made fields and forest luminous. But few among Jackson's men had time to notice the glory of the morning. It seemed to Harry that they were marching back almost as swiftly as they had come. Langdon was right and more. They were getting continuous practice not only in the art of living without food, sleep or rest, but also of going everywhere on a run instead of a walk. Those who survived it would be incomparable soldiers.

Winchester appeared and the people came forth rejoicing. Jackson gave orders for the disposition of the stores and then rode at once to a tent. He signalled to Harry also to dismount and enter. An orderly took the horses of both.

"Sit down at the table there," said Jackson. "I want to dictate to you some orders."

Harry sat down. He had forgotten to take off his cap and gloves, but he removed one gauntlet now, and picked up a pen which lay beside a little inkstand, a pad of coarse paper on the other side.

Jackson himself had not removed hat or gauntlets either, and the heavy cavalry cloak that he had worn on the ride remained flung over his shoulders. He dictated a brief order to his brigadiers, Loring, Edward Johnson, Garnett, the commander of the Stonewall Brigade, and Ashby, who led the cavalry, to prepare for a campaign and to see that everything was ready for a march in the morning.

Harry made copies of all the orders and sealed them.

"Deliver every one to the man to whom it is addressed," said Jackson, "and then report to me. But be sure that you say nothing of their contents to anybody."

The boy, still burning with zeal, hurried forth with the orders, delivered them all, and came back to the tent, where he found the general dictating to another aide. Jackson glanced at him and Harry, saluting, said:

"I have given all the orders, sir, to those for whom they were intended."

"Very well," said Jackson. "Wait and I shall have more messages for you to carry."

He turned to the second aide, but seeming to remember something, looked at his watch.

"Have you had any breakfast, Mr. Kenton?" he said.

"No, sir."

"Any sleep?"

"Yes, sir."

"When?"

"I slept well, sir, night before last."

Harry's reply was given in all seriousness. Jackson smiled. The boy's reply and his grave manner pleased him.

"I won't give you any more orders just now," he said. "Go out and get something to eat, but do not be gone longer than half an hour. You need sleep, too—but that can wait."

"I shall be glad to carry your orders, sir, now. The food can wait, too. I am not hungry."

Harry spoke respectfully. There was in truth an appealing note in his voice. Jackson gave him another and most searching glance.

"I think I chose well when I chose you," he said. "But go, get your breakfast. It is not necessary to starve to death now. We may have a chance at that later."

The faintest twinkle of grim humor appeared in his eyes and Harry, withdrawing, hastened at once to the Invincibles, where he knew he would have food and welcome in plenty.

St. Clair and Langdon greeted him with warmth and tried to learn from him what was on foot.

"There's a great bustle," said Langdon, "and I know something big is ahead. This is the last day of the Old Year, and I know that the New Year is going to open badly. I'll bet you anything that before to-morrow morning is an hour old this whole army will be running hot-foot over the country, more afraid of Stonewall Jackson than of fifty thousand of the enemy."

"But you've been in training for it," said Harry with a laugh.

"So I have, but I don't want to train too hard."

Harry ate and drank and was back at General Jackson's tent in twenty minutes. He had received a half hour but he was learning already to do better than was expected of him.

CHAPTER III.
STONEWALL JACKSON'S MARCH

Harry took some orders to brigadiers and colonels. He saw that concentration was going on rapidly and he shared the belief of his comrades that the army would march in the morning. He felt a new impulse of ambition and energy. It continually occurred to him that while he was doing much he might do more. He saw how his leader worked, with rapidity and precision, and without excitement, and he strove to imitate him.

The influence of Jackson was rapidly growing stronger upon the mind of the brilliant, sensitive boy, so susceptible to splendor of both thought and action. The general, not yet great to the world, but great already to those around him, dominated the mind of the boy. Harry was proud to serve him.

He saw that Jackson had taken no sleep, and he would take none either. Soon the question was forgotten, and he toiled all through the afternoon, glad to be at the heart of affairs so important.

Winchester was a sprightly little city, one of the best in the great valley, inhabited by cultivated people of old families, and Southern to the core. Harry and his young comrades had found a good welcome there. They had been in many houses and they had made many friends. The Virginians liked his bright face and manners. Now they could not fail to see that some great movement was afoot, and more than once his new friends asked him its nature, but he replied truthfully that he did not know. In the throb of great action Winchester disappeared from his thoughts. Every faculty was bent upon the plans of Jackson, whatever they might be.

The afternoon drew to a close and then the short winter twilight passed swiftly. The last night of the Old Year had come, and Harry was to enter at dawn upon one of the most vivid periods in the life of any boy that ever lived, a period paralleled perhaps only by that of the French lads who followed the young Bonaparte into the plains of Italy. Harry with all his dreams, arising from the enormous impression made upon him by Jackson, could not yet foresee what lay before him.

He was returning on foot from one of his shorter errands. He had ridden throughout the afternoon, but the time came when he thought the horse ought to rest, and with the coming of the twilight he had walked. He was not conscious of any weakness. His body, in a way, had become a mere mechanism. It worked, because the will acted upon it like a spring, but it was detached, separate from his mind. He took no more interest in it than he would in any other machine, which, when used up, could be cast aside, and be replaced with a new one.

He glanced at the camp, stretching through the darkness. Much fewer fires were burning than usual, and the men, warned to sleep while they could, had wrapped themselves already in their blankets. Then he entered the tent of Jackson with the reply to an order that he had taken to a brigadier.

The general stood by a wall of the tent, dictating to an aide who sat at the little table, and who wrote by the light of a small oil lamp. Harry saluted and gave him the reply. Jackson read it. As he read Harry staggered but recovered himself quickly. The overtaxed body was making a violent protest, and the vague feeling that he could throw away the old and used-up machine, and replace it with a new one was not true. He caught his breath sharply and his face was red with shame. He hoped that his general had not seen this lamentable weakness of his.

Jackson, after reading the reply, resumed his dictation. Harry was sure that the general had not seen. He had not noticed the weakness in an aide of his who should have no weakness at all! But Jackson had seen and in a few hours of contact he had read the brave, bright young soul of his aide. He finished the dictation and then turning to Harry, he said quietly:

"I can't think of anything more for you to do, Mr. Kenton, and I suppose you might as well rest. I shall do so myself in a half hour. You'll find blankets in the large tent just beyond mine. A half dozen of my aides sleep in it, but there are blankets enough for all and it's first come first served."

Harry gave the usual military salute and withdrew. Outside the tent, the body that he had used so cruelly protested not only a second time but many times. It was in very fact and truth detached from the will, because it no longer obeyed the will at all. His legs wobbled and bent like those of a paralytic, and his head fell forward through very weakness.

Luckily the tent was only a few yards away, and he managed to reach it and enter. It had a floor of planks and in the dark he saw three youths, a little older than himself, already sound asleep in their blankets. He promptly rolled himself in a pair, stretched his length against the cloth wall, and balmy sleep quickly came to make a complete reunion of the will and of the tired body which would be fresh again in the morning, because he was young and strong and recovered fast.

Harry slept hard all through the night and nature completed her task of restoring the worn fibers. He was roused shortly after dawn and the cooks were ready with breakfast for the army. He ate hungrily and when he would stop, one of his comrades who had slept with him in the tent told him to eat more.

"You need a lot to go on when you march with Jackson," he said. "Besides, you won't be certain where the next is coming from."

"I've learned that already," said Harry, as he took his advice.

A half hour later he was on his horse near Jackson, ready to receive his commands, and in the early hours of the New Year the army marched out of Winchester, the eager wishes of the whole population following it.

It was the brightest of winter mornings, almost like spring it seemed. The sky was a curving and solid sheet of sunlight, and the youths of the army were for the moment a great and happy family. They were marching to battle, wounds and death, but they were too young and too buoyant to think much about it.

Harry soon learned that they were going toward Bath and Hancock, two villages on the railway, both held by Northern troops. He surmised that Jackson would strike a sudden blow, surprise the garrisons, cut the railway, and then rush suddenly upon some greater force. A campaign in the middle of winter. It appealed to him as something brilliant and daring. The pulses which had beat hard so often lately began to beat hard again.

The army went swiftly across forest and fields. As the brigade had marched back the night before, so the whole army marched forward to-day. The fact that Jackson's men always marched faster than other men was forced again upon Harry's attention. He remembered from his reading an old comment of Napoleon's referring to war that there were only two or three men in Europe who knew the value of time. Now he saw that at least one man in America knew its value, and knew it as fully as Napoleon ever did.

The day passed hour by hour and the army sped on, making only a short halt at noon for rest and food. Harry joined the Invincibles for a few moments and was received with warmth by Colonel Leonidas Talbot, Lieutenant-Colonel Hector St. Hilaire and all his old friends.

"I am sorry to lose you, Harry," said Colonel Talbot, "but I am glad that you are on the immediate staff of General Jackson. It's an honor. I feel already that we're in the hands of a great general, and the feeling has gone through the whole army. There's an end, so far as this force is concerned, to doubt and hesitation."

"And we, the Southerners who are called the cavaliers, are led by a puritan," said Lieutenant-Colonel St. Hilaire. "Because if there ever was a puritan, General Jackson is one."

Harry passed on, intending to speak with his comrades, Langdon and St. Clair. He heard the young troops talking freely everywhere, never forgetting the fact that they were born free citizens as good as anybody, and never hesitating to comment, often in an unflattering way, upon their officers. Harry saw a boy who had just taken off his shoes and who was tenderly rubbing his feet.

"I never marched so fast before," he said complainingly. "My feet are sore all over."

"Put on your shoes an' shut up," said another boy. "Stonewall Jackson don't care nothin' about your feet. You're here to fight."

Harry walked on, but the words sank deep in his mind. It was an uneducated boy, probably from the hills, who had given the rebuke, but he saw that the character of Stonewall Jackson was already understood by the whole army, even to the youngest private. He found Langdon and St. Clair sitting together on a log. They were not tired, as they were mounted officers, but they were full of curiosity.

"What's passing through Old Jack's head?" asked Langdon, the irreverent and the cheerful.

"I don't know, and I don't suppose anybody will ever know all that's passing there."

"I'll wager my year's pay against a last year's bird nest that he isn't leading us away from the enemy."

"He certainly isn't doing that. We're moving on two little towns, Bath and Hancock, but there must be bigger designs beyond."

"This is New Year's Day, as you know," said St. Clair in his pleasant South Carolina drawl, "and I feel that Tom there is going to earn the year's pay that he talks so glibly about wagering."

"At any rate, Arthur," said Langdon, "if we go into battle you'll be dressed properly for it, and if you fall you'll die in a gentleman's uniform."

St. Clair smiled, showing that he appreciated Langdon's flippant comment. Harry glanced at him. His uniform was spotless, and it was pressed as neatly as if it had just come from the hands of a tailor. The gray jacket of fine cloth, with its rows of polished brass buttons, was buttoned as closely as that of a West Point cadet. He seemed to be in dress and manner a younger brother of the gallant Virginia captain, Philip Sherburne, and Harry admired him. A soldier who dressed well amid such trying obstacles was likely to be a soldier through and through. Harry was learning to read character from extraneous things, things that sometimes looked like trifles to others.

"I merely came over here to pass the time of day," he said. "We start again in two or three minutes. Hark, there go the bugles, and I go with them!"

He ran back, sprang on his horse a few seconds before Jackson himself was in the saddle, and rode away again.

The general sent him on no missions for a while, and Harry rode in silence. Observant, as always, he noticed the long ridges of the mountains, showing blue in the distance, and the occasional glimmer of water in the valley. It was beautiful, this valley, and he did not wonder that the Virginians talked of it so much. He shared their wrath because the hostile Northern foot already pressed a portion, and he felt as much eagerness as they to drive away the invader.

He also saw pretty soon that the long lines of the mountains, so blue and beautiful against the shining sun, were losing their clear and vivid tints. The sky above them was turning to gray, and their crests were growing pale. Then a wind chill and sharp with the edge of winter began to blow down from the slopes. It had been merely playing at summer that morning and, before the first day of January 1862, closed, winter rushed down upon Virginia, bringing with it the fiercest and most sanguinary year the New World ever knew — save the one that followed it, and the one that followed that.

The temperature dropped many degrees in an hour. Just as the young troops of Grant, marching to Donelson, deceived by a warm morning had cast aside their heavy clothing to be chilled to the bone before the day was over, so the equally young troops of Jackson now suffered in the same way, and from the same lack of thought.

Most of their overcoats and cloaks were in the wagons, and there was no time to get them, because Jackson would not permit any delays. They shivered and grumbled under their breath. Nevertheless the army marched swiftly, while the dark clouds, laden with snow and cold, marched up with equal swiftness from the western horizon.

A winter campaign! It did not seem so glorious now to many of the boys who in the warmth and the sunshine had throbbed with the thought of it. They inquired once more about those wagons containing their overcoats and blankets, and they learned that they had followed easier roads, while the troops themselves were taking short cuts through the forests and across the fields. They might be reunited at night, and they might not. It was not considered a matter of the first importance by Jackson.

Harry had been wise enough to retain his military cloak strapped to his saddle, and he wrapped it about his body, drawing the collar as high as he could. One of his gauntleted hands held the reins, and the other swung easily by his side. He would have given his cloak to some one of the shivering youths who marched on foot near him, but he knew that Jackson would not permit any such open breach of discipline.

The boy watched the leader who rode almost by his side. Jackson had put on his own cavalry cloak, but it was fastened by a single button at the top and it had blown open. He did not seem to notice the fact. Apparently he was oblivious of heat and cold alike, and rode on, bent a little forward in the saddle, his face the usual impenetrable mask. But Harry knew that the brain behind that brow never ceased to work, always thinking and planning, trying this combination and that, ready to make any sacrifice to do the work that was to be done.

The long shadows came, and the short day that had turned so cold was over, giving way to the night that was colder than the day. They were on the hills now and even the vigorous Jackson felt that it was time to stop until morning. The night had turned very dark, a fierce wind was blowing, and now and then a fine sift of snow as sharp as hail was blown against their faces.

The wagons with the heavy clothing, blankets and food had not come up, and perhaps would not arrive until the next day. Gloom as dark as the night itself began to spread among the young troops, but Jackson gave them little time for bemoaning their fate. Fires were quickly built from fallen wood. The men found warmth and a certain mental relief in gathering the wood itself. The officers, many of them boys themselves, shared in the work. They roamed through the forest dragging in fallen timber, and now and then, an old rail fence was taken panel by panel to join the general heap.

The fires presently began to crackle in the darkness, running in long, irregular lines, and the young soldiers crowded in groups about them. At the same time they ate the scanty rations they carried in their knapsacks, and wondered what had become of the wagons. Jackson sent detachments to seek his supply trains, but Harry knew that he would not wait for it in the morning. The horses drawing the heavy loads over the slippery roads would need rest as badly as the men, and Jackson would go on. If food was not there—well then his troops must march on empty stomachs.

Youth changes swiftly and the high spirits with which the soldiers had departed in the morning were gone. The night had become extremely cold. Fierce winds whistled down from the crests of the mountains and pierced their clothing with myriads of little icy darts. They crept closer and closer to the fire. Their faces burned while their backs froze, and the menacing wind, while it chilled them to the marrow with its breath, seemed to laugh at them in sinister fashion. They thought with many a lament of their warm quarters in Winchester.

Harry shared the common depression to a certain extent. He had recalled that morning how the young Napoleon started on his great campaign of Italy, and there had been in his mind some idea that it would be repeated in the Virginia valleys, but he recalled at night that the soldiers of the youthful Bonaparte had marched and fought in warm days in a sunny country. It was a different thing to conduct a great campaign, when the clouds heavy with snow were hovering around the mountain tops, and the mercury was hunting zero. He shivered and looked apprehensively into the chilly night. His apprehension was not for a human foe, but for the unbroken spirits of darkness and mystery that can cow us all.

No tents were pitched. Jackson shared the common lot, sitting by a fire with some of the higher officers, while three or four other young aides were near. The sifts of snow turned after a while into a fine but steady snow, which continued half an hour. The backs of the soldiers were covered with white, while their faces burned. Then there was a shuffling sound at every fire, as the men turned their backs to the blaze and their faces to the forest.

Harry watched General Jackson closely. He was sitting on a fallen log, which the soldiers had drawn near to one of the largest fires, and he was staring intently into the coals. He did not speak, nor did he seem to take any notice of those about him. Harry knew, too, that he was not seeing the coals, but the armies of the enemy on the other side of the cold mountain.

Jackson after a while beckoned to the young aides and he gave to every one in turn the same command.

"Mount and make a complete circuit of the army. Report to me whether all the pickets are watchful, and whether any signs of the enemy can be seen."

Harry had tethered his horse in a little grove near by, where he might be sheltered as much as possible from the cold, and the faithful animal which had not tasted food that day, whimpered and rubbed his nose against his shoulder when he came.

"I'm sorry, old boy," whispered Harry, "I'd give you food if I could, but since I can't give you food I've got to give you more work."

He put on the bridle, leaped into the saddle, which had been left on the horse's back, and rode away on his mission. The password that night was "Manassas," and Harry exchanged it with the pickets who curved in a great circle through the lone, cold forest. They were always glad to see him. They were alone, save when two of them met at the common end of a beat, and these youths of the South were friendly, liking to talk and to hear the news of others.

Toward the Northern segment of the circle he came to a young giant from the hills who was walking back and forth with the utmost vigor and shaking himself as if he would throw off the cold. His brown face brightened with pleasure when he saw Harry and exchanged the password.

"Two or three other officers have been by here ridin' hosses," he said in the voice of an equal speaking to his equal, "an' they don't fill me plum' full o' envy a-tall, a-tall. I guess a feller tonight kin keep warmer walkin' on the ground than ridin' on a hoss. What might your name be, Mr. Officer?"

"Kenton. I'm a lieutenant, at present on the staff of General Jackson. What is yours?"

"Seth Moore, an' I'm always a private, but at present doin' sentinel duty, but wishin' I was at home in our double log house 'tween the blankets."

"Have you noticed anything, Seth?" asked Harry, not at all offended by the nature of his reply.

"I've seen some snow, an' now an' then the cold top of a mountain, an' —"

"An' what, Seth?"

"Do you see that grove straight toward the north four or five hundred yards away?"

"Yes, but I can make nothing of it but a black blur. It's too far away to tell the trunks of the trees apart."

"It's too fur fur me, too, an' my eyes are good, but ten or fifteen minutes ago, leftenant, I thought I saw a shadder at the edge of the grove. It 'peared to me that the shadder was like that of a horse with a man on it. After a while it went back among the trees an' o' course I lost it thar."

"You feel quite sure you saw the shadow, Seth?"

"Yes, leftenant. I'm shore I ain't mistook. I've hunted 'coons an' 'possums at night too much to be mistook about shadders. I reckon, if I may say so, shadders is my specialty, me bein' somethin' o' a night owl. As shore as I'm standin' here, leftenant, and as shore as you're settin' there on your hoss, a mounted man come to the edge of that wood an' stayed thar a while, watchin' us. I'd have follered him, but I couldn't leave my beat here, an' you're the first officer I've saw since. It may amount to nothin, an' then again it mayn't."

"I'm glad you told me. I'll go into the grove myself and see if anybody is there now."

"Leftenant, if I was you I'd be mighty keerful. If it's a spy it'll be easy enough for him under the cover of the trees to shoot you in the open comin' toward him."

Harry knew that Jackson planned a surprise of some kind and Seth Moore's words about the mounted man alarmed him. He did not doubt the accuracy of the young mountaineer's eyesight, or his coolness, and he resolved that he would not go back to headquarters until he knew more about that "shadow." But Moore's advice about caution was not to be unheeded.

"If you keep in the edge of our woods here," said Moore, "an' ride along a piece you'll come to a little valley. Then you kin go up that an' come into the grove over thar without being seed."

"Good advice. I'll take it."

Harry loosened one of the pistols in his belt and rode cautiously through the wood as Seth Moore had suggested. The ground sloped rapidly, and soon he reached the narrow but deep little valley with a dense growth of trees and underbrush on either side. The valley led upward, and he came into the grove just as Moore had predicted.

This forest was of much wider extent than he had supposed. It stretched northward further than he could see, and, although it was devoid of undergrowth, it was very dark among the trees. He rode his horse behind the trunk of a great oak, and, pausing there, examined all the forest within eyeshot.

He saw nothing but the long rows of tree trunks, white on the northern side with snow, and he heard nothing but the cold rustle of wind among boughs bare of branches. Yet he had full confidence in the words of Seth Moore. He could neither see him nor hear him, but he was sure that somebody besides himself was in the wood. Once more the soul and spirit of his great ancestor were poured into him, and for the moment he, too, was the wilderness rover, endowed with nerves preternaturally acute.

Hidden by the great tree trunks he listened attentively. His horse, oppressed by the cold and perhaps by the weariness of the day, was motionless and made no sound. He waited two or three minutes and then he was sure that he heard a slight noise, which he believed was made by the hoofs of a horse walking very slowly. Then he saw the shadow.

It was the dim figure of a man on horseback, moving very cautiously at some distance from Harry. He urged his own horse forward a little, and the shadow stopped instantly. Then he knew that he had been seen, and he sat motionless in the saddle for an instant or two, not knowing what to do.

After all, the man on horseback might be a friend. He might be some scout from a band of rangers, coming to join Jackson; and not yet sure that the army in the woods was his. Recovering from his indecision he rode forward a little and called:

"Who are you?"

The shadow made no reply, and horse and rider were motionless. They seemed for an instant to be phantoms, but then Harry knew that they were real. He was oppressed by a feeling of the weird and menacing. He would make the sinister figure move and his hand dropped toward his pistol belt.

"Stop, I can fire before you!" cried the figure sharply, and then Harry suddenly saw a pistol barrel gleaming across the stranger's saddle bow.

Harry checked his hand, but he did not consider himself beaten by any means. He merely waited, wary and ready to seize his opportunity.

"I don't want to shoot," said the man in a clear voice, "and I won't unless you make me. I'm no friend. I'm an enemy, that is, an official enemy, and I think it strange, Harry Kenton, almost the hand of fate, that you and I come face to face again under such circumstances."

Harry stared, and then the light broke. Now he remembered both the voice and the figure.

"Shepard!" he exclaimed.

"It's so. We're engaged upon the same duty. I've just been inspecting the army of General Jackson, calculating its numbers, its equipment, and what it may do. Keep your hand away from that pistol. I might not hit you, but the chances are that I would. But as I said, I don't want to shoot. It wouldn't help our cause or me any to maim or kill you. Suppose we call it peace between us for this evening."

"I agree to call it peace because I have to do it."

Shepard laughed, and his laugh was not at all sarcastic or unpleasant.

"Why a rage to kill?" he said. "You and I, Harry Kenton, will find before this war is over that we'll get quite enough of fighting in battles without seeking to make slaughter in between. Besides, having met you several times, I've a friendly feeling for you. Now turn and ride back to your own lines and I'll go the other way."

The blood sprang into Harry's face and his heart beat hard. There was something dominating and powerful in the voice. It now had the tone of a man who spoke to one over whom he ruled. Yet he could do nothing. He saw that Shepard was alert and watchful. He felt instinctively that his foe would fire if he were forced to do so and that he would not miss. Then despite himself, he felt admiration for the man's skill and power, and a pronounced intellectual quality that he discovered in him.

"Very well," he replied, "I'll turn and go back, but I want to tell you, Mr. Shepard, that while you have been estimating what General Jackson's army can do you must make that estimate high."

"I've already done so," called Shepard — Harry was riding away as he spoke. The boy at the edge of the wood looked back, but the shadow was already gone. He rode straight across the open and Seth Moore met him.

"Did you find anything?" the young mountaineer asked.

"Yes, there was a mounted man in a blue uniform, a spy, who has been watching, but he made off. You had good eyes, Seth, and I'm going to report this at once to General Jackson."

Harry knew that he was the bearer of an unpleasant message. General Jackson was relying upon surprise, and it would not please him to know that his movements were watched by an active and intelligent scout or spy. But the man had already shown his greatness by always insisting upon hearing the worst of everything.

He found the chief, still sitting before one of the fires and reported to him fully. Jackson listened without comment, but at the end he said to two of the brigadiers who were sitting with him:

"We march again at earliest dawn. We will not wait for the wagons."

Then he added to Harry:

"You've done good service. Join the sleepers, there."

He pointed to a group of young officers rolled in their blankets, and Harry obeyed quickly.

CHAPTER IV.
WAR AND WAITING

Harry slept like one dead, but he was awakened at dawn, and he rose yet heavy with sleep and somewhat stiff from the severe exertions of the day before. But it all came back in an instant, the army, the march, and the march yet to come.

They had but a scanty breakfast, the wagons not yet having come up, and in a half hour they started again. They grumbled mightily at first, because the day was bleak beyond words, heavy with clouds, and sharp with chill. The country seemed deserted and certainly that somber air was charged with no omens of victory.

But in spite of everything the spirits of the young troops began to rise. They took a pride in this defiance of nature as well as man. They could endure cold and hunger and weariness as they would endure battle, when it came. They went on thus three days, almost without food and shelter. Higher among the hills the snow sometimes beat upon them in a hurricane, and at night the winds howled as if they had come down fresh from the Arctic.

The spirits of the young troops, after rising, fell again, and their feet dragged. Jackson, always watching, noticed it. Beckoning to several of his staff, including Harry, he rode back along the lines, giving a word of praise here and two words of rebuke there. They came at last to an entire brigade, halted by the roadside, some of the men leaning against an old rail fence.

Jackson looked at the men and his face darkened. It was his own Stonewall Brigade, the one of which he was so proud, and which he had led in person into the war. Their commander was standing beside a tree, and riding up to him he demanded fiercely:

"What is the meaning of this? Why have you stopped?"

"I ordered a stop of a little while for the men to cook their rations," replied General Garnett.

Jackson's face darkened yet further, and the blue eyes were menacing.

"There is no time for that," he said sharply.

"But the men can't go any farther without them. It's impossible."

"I never found anything impossible with this brigade."

Jackson shot forth the words as if they were so many bullets, gave Garnett a scornful look and rode on. Harry followed him, as was his duty, but more slowly, and looked back. He saw a deep red flush show through Garnett's sunburn. But the preparations for cooking were stopped abruptly. Within three minutes the Stonewall Brigade was in line again, marching resolutely over the frozen road. Garnett had recognized that the impossible was possible—at least where Jackson led.

Not many stragglers were found as they rode on toward the rear, but every regiment increased its speed at sight of the stern general. After circling around the rear he rode back toward the front, and he left Harry and several others to go more slowly along the flanks and report to him later.

When Harry was left alone he was saluted with the usual good-humored chaff by the soldiers who again demanded his horse of him, or asked him whether they were to fight or whether they were training to be foot-racers. Harry merely smiled, and he came presently to the Invincibles, who were trudging along stubbornly, with the officers riding on their flanks. Langdon was as cheerful as usual.

"Things have to come to their worst before they get better," he said to Harry, "and I suppose we've about reached the worst. A sight of the enemy would be pleasant, even if it meant battle."

"We're marching on Bath," said Harry, "and we ought to strike it to-night, though I'm afraid the Yankees have got warning of our coming."

He was thinking of Shepard, who now loomed very large to him. The circumstances of their meetings were always so singular that this Northern scout and spy seemed to him to possess omniscience.

Beyond a doubt he would notify every Northern garrison he could reach of Jackson's coming.

Suddenly the band of South Carolinians, who were still left in the Invincibles, struck up a song:

"Ho, woodsmen of the mountain-side!
Ho, dwellers in the vales!
Ho, ye who by the chafing tide
Have roughened in the gales!
Leave barn and byre, leave kin and cot,
Lay by the bloodless spade:
Let desk and case and counter rot,
And burn your books of trade!"

All the Invincibles caught the swing and rush of the verses, and regiments before them and behind them caught the time, too, if not the words. The chant rolled in a great thundering chorus through the wintry forest. It was solemn and majestic, and it quickened the blood of these youths who believed in the cause for which they fought, just as those on the other side believed in theirs.

"It was written by one of our own South Carolinians," said St. Clair, with pride. "Now here goes the second verse! Lead off, there, Langdon! They'll all catch it!"

"The despot roves your fairest lands;
And till he flies or fears,
Your fields must grow but armed bands
Your sheaves be sheaves of spears:
Give up to mildew and to rust
The useless tools of gain
And feed your country's sacred dust
With floods of crimson rain!"

Louder and louder swelled the chorus of ten thousand marching men. It was not possible for the officers to have stopped them had they wished to do so, and they did not wish it. Stonewall Jackson, who had read and studied much, knew that the power of simple songs was scarcely less than that of rifle and bayonet, and he willingly let them sing on. Now and then, a gleam came from the blue eyes in his tanned, bearded face.

Harry, sensitive and prone to enthusiasm, was flushed in every vein by the marching song. He seemed to himself to be endowed with a new life of vigor and energy. The invader trod the Southern land and they must rush upon him at once. He was eager for a sight of the blue masses which they would certainly overcome.

He returned to his place near the head of the column with the staff of the commander. Night was now close at hand, but Bath was still many miles away. It was colder than ever, but the wagons had not yet come up and there were no rations and tents. Only a few scraps of food were left in the knapsacks.

"Ride to Captain Sherburne," said General Jackson to Harry, "and tell him to go forward with his men and reconnoiter."

"May I go with him, sir?"

"Yes, and then report to me what he and his men find."

Harry galloped gladly to the vanguard, where the gallant young captain and his troop were leading. These Virginians preserved their fine appearance. If they were weary they did not show it. They sat erect in their saddles and the last button on their uniforms was in place. Their polished spurs gleamed in the wintry sun.

They set off at a gallop, Harry riding by the side of Captain Sherburne. Blood again mounted high with the rapid motion and the sense of action. Soon they left the army behind, and, as the road was narrow and shrouded in forest, they could see nothing of it. Its disappearance was as complete as if it had been swallowed up in a wilderness.

They rode straight toward Bath, but after two or three miles they slackened speed. Harry had told Sherburne of the presence of Shepard the night before, and the captain knew that they must be cautious.

Another mile, and at a signal from the captain the whole troop stopped. They heard hoofbeats on the road ahead of them, and the sound was coming in their direction.

"A strong force," said Captain Sherburne.

"Probably larger than ours, if the hoofbeats mean anything," said Harry.

"And Yankees, of course. Here they are!"

A strong detachment of cavalry suddenly rounded a curve in the road and swept into full view. Then the horsemen stopped in astonishment at the sight of the Confederate troop.

There was no possibility of either command mistaking the other for a friend, but Sherburne, despite his youth, had in him the instinct for quick perception and action which distinguished the great cavalry leaders of the South like Jeb Stuart, Turner Ashby and others. He drew his men back instantly somewhat in the shelter of the trees and received the Union fire first.

As Sherburne had expected, few of the Northern bullets struck home. Some knocked bark from the trees, others kicked up dirt from the frozen road, but most of them sang vainly through the empty air and passed far beyond. Now the Southerners sent their fire full into the Union ranks, and, at Sherburne's shouted command, charged, with their leader at their head swinging his sword in glittering circles like some knight of old.

The Southern volley had brought down many horses and men, but the Northern force was double in numbers and many of the men carried new breech-loading rifles of the best make. While unused to horses and largely ignorant of the country, they had good officers and they stood firm. The Southern charge, meeting a second volley from the breech-loading rifles, broke upon their front.

Harry, almost by the side of Sherburne, felt the shock as they galloped into the battle smoke, and then he felt the Virginians reel. He heard around him the rapid crackle of rifles and pistols, sabers clashing together, the shouts of men, the terrible neighing of wounded horses, and then the two forces drew apart, leaving a sprinkling of dead and wounded between.

It was a half retreat by either, the two drawing back sixty or seventy yards apiece and then beginning a scattered and irregular fire from the rifles. But Sherburne, alert always, soon drew his men into the shelter of the woods, and attempted an attack on his enemy's flank.

Some destruction was created in the Union ranks by the fire from the cover of the forest, but the officers of the opposing force showed skill, too. Harry had no doubt from the way the Northern troops were handled that at least two or three West Pointers were there. They quickly fell back into the forest on the other side of the road, and sent return volleys.

Harry heard the whistle and whizz of bullets all about them. Bark was clipped from trees and dry twigs fell. Yet little damage was done by either. The forest, although leafless, was dense, and trunks and low boughs afforded much shelter. Both ceased fire presently, seeming to realize at the same moment that nothing was being done, and hovered among the trees, each watching for what the other would try next.

Harry kept close to Captain Sherburne, whose face plainly showed signs of deep disgust. His heart was full of battle and he wished to get at the enemy. But prudence forbade another charge upon a force double his numbers and now sheltered by a wood. At this moment it was the boy beside him who was cooler than he.

"Captain Sherburne," he suggested mildly, "didn't General Jackson merely want to find out what was ahead of him? When the army comes up it will sweep this force out of its way."

"That's so," agreed Sherburne reluctantly, "but if we retire they'll claim a victory, and our men will be depressed by the suspicion of defeat."

"But the Yankees are retiring already. Look, you can see them withdrawing! They were on the same business that we were, and it's far more important for them to be sure that Jackson is advancing than it is for us to know that an enemy's in front."

"You're right. We knew already that he was there, and we were watching to get him. It's foolish for us to stay here, squabbling with a lot of obstinate Yankees. We'll go back to Jackson as fast as we can. You're a bright boy, Harry."

He dropped a hand affectionately on Harry's shoulder, then gave the order to the men and they turned their horses' heads toward the army. At the same time they saw with their own eyes the complete withdrawal of the Union troops, and the proud Virginians were satisfied. It was no defeat. It was merely a parting by mutual consent, each moving at the same instant, that is, if the Yankees didn't go first.

They galloped back over the frozen road, and Captain Sherburne admitted once more to himself the truth of Harry's suggestion. Already the twilight was coming, and again it was heavy with clouds. In the east all the peaks and ridges were wrapped about with them, and the captain knew that they meant more snow. Heavy snow was the worst of all things for the advance of Jackson.

Captain Sherburne gave another signal to his men and they galloped faster. The hoofbeats of nearly two hundred horses rang hard on the frozen road, but with increased speed pulses throbbed faster and spirits rose. The average age of the troops was not over twenty, and youth thought much of action, little of consequences.

They saw in a half hour the heads of columns toiling up the slopes, and then Jackson riding on Little Sorrel, his shoulders bent forward slightly, the grave eyes showing that the great mind behind them was still at work, planning, planning, always planning. Their expression did not change when Sherburne, halting his horse before him, saluted respectfully.

"What did you find, Captain Sherburne?" he asked.

"The enemy, sir. We ran into a force of cavalry about four hundred strong."

"And then?"

"We had a smart little skirmish with them, sir, and then both sides withdrew."

"Undoubtedly they went to report to their people, as you have come to report to yours. It looks as if our attempt to surprise Bath might fail, but we'll try to reach it to-night. Lieutenant Kenton, ride back and give the brigade commanders orders to hasten their march."

He detached several others of his staff for the same duty, and in most cases wrote brief notes for them. Harry noticed how he took it for granted that one was always willing to do work, and yet more work. He himself had just ridden back from battle, and yet he was sent immediately on another errand. He noticed, too, how it set a new standard for everybody. This way Jackson had of expecting much was rapidly causing his men to offer much as a matter of course.

While Jackson was writing the notes to the brigadiers he looked up once or twice at the darkening skies. The great mass of clouds, charged with snow that had been hovering in the east, was now directly overhead. When he had finished the last note it was too dark for him to write any more without help of torch. As he handed the note to the aide who was to take it, a great flake of snow fell upon his hand.

Harry found that the brigades could move no faster. They were already toiling hard. The twilight had turned to night, and the clouds covered the whole circle of the heavens. The snow, slow at first, was soon falling fast. The soldiers brushed it off for a while, and then, feeling that it was no use, let it stay. Ten thousand men, white as if wrapped in winding sheets, marched through the mountains. Now and then, a thin trickle of red from a foot, encased in a shoe worn through, stained the snow.

The wind was not blowing, and the night, reinforced by the clouds, became very dark, save the gleam from the white covering of snow upon the earth. Torches began to flare along the line, and still Jackson marched. Harry knew what was in his mind. He wished to reach Bath that night and fall upon the enemy when he was not expected, even though that enemy had been told that Jackson was coming. The commander in front, whoever he might be, certainly would expect no attack in the middle of the night and in a driving snowstorm.

But the fierce spirit of Jackson was forced to yield at last. His men, already the best marchers on the American continent, could go no farther. The order was given to camp. Harry more than guessed how bitter was the disappointment of his commander, and he shared it.

The men, half starved and often stiff with cold, sank down by the roadside. They no longer asked for the wagons containing their food and heavy clothing, because they no longer expected them. They passed from high spirits to a heavy apathy, and now they did not seem to care what happened. But the officers roused them up as much as possible, made them build fires with every piece of wood they could find, and then let them wrap themselves in their blankets and go to sleep — save for the sentinels.

All night long the snow beat on Jackson's army lying there among the mountains, and save for a few Union officers not far away, both North and South wondered what had become of it.

It was known at Washington and Richmond that Jackson had left Winchester, and then he had dropped into the dark. The eyes of the leaders at both capitals were fixed upon the greater armies of McClellan and Johnston, and Stonewall Jackson was not yet fully understood by either. Nevertheless, the gaunt and haggard President of the North began to feel anxiety about this Confederate leader who had disappeared with his army in the mountains of Northern Virginia.

The telegraph wires were not numerous then, but they were kept busy answering the question about Jackson. Banks and the other Union leaders in the valley sent reassuring replies. Jackson would not dare to attack them. They had nearly three times as many men as he, and it did not matter what had become of him. If he chose to come, the sooner he came, the sooner he would be annihilated. McClellan himself laughed at the fears about Jackson. He was preparing his own great army for a march on Richmond, one that would settle everything.

But the army of Jackson, nevertheless, rose from the snow the next morning, and marched straight on the Union garrison. The rising was made near Bath, and the army literally brushed the snow from itself before eating the half of a breakfast, and taking to the road again, Jackson, on Little Sorrel, leading them. Harry, as usual, rode near him.

Harry, despite exertions and hardships which would have overpowered him six months before, did not feel particularly hungry or weary that morning. No one in the army had caught more quickly than he the spirit of Stonewall Jackson. He could endure anything, and in another hour or two they would pass out of this wilderness of forest and snow, and attack the enemy. Bath was just ahead.

A thrill passed through the whole army. Everybody knew that Jackson was about to attack. While the first and reluctant sun of dawn was trying to pierce the heavy clouds, the regiments, spreading out to right and left to enclose Bath, began to march. Then the sun gave up its feeble attempts, the clouds closed in entirely, the wind began to blow hard, and with it came a blinding snow, and then a bitter hail.

Harry had been sent by Jackson to the right flank with orders and he was to remain there, unless it became necessary to inform the commander that some regiment was not doing its duty. But he found them all marching forward, and, falling in with the Invincibles, he marched with them. Yet it was impossible for the lines to retain cohesion or regularity, so fierce was the beat of the storm.

It was an alternation of blinding snow and of hail that fairly stung. Often the officers could not see the men thirty yards distant, and there was no way of knowing whether the army was marching forward in the complete half circle as planned. Regiments might draw apart, leaving wide gaps between, and no one would know it in all that hurricane.

Harry rode by the side of Colonel Leonidas Talbot and Lieutenant-Colonel Hector St. Hilaire, who were leading the Invincibles in person. Both had gray military cloaks drawn around them, but Harry saw that they were shivering with cold as they sat on their horses, with the snow accumulating on their shoulders and on the saddles around them. In truth, the foot cavalry had rather the better of it, as the hard marching kept up the circulation.

"Not much like the roses of Charleston," said Colonel Talbot, faintly smiling.

"But I'm glad to be here," said Harry, "although I will admit, sir, that I did not expect a campaign to the North Pole."

"Neither did I, but I'm prepared for anything now, under the commander that we have. Bear in mind, my young friend, that this is for your private ear only."

"Of course, sir! What was that? Wasn't it a rifle shot?"

"The report is faint, but it was certainly made by a rifle. And hark, there are others! We've evidently come upon their outposts! Confound this storm! It keeps us from seeing more than twenty yards in front of us!"

The scattered rifle fire continued, and the weary soldiers raised their heads which they had bent to shelter their eyes from the driving snow and hail. Pulses leaped up again, and blood sparkled. The whole army rushed forward. The roofs of houses came into view, and there was Bath.

But the firing had been merely that of a small rear guard, skirmishers who surrendered promptly. The garrison, warned doubtless by Shepard, and then the scouting troop, had escaped across the river, but Jackson's wintry march was not wholly in vain. The fleeing Union troops had no time either to carry away or destroy the great stores of supplies, accumulated there for the winter, and the starving and freezing Southerners plunged at once into the midst of plenty, ample compensation to the young privates.

The population, ardently Southern, as everywhere in these Virginia towns, welcomed the army with wild enthusiasm. Officers and soldiers were taken into the houses, as many as Bath could hold, and enormous fires were built in the open spaces for the others. They also showed the way at once to the magazines, where the Union supplies were heaped up.

Harry, at the direction of his general, went with one of the detachments to seize these. Their first prize was an old but large storehouse, crammed full of the things they needed most. The tall mountain youth, Seth Moore, was one of his men, and he proved to be a prince of looters.

"Blankets! blankets!" cried Moore. "Here they are, hundreds of 'em! An' look at these barrels! Bacon! Beef! Crackers! An' look at the piles of cheese! Oh, Lieutenant Kenton, how my mouth waters! Can't I bite into one o' them cheeses?"

"Not yet," said Harry, whose own mouth was watering, too, "but you can, Seth, within ten minutes at the farthest. The whole army must bite at once."

"That's fa'r an' squar', but ain't this richness! Cove oysters, cans an' cans of 'em, an' how I love 'em! An' sardines, too, lots of 'em! Why, I could bite right through the tin boxes to get at 'em. An' rice, an' hominy, an' bags o' flour. Why, the North has been sendin' whole train loads of things down here for us to eat!"

"And she has been sending more than that," said Harry. "Here are five or six hundred fine breech-loading rifles, and hundreds of thousands of cartridges. She's been sending us arms and ammunition with which to fight her!"

His boyish spirit burst forth. Even though an officer, he could not control them, and he was radiant as the looting Seth Moore himself. He went out to report the find and to take measures concerning it. On his way he met hundreds of the Southern youths who had already put on heavy blue overcoats found in the captured stores. The great revulsion had come. They were laughing and cheering and shaking the hands of one another. It was a huge picnic, all the more glorious because they had burst suddenly out of the storm and the icy wilderness.

But order was soon restored, and wrapped in warm clothing they feasted like civilized men, the great fires lighting up the whole town with a cheerful glow. Harry was summoned to new duties. He was also a new man. Warmth and food had doubled his vitality, and he was ready for any errand on which Jackson might send him.

While it was yet snowing, he rode with a half dozen troopers toward the Potomac. On the other side was a small town which also held a Union garrison. Scouting warily along the shores, Harry discovered that the garrison was still there. Evidently the enemy believed in the protection of the river, or many of their leaders could not yet wholly believe that Jackson and his army, making a forced march in the dead of winter, were at hand.

But he had no doubt that his general would attend to these obstinate men, and he rode back to Bath with the news. Jackson gave his worn troops a little more rest. They were permitted to spend all that day and night at Bath, luxuriating and renewing their strength and spirits.

Harry slept, for the first time in many nights, in a house, and he made the most of it, because he doubted whether he would have another such chance soon. Dawn found the army up and ready to march away from this place of delight.

They went up and down the Potomac three or four days, scattering or capturing small garrisons, taking fresh supplies and spreading consternation among the Union forces in Northern Virginia and Maryland. It was all done in the most bitter winter weather and amid storms of snow and hail. The roads were slippery with sleet, and often the cavalry were compelled to dismount and lead their horses long distances. There was little fighting because the Northern enemy was always in numbers too small to resist, but there was a great deal of hard riding and many captures.

News of Jackson's swoop began to filter through to both Richmond and Washington. In Richmond they wondered and rejoiced. In Washington they wondered, but did not rejoice. They had not expected there any blow to be struck in the dead of winter, and Lincoln demanded of his generals why they could not do as well. Distance and the vagueness of the news magnified Jackson's exploits and doubled his numbers. Eyes were turned with intense anxiety toward that desolate white expanse of snow and ice, in the midst of which he was operating.

Jackson finally turned his steps toward Romney, which had been the Union headquarters, and his men, exhausted and half starved, once more dragged themselves over the sleety roads. Winter offered a fresh obstacle at every turn. Even the spirits of Harry, who had borrowed so much from the courage of Jackson, sank somewhat. As they pulled themselves through the hills on their last stage toward Romney, he was walking. His horse had fallen three times that day on the ice, and was now too timid to carry his owner.

So Harry led him. The boy's face and hands were so much chapped and cracked with the cold that they bled at times. But he wasted no sympathy on himself. It was the common fate of the army. Jackson and his generals, themselves, suffered in the same way. Jackson was walking, too, for a while, leading his own horse.

Harry was sent back to bring up the Invincibles, as Romney was now close at hand, and there might be a fight. He found his old colonel and lieutenant-colonel walking over the ice. Both were thin, and were black under the eyes with privation and anxiety. These were not in appearance the men whom he had known in gay and sunny Charleston, though in spirit the same. They gave Harry a welcome and hoped that the enemy would wait for them in Romney.

"I don't think so," said Harry, "but I've orders for you from General Jackson to bring up the Invincibles as fast as possible."

"Tell General Jackson that we'll do our best," said Colonel Talbot, as he looked back at his withered column.

They seemed to Harry to be withered indeed, they were so gaunt with hardship and drawn up so much with cold. Many wore the blue Northern overcoats that they had captured at Bath, and more had tied up their throats and ears in the red woolen comforters of the day, procured at the towns through which they passed. They, too, were gaunt of cheek and black under the eye like their officers.

The Invincibles under urging increased their speed, but not much. Little reserve strength was left in them. Langdon and St. Clair, who had been sent along the line, returned to Colonel Talbot where Harry was still waiting.

"They're not going as fast as a railroad train," said Langdon in an aside to Harry, "but they're doing their best. You can't put in a well more than you can take out of it, and they're marching now not on their strength, but their courage. Still, it might be worse. We might all be dead."

"But we're not dead, by a big margin, and I think we'll make another haul at Romney."

"But Old Jack won't let us stay and enjoy it. I never saw a man so much in love with marching. The steeper the hills and mountains, the colder the day, the fiercer the sleet and snow, the better he likes it."

"The fellow who said General Jackson didn't care anything about our feet told the truth," said St. Clair, thoughtfully. "The general is not a cruel man, but he thinks more of Virginia and the South, and our cause, than he does of us. If it were necessary to do so to win he'd sacrifice us to the last man and himself with us."

"And never think twice before doing it. You've sized him up," said Harry. The army poured into Romney and found no enemy. Again a garrison had escaped through the mountain snows when the news reached it that Jackson was at hand. But they found supplies of food, filled their empty stomachs, and as Langdon had foretold, quickly started anew in search of another enemy elsewhere.

But the men finally broke down under the driving of the merciless Jackson. Many of them began to murmur. They had left the bleeding trail of their feet over many an icy road, and some said they were ready to lie down in the snow and die before they would march another mile. A great depression, which was physical rather than mental, a depression born of exhaustion and intense bodily suffering, seized the army.

Jackson, although with a will of steel, was compelled to yield. Slowly and with reluctance, he led his army back toward Winchester, leaving a large garrison in Romney. But Harry knew what he had done, although nothing more than skirmishes had been fought. He had cleared a wide region of the enemy. He had inspired enthusiasm in the South, and he had filled the North with alarm. The great movement of McClellan on Richmond must beware of its right flank. A dangerous foe was there who might sting terribly, and men had learned already that none knew when or whence Jackson might come.

A little more than three weeks after their departure Harry and his friends and the army, except the portion left in garrison at Romney, returned to Winchester, the picturesque and neat little Virginia city so loyal to the South. It looked very good indeed to Harry as he drew near. He liked the country, rolling here and there, the hills crested with splendid groves of great trees. The Little North Mountain a looming blue shadow to the west, and the high Massanutton peaks to the south seemed to guard it round. And the valley itself was rich and warm with the fine farms spread out for many miles. Despite the engrossing pursuit of the enemy and of victory and glory, Harry's heart thrilled at the sight of the red brick houses of Winchester.

Here came a period of peace so far as war was concerned, but of great anxiety to Harry and the whole army. The government at Richmond began to interfere with Jackson. It thought him too bold, even rash, and it wanted him to withdraw the garrison at Romney, which was apparently exposed to an attack by the enemy in great force. It was said that McClellan had more than two hundred thousand men before Washington, and an overwhelming division from it might fall at any time upon the Southern force at Romney.

Harry, being a member of Jackson's staff, and having become a favorite with him, knew well his reasons for standing firm. January, which had furnished so fierce a month of winter, was going. The icy country was breaking up under swift thaws, and fields and destroyed roads were a vast sea of mud in which the feet of infantry, the hoofs of horses and the wheels of cannon would sink deep.

Jackson did not believe that McClellan had enough enterprise to order a march across such an obstacle, but recognizing the right of his government to expect obedience, he sent his resignation to Richmond. Harry knew of it, his friends knew of it, and their hearts sank like plummets in a pool.

Another portion of the Invincibles had been drawn off to reinforce Johnston's army before Richmond, as they began to hear rumors now that McClellan would come by sea instead of land, and their places were filled with more recruits from the valley of Virginia. Scarcely a hundred of the South Carolinians were left, but the name, "The Invincibles" and the chief officers, stayed behind. Jackson had been unwilling to part with Colonel Talbot and Lieutenant-Colonel

St. Hilaire, experienced and able West Pointers. Langdon and St. Clair also stayed.

Harry talked over the resignation with these friends of his, and they showed an anxiety not less than his own. It had become evident to the two veteran West Pointers that Jackson was the man. Close contact with him had enabled them to read his character and immense determination.

"I hope that our government at Richmond will decline this resignation and give him a free hand," said Colonel Talbot to Harry. "It would be a terrible loss if he were permitted to drop out of the army. I tell you for your own private ear that I have taken it upon me to Write a letter of protest to President Davis himself. I felt that I could do so, because Mr. Davis and myself were associated closely in the Mexican War."

The answer came in time from Richmond. Stonewall Jackson was retained and a freer hand was given to him. Harry and all his comrades felt an immense relief, but he did not know until long afterward how near the Confederacy had come to losing the great Jackson.

Benjamin, the Secretary of War, and President Davis both were disposed to let him go, but the powerful intervention of Governor Letcher of Virginia induced them to change their minds. Moreover, hundreds of letters from leading Virginians who knew Jackson well poured in upon him, asking him to withdraw the resignation. So it was arranged and Jackson remained, biding his time for the while at Winchester, until he could launch the thunderbolt.

A pleasant month for Harry, and all the young staff officers passed at Winchester. The winter of intense cold had now become one of tremendous rain. It poured and it poured, and it never ceased to pour. Between Winchester and Washington and McClellan's great army was one vast flooded area, save where the hills and mountains stood.

But in Winchester the Southern troops were warm and comfortable. It was a snug town within its half circle of mountains. Its brick and wooden houses were solid and good. The young officers when they went on errands trod on pavements of red brick, and oaks and elms and maples shaded them nearly all the way.

When Harry, who went oftenest on such missions, returned to his general with the answers, he walked up a narrow street, where the silver maples, which would soon begin to bud under the continuous rain, grew thickest, and came to a small building in which other officers like himself wrote at little tables or waited in full uniform to be sent upon like errands. If it were yet early he would find Jackson there, but if it were late he would cross a little stretch of grass to the parsonage, the large and solid house, where the Presbyterian minister, Dr. Graham, lived, and where Jackson, with his family, who had joined him, now made his home in this month of waiting.

It was here that Harry came one evening late in February. It had been raining as usual, and he wore one of the long Union overcoats captured at Bath, blue then but a faded grayish brown now. However, the gray Confederate uniform beneath it was neat and looked fresh. Harry was always careful about his clothing, and the example of St. Clair inspired him to greater efforts. Besides, there was a society in Winchester, including many handsome young women of the old Virginia families, and even a budding youth who was yet too young for serious sentimentalism, could not ignore its existence.

It was twilight and the cold rain was still coming down steadily, as Harry walked across the grass, and looked out of the wet dusk at the manse. Lights were shining from every window, and there was warmth around his heart. The closer association of many weeks with Jackson had not only increased his admiration, but also had given the general a great place in the affection that a youth often feels for an older man whom he deems a genius or a hero.

Harry walked upon a little portico, and taking off the overcoat shook out the rain drops. Then he hung it on a hook against the wall of the house. The door was open six inches or so, and a ribbon of brilliant light from within fell across the floor of the portico.

Harry looked at the light and smiled. He was young and he loved gayety. He smiled again when he heard within the sound of laughter. Then he pushed the door farther open and entered. Now the laughter rose to a shout, and it was accompanied by the sound of footsteps. A man, thick of hair and beard, was running down a stairway. Perched high upon his shoulders was a child of three or four years, with both hands planted firmly in the thick hair. The small feet crossed over the man's neck kicked upon his chest, but he seemed to enjoy the sport as much as the child did.

Harry paused and stood at attention until the man saw him. Then he saluted respectfully and said to General Jackson:

"I wish to report to you, sir, that I delivered the order to General Garnett, as you directed, and here, sir, is his reply."

He handed a note to the general, who read it, thrust it into his pocket, and said:

"That ends your labors for the day, Lieutenant Kenton. Come in now and join us."

He picked up the child again, and carrying it in his arms, led the way into an inner room, where he gave it to a nurse. Then they passed into the library, where Dr. Graham, several generals and two or three of Winchester's citizens were gathered.

All gave Harry a welcome. He knew them well, and he looked around with satisfaction at the large room, with its rows and rows of books, bound mostly in dark leather, volumes of theology, history, essays, poetry, and of the works of Walter Scott and Jane Austen. Jackson himself was a rigid Presbyterian, and he and Dr. Graham had many a long talk in this room on religion and other topics almost equally serious.

But to-night they were in a bright mood. A mountaineer had come in with four huge wild turkeys, which he insisted upon giving to General Jackson himself, and guests had been asked in to help eat them.

Nearly twenty people sat around the minister's long table. The turkeys, at least enough for present needs, were cooked beautifully, and all the succulent dishes which the great Virginia valleys produce so fruitfully were present. General Jackson himself, at the request of the minister, said grace, and he said it so devoutly and so sincerely that it always impressed the hearers with a sense of its reality.

It was full dusk and the rain was beating on the windows, when the black attendants began to serve the guests at the great board. Several ladies, including the general's wife, were present. The room was lighted brilliantly, and a big fire burned in the wide fireplace at the end. To Harry, three seats away from General Jackson, there was a startling contrast between the present moment and that swift campaign of theirs through the wintry mountains where the feet of the soldiers left bloody trails on the ice and snow.

It was a curious fact that for a few instants the mountain and the great cold were real and this was but fancy. He looked more than once at the cheerful faces and the rosy glow of the fire, before he could convince himself that he was in truth here in Winchester, with all this comfort, even luxury, around him.

Sitting next to him was a lady of middle age, Mrs. Howard, of prominence in the town and a great friend of the Grahams. Harry realized suddenly that while the others were talking he had said nothing, and he felt guilty of discourtesy. He began an apology, but Mrs. Howard, who had known him very well since he had been in Winchester, learning to call him by his first name, merely smiled and the smile was at once maternal and somewhat sad.

"No apologies are needed, Harry," she said in a low tone that the others might not hear. "I read your thoughts. They were away in the mountains with a marching army. All this around us speaks of home and peace, but it cannot last. All of you will be going soon."

"That's true, Mrs. Howard, I was thinking of march and battle, and I believe you're right in saying that we'll all go soon. That is what we're for."

She smiled again a little sadly.

"You're a good boy, Harry," she said, "and I hope that you and all your comrades will come back in safety to Winchester. But that is enough croaking from an old woman and I'm ashamed of myself. Did you ever see a happier crowd than the one gathered here?"

"Not since I was in my father's house when the relatives would come to help us celebrate Christmas."

"When did you hear from your father?" asked Mrs. Howard, whose warm sympathies had caused Harry to tell her of his life and of his people whom he had left behind in Kentucky.

"Just after the terrible disaster at Donelson. He was in the fort, but he escaped with Forrest's cavalry, and he went into Mississippi to join the army under Albert Sidney Johnston. He sent a letter for me to my home, Pendleton, under cover to my old teacher, Dr. Russell, who forwarded it to me. It came only this morning."

"How does he talk?"

"Hopefully, though he made no direct statement. I suppose he was afraid to do so lest the letter fall into the hands of the Yankees, but I imagine that General Johnston's army is going to attack General Grant's."

"If General Johnston can win a victory it will help us tremendously, but I fear that man, Grant. They say that he had no more men at Donelson than we, but he took the fort and its garrison."

"It's true. Our affairs have not been going well in the West."

Harry was downcast for a few moments. Much of their Western news had come through the filter of Richmond, but despite the brighter color that the Government tried to put on it, it remained black. Forts and armies had been taken. Nothing had been able to stop Grant. But youth again came to Harry. He could not resist the bright light and the happy talk about him. Bitter thoughts fled.

General Jackson was in fine humor. He and Dr. Graham had started to discuss a problem in Presbyterian theology in which both were deeply interested, but they quickly changed it in deference to the younger and lighter spirits about them. Harry had never before seen his general in so mellow a vein. Perhaps it was the last blaze of the home-loving spirit, before entering into that storm of battle which henceforth was to be his without a break.

The general, under urging, told of his life as an orphan boy in his uncle's rough home in the Virginia wilderness, how he had been seized once by the wanderlust, then so strong in nearly all Americans, and how he and his brother had gone all the way down the Ohio to the Mississippi, where they had camped on a little swampy island, earning their living by cutting wood for the steamers on the two rivers.

"How old were you two then, General?" asked Dr. Graham.

"The older of us was only twelve. But in those rough days boys matured fast and became self-reliant at a very early age. We did not run away. There wasn't much opposition to our going. Our uncle was sure that we'd come back alive, and though we arrived again in Virginia, five or six hundred miles from our island in the river, all rags and filled with fever, we were not regarded as prodigal sons. It was what hundreds, yes, thousands of other boys did. In our pleasant uplands we soon got rid of both rags and fever."

"And you did not wish to return to the wilderness?"

"The temptation was strong at times, but it was defeated by other ambitions. There was school and I liked sports. These soon filled up my life."

Harry knew much more about the life of Jackson, which the modesty of his hero kept him from telling. Looking at the strong, active figure of the man so near him he knew that he had once been delicate, doomed in childhood, as many thought, to consumption, inherited from his mother. But a vigorous life in the open air had killed all such germs. He was a leader in athletic sports. He was a great horseman, and often rode as a jockey for his uncle in the horse races which the open-air Virginians loved so well, and in which they indulged so much. He could cut down a tree or run a saw-mill, or drive four horses to a wagon, or seek deer through the mountains with the sturdiest hunter of them all. And upon top of this vigorous boyhood had come the long and severe training at West Point, the most thorough and effective military school the world has ever known.

Harry did not wonder, as he looked at his general, that he could dare and do so much. He might be awkward in appearance, he might wear his clothes badly, but the boy at ten years had been a man, doing a man's work and with a man's soul. He had come into the field, no parade soldier, but with a body and mind as tough and enduring as steel, the whole surcharged and heated with a spirit of fire.

Both Harry and Mrs. Howard had become silent and were watching the general. For some reason Jackson was more moved than usual. His manner did not depart from its habitual gravity. He made no gestures, but the blue eyes under the heavy brows were irradiated by a peculiar flashing light.

The long dinner went on. It was more of a festival than a banquet, and Harry at last gave himself up entirely to its luxurious warmth. The foreboding that their mellow days in the pleasant little city were over, was gone, but it was destined to come again. Now, after the dinner was finished, and the great table was cleared away, they sat and talked, some in the dining room and some in the library.

It was still raining, that cold rain which at times turns for a moment or two to snow, and it dashed in gusts against the window panes. Harry was with some of the younger people in the library, where they were playing at games. The sport lagged presently and he went to a window, where he stood between the curtain and the glass.

He saw the outside dimly, the drenched lawn, and the trees beyond, under which two or three sentinels, wrapped closely in heavy coats, walked to and fro. He gazed at them idly, and then a shadow passed between him and them. He thought at first that it was a blurring of the glass by some stronger gust of rain, but the next moment his experience told him that it could not be so. He had seen a shadow, and the shadow was that of a man, sliding along against the wall of the house, in order that he might not be seen by a sentinel.

Harry's suspicions were up and alive in an instant. In this border country spies were numerous. It was easy to be a spy where people looked alike and spoke the same language with the same accent. His suspicions, too, centered at once upon Shepard, whom he knew to be so daring and skillful.

The lad was prompt to act. He slipped unnoticed into the hall, put on his greatcoat, felt of the pistol in his belt, opened the front door and stepped out into the dark and the rain.

CHAPTER V.
THE NORTHERN ADVANCE

Harry flattened himself against the wall and all his training and inherited instincts came promptly to his service. He knew that he, too, would be in the shadow there, where it was not likely that the sentinels could see him owing to the darkness of the night. Then he moved cautiously toward the window where he had seen the outline.

The cold rain beat on his face and he saw the figures of the sentinels moving back and forth, but, black against the black wall, he was confident that he could not be seen by them. Half way to the window, his eyes now having gotten used to the darkness, he knelt down and examined the earth, made soft by the rains. He distinctly saw footprints, undoubtedly those of a man, leading by the edge of the wall, and now he knew that he had not been mistaken.

Harry came to the window himself, and, glancing in, he saw that the merriment was going on unabated. He continued his search, following the revealing foot prints. He went nearly all the way around the house and then lost them among heavy shrubbery. He surmised that at this point the spy — he was sure that it was a spy and sure, too, that it was Shepard — had left the place, passing between the sentinels in the rainy dark.

He spoke to the sentinels, who knew him well, and they were quite confident that nobody had come within their lines. But Harry, while keeping his own counsel, held another opinion and he was equally positive about it. He was returning to the house, when he heard the tread of hoofs, and then a horseman spoke with the sentinels. He looked back and recognized Sherburne.

The young captain was holding himself erect in the saddle, but his horse and his uniform were covered with red mud. There were heavy black lines under his eyes and his face, despite his will, showed strong signs of weariness. Sure that his mission was important, Harry went to him at once.

"Is General Jackson inside?" asked Sherburne.

"Yes, and he has not yet gone to bed," replied Harry, looking at the lighted windows.

"Then ask him if I can see him at once. He sent my troop and me on a scout toward Romney this morning. I have news, news that cannot wait."

"Of course, he'll see you. Come inside."

Sherburne slipped from his horse. Harry noticed that it was not his usual elastic spring. He seemed almost to fall to the ground, and the horse, no hand on the reins, still stood motionless, his head drooping. It was evident that Sherburne was in the last stages of exhaustion, and now that he came nearer his face showed great anxiety as well as weariness.

Harry opened the door promptly and pushed him inside. Then he helped him off with his wet and muddy overcoat, pushed him into a chair, and said:

"I'll announce you to General Jackson, and he'll see you at once."

Harry knew that Jackson would not linger a second, when a messenger of importance came, and he went into the library where the minister and the general stood talking. General Jackson held in one hand a large leather-covered volume, and with the forefinger of the other hand he was pointing to a paragraph in it. The minister was saying something that Harry did not catch, but he believed that they were arguing some disputed point of Presbyterian doctrine.

When Jackson saw Harry he closed the book instantly, and put it on the shelf. He had seen in the eyes of his aide that he was coming with no common message.

"Captain Sherburne is in the hall, sir," said the boy. "He has come back from the scout toward Romney."

"Bring him in."

The minister quietly slipped out, as Sherburne entered, but Jackson bade Harry remain, saying that he might have orders for him to carry.

"What have you to tell me, Captain Sherburne?" asked Jackson.

"We saw the patrols of the enemy, and we took two prisoners. We learned that McClellan's army is showing signs of moving, and we saw with our own eyes that Banks and Shields are preparing for the same. They threaten us here in Winchester."

"What force do you think Banks has?"

"He must have forty thousand men."

"A good guess. The figures of my spies say thirty-eight thousand, and we can muster scarcely five thousand here. We must move."

Jackson spoke without emotion. His words were cold and dry, even formal. Harry's heart sank. If eight times their numbers were advancing upon them, then they must abandon Winchester. They must leave to the enemy this pleasant little city, so warmly devoted to the Southern cause and confess weakness and defeat to these friends who had done so much for them during their stay.

He felt the full bitterness of the blow. The people of the South— little immigration had gone there—were knit together more closely by ties of kinship than those of the North. Harry through the maternal line was, like most Kentuckians, of Virginia descent, and even here in Winchester he had found cousins, more or less removed it was true, but it was kinship, nevertheless, and they had made the most of it. It would have been easier for him were strangers instead of friends to see their retreat.

"Captain Sherburne, you will go to your quarters and sleep. It is obvious that you need rest," said Jackson. "Mr. Kenton, you will wait and take the orders that I am going to write."

Sherburne saluted and withdrew promptly. Jackson turned to a shelf of the library on which lay pen, ink and paper, and standing before it rapidly wrote several notes. It was his favorite attitude— habit of his West Point days—to write or read standing.

It took him less than five minutes to write the notes, and he handed them to Harry to deliver without delay to the brigade commanders. His tones were incisive and charged with energy. Harry felt the electric thrill pass to himself, and with a quick salute he was once more out in the rain.

Some of the brigadiers were asleep, and grumbled when Harry awoke them, but the orders soon sent the last remnants of sleep flying. The boy did not linger, but returned quickly to the manse, where

General Jackson met him at the door. Other aides were coming or going, but all save one or two windows of the house were dark now, and the merrymaking was over.

"You have delivered the orders?" asked Jackson.

"Yes, sir, all of them."

Harry also told then of the face that he had seen at the window and his belief concerning its identity.

"Very likely," said Jackson, "but we cannot pursue him now. Now go to headquarters and sleep, but I shall want you at dawn."

Harry was ready before the first sunlight, and that day consternation spread through Winchester. The enemy was about to advance in overwhelming force, and Jackson was going to leave them. Johnston was retreating before McClellan, and Jackson in the valley must retreat before Banks.

There could be no doubt about the withdrawal of Jackson. The preparations were hurried forward with the utmost vigor. A train took the sick to Staunton, and in one of the coaches went Mrs. Jackson to her father's home. Town and camp were filled with talk of march and battle, and the younger rejoiced. They felt that a month of waiting had made them rusty.

Amid all the bustle Jackson found time to attend religious services, and also ordered every wagon that reached the camp with supplies to be searched. If liquor were found it was thrown at once upon the ground. The soldiers, even the recruits, knew that they were to follow a God-fearing man. Oliver Cromwell had come back to earth. But most of the soldiers were now disciplined thoroughly. The month they had spent at Winchester after the great raid had been devoted mostly to drill.

The day of departure came and the army, amid the good wishes of many friends in Winchester, filed out of the town. The great rains, which, it had seemed, would never cease, had ceased at last. There was a touch of spring in the air, and in sheltered places the grass was taking on deep tints of green.

During all the days of preparation Jackson had said nothing about his plan of retreat. The Virginians, lining the streets and watching so anxiously, did not know where he would seek refuge. And suddenly as they watched, a cheer, tremendous and involuntary, burst from them.

The heads of Jackson's columns were turned north. He was not marching away from the enemy. He was marching toward him. But the burst of elation was short. Even the civilians in Winchester knew that Jackson was hugely outnumbered.

Harry himself was astonished, and he gazed at his leader. What fathomless purpose lay beneath that stern, bearded face? Jackson's eyes expressed nothing. He and he alone knew what was in his mind.

But the troops asked no word from their leaders. The fact that their faces were turned toward the north was enough for them. They knew, too, of the heavy odds that were against them, but they were not afraid.

As Harry watched the young soldiers, many of whom sang as they marched, his own enthusiasm rose. He had seen companies in brilliant uniforms at Richmond, but no parade soldiers were here. There were few glimpses of color in the columns, but the men marched with a strong, elastic step. They had all been born upon the farms or in the little villages, and they were familiar with the hills and forests. They had been hunters, too, as soon as their arms were strong enough to hold rifle or shot gun. Most of them had killed deer or bear in the mountains, and all of them had known how to ride from earliest childhood. They had endured every hardship and they knew how to take care of themselves in any kind of country and in any kind of weather.

Harry smiled as he looked at their uniforms. How different they were from some of the gay young companies of Charleston! These uniforms had been spun for them and made for them by their own mothers and wives and sisters or sweethearts. They were all supposed to be gray, but there were many shades of gray, sometimes verging to a light blue, with butternut as the predominant color. They wore gray jackets, short of waist and single-breasted. Caps were giving way to soft felt hats, and boots had already been supplanted by broad, strong shoes, called brogans.

Many of the soldiers carried frying pans and skillets hung on the barrels of their rifles, simple kitchen utensils which constituted almost the whole of their cooking equipment. Their blankets and rubber sheets for sleeping were carried in light rolls on their backs. A toothbrush was stuck in a buttonhole. On their flanks or in front rode the cavalry, led by the redoubtable Turner Ashby, and there was in all their number scarcely a single horseman who did not ride like the Comanche Indian, as if he were born in the saddle. Ashby was a host in himself. He had often ridden as much as eighty miles a day to inspect his own pickets and those of the enemy, and it was told of him that he had once gone inside the Union lines in the disguise of a horse doctor.

The Northern cavalry, unused to the saddle, compared very badly with those of the South in the early years of the war. Ashby's men, moreover, rode over country that they had known all their lives. There was no forest footpath, no train among the hills hidden from them. But the cannon of Jackson's army was inferior. Here the mechanical genius of the North showed supreme.

Such was the little army of Jackson, somber to see, which marched forth upon a campaign unrivalled in the history of war. The men whom they were to meet were of staunch stock and spirit themselves. Banks, their commander, had worked in his youth as a common laborer in a cotton mill, and had forced himself up by vigor and energy, but Shields was a veteran of the Mexican War. Most of the troops had come from the west, and they, too, were used to every kind of privation and hardship.

Harry's duties carried him back and forth with the marching columns, but he lingered longest beside the Invincibles, only a regiment now, and that regiment composed almost wholly of Virginians. St. Clair was still in the smartest of uniforms, a contrast to the others, and as he nodded to Harry he told him that the troops expected to meet the enemy before night.

"I don't know how they got that belief," he said, "but I know it extends to all our men. What about it, Harry?"

"Stonewall Jackson alone knows, and he's not telling."

"They say that Banks is coming with ten to one!" said Langdon, "but it might be worse than that. It might be a hundred to one."

"It's hardly as bad as ten to one, Tom," said Harry with a laugh. "Ashby's men say it's only eight to one, and they know."

"It's all right, then," said Langdon, squaring his shoulders, and looking ferocious. "Ten to one would be a little rough on us, but I don't mind eight to one at all! at all! They say that the army of Banks is not many miles away. Is it so, Harry?"

"I suppose so. That's the news the cavalry bring in."

Harry rode on, saluting Colonel Talbot and Lieutenant-Colonel St. Hilaire as he passed. They returned the salutes, but said nothing, and in a few minutes he was with General Jackson again.

It was now March, and the spring was making headway in the great valley. The first flush of green was over everything. The snows were gone, the rains that followed were gone, too, and the earth was drying rapidly under the mild winds that blew from the mountains. It was evident to all that the forces of war were unloosed with the departure of winter.

The day was filled with excitement for Harry. The great Federal army was now so near that the rival pickets were almost constantly in touch. Only stern orders from Jackson kept his fiery cavalry from making attacks which might have done damage, but not damage enough. Banks, the Union leader, eminent through politics rather than war, having been Governor of Massachusetts, showed the utmost caution. Feeling secure in his numbers he resolved to risk nothing until he gained his main object — Winchester — and the efforts of Turner Ashby and his brilliant young lieutenants like Sherburne, could not lead him into any trap.

Night came and the Southern army stopped for supper and rest. The Northern army was then only four miles from Winchester, and within a half hour hostile pickets had been firing at one another. Yet the men ate calmly and lay down under the trees. Jackson called a council in a little grove. General Garnett, the commander of the Stonewall Brigade, all the colonels of the regiments, and the most trusted young officers of his staff were present. A little fire of fallen wood lighted up the anxious and earnest faces.

Jackson spoke rapidly. Harry had never before seen him show so much emotion and outward fire. He wanted to bring up all his men and attack the Union army at once. He believed that the surprise and the immense dash of the Southern troops would overcome the great odds. But the other officers shook their heads sadly. There had been a confusion of orders. Their own troops had been scattered and their supply trains were far away. If they attacked they would surely fall.

Jackson reluctantly gave up his plan and walked gloomily away. But he turned presently and beckoned to Harry and others of his staff. His eyes were shining. Some strange mood seemed to possess him.

"Mount at once, gentlemen," he said, "and ride with me. I'm going to Winchester."

One or two of the officers opened their mouths to protest, but checked the words when they saw Jackson's stern face. They sprang into the saddle, and scorning possible attack or capture by roving Union cavalry, galloped to the town.

Jackson drew rein before the manse, where Dr. Graham was already standing at the open door to meet him, runners from the town carrying ahead the news that Jackson was returning with his staff. It seemed that something the general had said to the minister the day before troubled him. Harry inferred from the words he heard that Jackson had promised the minister too much and now he was stung by conscience. Doubtless he had told Dr. Graham that he would never let the Federals take Winchester, and he had come to apologize for his mistake. Harry was not at all surprised. In fact, as he came to know him thoroughly, he was never surprised at anything this strange man and genius did.

Harry's surmise was right. Jackson was torn with emotion at being compelled to abandon Winchester, and he wanted to explain how it was to the friend whom he liked so well. He had thoughts even yet of striking the enemy that night and driving him away. Looking the minister steadily in the face, but not seeing him, seeing instead a field of battle, he said slowly, biting each word:

"I—will—yet—carry—out—this plan. I—will—think. It—must be done."

The minister said nothing, standing and staring at the general like one fascinated. He had never seen Jackson that way before. His face was lined with thought and his eyes burned like coals of fire. His hand fiercely clinched the hilt of his sword. He, who showed emotion so rarely, was overcome by it now.

But the fire in his eyes died, his head sank, and his hand fell from his sword.

"No, no," he said sadly. "I must not try it. Too many of my brave men would fall. I must withdraw, and await a better time."

Saying good-by to his friend he mounted and rode in silence from Winchester again, and silently the people saw him go. His staff followed without a word. When they reached a high hill overlooking the town Jackson paused and the others paused with him. All turned as if by one accord and looked at Winchester.

The skies were clear and a silver light shone over the town. It was a beautiful, luminous light and it heightened the beauty of spire, roof, and wall. Jackson looked at it a long time, the place where he had spent such a happy month, and then, his eye blazing again, he lifted his hand and exclaimed with fierce energy:

"That is the last council of war I will ever hold!"

Harry understood him. He knew that Jackson now felt that the council had been too slow and too timid. Henceforth he would be the sole judge of attack and retreat. But the general's emotion was quickly suppressed. Taking a last look at the little city that he loved so well, he rode rapidly away, and his staff followed closely at his heels.

That was a busy and melancholy night. The young troops, after all, were not to fight the enemy, but were falling back. Youth takes less account than age of odds, and they did not wish to retreat. Harry who had seen that look upon Jackson's face, when he gazed back at Winchester, felt that he would strike some mighty counter-blow, but he did not know how or when.

The army withdrew slowly toward Strasburg, twenty-five miles away, and the next morning the Union forces in overwhelming numbers occupied Winchester. Meantime the North was urging McClellan with his mighty army to advance on Richmond, and Stonewall Jackson and his few thousands who had been driven out of Winchester were forgotten. The right flank of McClellan, defended by Banks and forty thousand men, would be secure.

There was full warrant for the belief of McClellan. It seemed to Harry as they retreated up the valley that they were in a hopeless checkmate. What could a few thousand men, no matter how brave and hardy, do against an army as large as that of Banks? But he was cheered somewhat by the boldness and activity of the cavalry under Ashby. These daring horsemen skirmished continually with the enemy, and Harry, as he passed back and forth with orders, saw much of it.

Once he drew up with the Invincibles, now a Virginia instead of a South Carolina regiment, and sitting on horseback with his old friends, watched the puffs of smoke to the rear, where Ashby's men kept back the persistent skirmishers of the North.

"Colonel," said Harry to Colonel Talbot, "what do you think of it? Shall we ever make headway against such a force? Or shall we be compelled to retreat until we make a junction with the main army under General Johnston?"

Colonel Talbot glanced back at the puffs of white smoke, and suddenly his eyes seemed to flash with the fire that Harry had seen in Jackson's when he looked upon the Winchester that he must leave.

"No, Harry, I don't believe we'll keep on retreating," he replied. "I was with General Taylor when he fell back before the Mexican forces under Santa Anna which outnumbered him five to one. But at Buena Vista he stopped falling back, and everybody knows the glorious victory we won there over overwhelming odds. The Yankees are not Mexicans. Far from it. They are as brave as anybody. But Stonewall Jackson is a far greater general than Zachary Taylor."

"I'm hoping for the best," said Harry.

"We'll all wait and see," said the colonel.

They stopped falling back at Mount Jackson, twenty-five miles from Winchester, and the army occupied a strong position. Harry felt instinctively that they would fall back no more, and his spirits began to rise again. But the facts upon which his hopes were based were small. Jackson had less than five thousand men, and in the North he was wiped off the map. It was no longer necessary for cabinet members and generals to take him into consideration.

Jackson now out of the way, the main portion of the army under Banks was directed to march eastward to Manassas, while a heavy detachment still more than double Jackson's in numbers remained in the valley. Meanwhile McClellan, with his right flank clear, was going by sea to Richmond, goaded to action at last by the incessant demands of a people which had a right to expect much of his great and splendidly equipped army.

Harry was with Stonewall Jackson when the news of these movements reached them, brought by Philip Sherburne, who, emulating his commander, Turner Ashby, seemed never to rest or grow weary.

"General Banks is moving eastward to cover the eastern approaches to Washington," said the young captain, "while General Shields with 12,000 men is between us and Winchester."

"So," said Jackson. Sherburne looked at him earnestly, but he gave no sign.

"Ride back to your chief and tell him I thank him for his vigilance and to report to me promptly everything that he may discover," said Jackson. "You may ride with him also, Mr. Kenton, and return to me in an hour with such news as you may have."

Harry went gladly. Sometimes he longed to be at the front with Turner Ashby, there where the rifles were often crackling.

"What will he do? Will he turn now?" said Sherburne anxiously to Harry.

"I heard General Jackson say that he would never hold another council of war, and he's keeping his word. Nobody knows his plans, but I think he'll attack. I feel quite sure of it, captain."

They came soon to a field in which Turner Ashby was sitting on a horse, examining points further down the valley with a pair of powerful glasses. Sherburne reported briefly and Ashby nodded, but did not take the glasses from his eyes. Harry also looked down the valley and his strong sight enabled him to detect tiny, moving figures which he knew were those of Union scouts and skirmishers.

Despite his youth and the ardor of battle in his nostrils, Harry felt the tragedy of war in this pleasant country. It was a noble landscape, that of the valley between the blue mountains. Before him stretched low hills, covered here and there with fine groups of oak or pine without undergrowth. Houses of red brick, with porticoes and green shutters, stood in wide grounds. Most of them were inhabited yet, and their owners always brought information to the soldiers of the South, never to those of the North.

The earth had not yet dried fully from the great rains, and horses and cannon wheels sank deep in the mud, whenever they left the turnpike running down the center of the valley and across which a

Northern army under Shields lay. The men in blue occupied a wide stretch of grassy fields on the east, and on the west a low hill, with a small grove growing on the crest. Dominating the whole were the lofty cliffs of North Mountain on the west. The main force of the North, strengthened with cannon, lay to the east of the turnpike. But on the hill to the west were two strong batteries and near it were lines of skirmishers. Shields, a veteran of the Mexican war himself, was not present at this moment, but Kimball, commanding in his absence, was alert and did not share the general belief that Stonewall Jackson might be considered non-existent.

Harry, things coming into better view, the longer he looked, saw much of the Union position, and Turner Ashby presently handed him the glasses. Then he plainly discerned the guns and a great mass of infantry, with the colors waving above them in the gentle breeze.

"They're there," said Turner Ashby, dryly. "If we want to attack they're waiting."

Harry rode back to Jackson, and told him that the whole Union force was in position in front, and then the boy knew at once that a battle was coming. The bearded, silent man showed no excitement, but sent orders thick and fast to the different parts of his army. The cavalry led by Ashby began to press the enemy hard in front of a little village called Kernstown. A regiment with two guns led the advance on the west of the turnpike, and the heavier mass of infantry marched across the fields on the left.

Harry, as his duty bade him, kept beside his general, who was riding near the head of the infantry. The feet of men and horses alike sank deep in the soft earth of the fields, but they went forward at a good pace, nevertheless. Their blood was hot and leaping. There was an end to retreats. They saw the enemy and they were eager to rush upon him.

The pulses in Harry's temples were beating hard. He already considered himself a veteran of battle, but he could not see it near without feeling excitement. A long line of fire had extended across the valley. White puffs of smoke arose like innumerable jets of steam. The crackle of the rifles was incessant and at the distance sounded like the ripping of heavy cloth.

Then came a deep heavy crash that made the earth tremble. The two batteries on the hill had opened at a range of a mile on Jackson's infantry. Those men of the North were good gunners and Harry heard the shells and solid shot screaming and hissing around. Despite his will he could not keep from trembling for a while, but presently it ceased, although the fire was growing heavier.

But the Southern infantry were so far away that the artillery fire did not harm. Ever urged on by Jackson, they pressed through fields and marshy ground, their destination a low ridge from which, as a place of advantage, they could reply to the Union batteries. From the east and from a point near a church called the Opequon came the thunder of their own guns advancing up the other side of the turnpike.

Now the great marching qualities of Jackson's men were shown. Not in vain had they learned to be foot cavalry. They pressed forward through the deep mud and always the roar of the increasing fire called them on. Before them stretched the ridge and Harry was in fear lest the enemy spring forward and seize it first.

But no foe appeared in front of them in the fields, and then with a rush they were at the foot of the ridge. Another rush and they had climbed it. Harry from its crest saw the wide field of combat and he knew that the greater battle had just begun.

CHAPTER VI.
KERNSTOWN

The long winding lines of the two armies spread over a maze of fields, woods and thickets, with here and there a stone wall and scattered low hills, which could be used as points of strength. Jackson's men, led by able officers, were pushing forward with all their might. The woods, the thickets and the mud nullified to some extent the superior power of the Northern artillery, but the rifles were pouring forth shattering volleys, many at close range.

Harry felt his horse stagger just after he reached the crest of the hill, but he took no notice of it until a few minutes later, when the animal began to shiver. He leaped clear just in time, for when the shiver ceased, the horse plunged forward, fell on his side and lay dead. As Harry straightened himself on his feet a bullet went through the brim of his cap, and another clipped his epaulet.

"Those must be western men shooting at you, Harry," said a voice beside him. "But it could have been worse. You're merely grazed, when you could have been hit and hit deep."

It was Langdon, cool and imperturbable, who was speaking. He was regarding Harry rather quizzically, as the boy mechanically brushed the mud from his clothes.

"Force of habit," said Langdon, and then he suddenly grasped Harry and pulled him to his knees. There was a tremendous crash in front of them, and a storm of bullets swept over their heads.

"I saw a Yankee officer give the word, and then a million riflemen rose from the bushes and fired straight at us!" shouted Langdon. "You stay here! See the Invincibles are all about you!"

Harry saw that he had in truth fallen among the Invincibles. There was St. Clair, immaculate, a blazing red spot in either cheek, gazing at the great swarms of riflemen in front. Colonel Leonidas Talbot and Lieutenant-Colonel Hector St. Hilaire, those veteran West Pointers, were stalking up and down in front of their lines, fiercely bidding their men to lie down. But Harry knew that his duty was elsewhere.

"I belong to the general!" he exclaimed. "I must join him!"

Casting one glance of regret at the fallen horse that had served him so well he rushed toward General Jackson, who with the rest of his staff had dismounted. The general, showing no emotion or anxiety, was watching the doubtful combat.

Along the whole line the battle was deepening. The able West Pointers on the Northern side were hurrying forward fresh troops. Shields himself was coming with new battalions. The men from Ohio and the states further west, expert like the Southerners in the use of the rifle, and confident of victory, were pouring a heavy and unbroken fire upon the thinner Southern lines. They, too, knew the value of cover and, cool enough to think about it, they used every thicket, and grove and ridge that they could reach.

The roar of the battle was heard plainly in Winchester, and the people of the town, although it was now held by the North, wished openly for the success of the South. The Northern troops, as it happened, nearly all through the war, were surrounded by people who were against them. The women at the windows and on the house tops looked eagerly for the red flare in the South which should betoken the victorious advance of Jackson, sweeping his enemies before him.

But Jackson was not advancing. All the valor and courage of the South so far had been in vain. Harry, standing near his commander, and awaiting any order that might be given him, saw new masses of the enemy advancing along every road and through the fields. The Union colors, held aloft in front of the regiments, snapped defiantly in the wind. And those western riflemen, from their cover, never ceased to pour showers of bullets upon the Southern lines. They had already cut a swath of dead, and many wounded were dragging themselves to the rear.

It seemed to Harry, looking over the field, that the battle was lost. The Northern troops were displaying more tenacity than the Southern officers had expected. Moreover, they were two to one, in strong positions, and with a much superior artillery. As he looked he saw one of the Virginia regiments reel back before the attack of much greater numbers and retreat in some disorder. The victors came on, shouting in triumph, but in a few minutes their officers rallied them, another Virginia regiment rushed to their relief, and the two, united, hurled themselves upon the advancing enemy. The Union troops were driven back with great loss, and Harry noticed that the fire from their two great batteries was weakening. He could not keep from shouting in joy, but he was glad that the sound of his voice was drowned in the thunder of the battle.

General Jackson had no orders for him at present, and Harry watched with extraordinary fascination the battle which was unrolling itself in film after film before him. He saw a stone fence running down the center of a field, and then he saw beyond it a great mass of Northern infantry advancing with bayonets shining and colors waving. From his own side a regiment was running toward it.

Who would reach the fence first? The pulses in Harry's temple beat so hard that they hurt. He could not take his eyes from that terrible race, a race of human beings, a race of life and death. The sun blazed down on the rival forces as they sped across the field. But the Southerners reached the wall first. Not in vain had Jackson trained his foot cavalry to march faster anywhere than any other troops in the world.

Harry saw the Virginians sink down behind the fence, the crest of which a moment later blazed with fire for a long distance. He saw the whole front line of the Northern troops disappear, while those behind were thrown into confusion. The Southerners poured in a second volley before they could recover and the whole force broke and retreated. Other troops were brought up but in the face of everything the Virginians held the fence.

But Shields was an able officer. Moreover he and Jackson had been thrown together in former years, and he knew him. He divined some of the qualities of Jackson's mind, and he felt that the Southern general, the field being what it was, was going to push hardest at the center. He accumulated his own forces there in masses that increased continually. He had suffered a wound the previous day in a skirmish, and he could not be at the very front, but he delivered his orders through Kimball, who was in immediate command upon the field.

Five regiments in reserve were suddenly hurled forward and struck the Confederates a tremendous blow.

Harry saw these regiments emerge from the woods and thickets and he saw the gray lines reel before them. Jackson, pointing toward this new and furious conflict, said to Harry:

"Jump on the horse there and tell the officer in command that he must stand firm at all hazards!"

Harry sprang upon a horse not his own, and galloped away. The moment he came into view the western riflemen began to send bullets toward him. His horse was struck, but went on. Another bullet found him, and then a third, which was mortal. Harry leaped clear of the second horse that had been killed under him, and ran toward the officer in charge of the stricken troops. But they were retreating already. They moved slowly, but they moved backward.

Harry joined with the officers in their entreaties to the men to stand, but the pressure upon them was too great. General Garnett, the commander of the Stonewall Brigade, had given an order of his own accord to retreat, and all that part of the line was falling back. The Northern leader, seeing the breach, continually pushed forward fresh troops and more cannon, while the deadly riflemen in the thickets did more harm than the great guns.

The Southerners were compelled to fall back. One gun was lost. Jackson from the crest of the hill had seen with amazement the retreat of the famous Stonewall Brigade that he had once led in person. He galloped across the field, reckless of bullets, and fiercely bade Garnett turn and hold his ground. A drummer stood near and Jackson, grasping him by the shoulder with a firm right hand, fairly dragged him to the crest of a little hill, and bade him beat the rally.

While Jackson still held him he gave the call to stand and fight. But the Southerners could not. The men in blue, intoxicated with victory, pushed forward in thousands and thousands. Their heavy masses overbore all resistance. Jackson, Garnett, Harry and all the officers, young and old were swept from the field by that flood, crested with fire and steel. It was impossible to preserve order and cohesion. The broken regiments were swept back in a confused mass.

Jackson galloped about, trying to rally his men, and his staff gave all the help they could. Harry was on foot once more, waving the sword of which he was so proud. But nothing could stay the tremendous pressure of the Union army. Their commanders always pushed them forward and always fresh men were coming. Skilled cannoneers sent grape shot, shell and round shot whistling through the Southern ranks. The Northern cavalry whipped around the Southern flanks and despite the desperate efforts of Ashby, Sherburne, and the others, began to clip off its wings.

Harry often wondered afterward how his life was preserved. It seemed impossible that he could have escaped such a storm from rifle and cannon, but save for the slight scratches, sustained earlier in the action, he remained untouched. He did not think of it at the time, only of the avalanche that was driving them back. He saw before him a vast red flame, through which bayonets and faces of men showed, ever coming nearer.

Now the North was sure of victory. The shouts of joy ran up and down their whole front. The batteries were pushed nearer and nearer, and sent in terrible volleys at short range. The riflemen who had done such deadly work rose from the woods and thickets, and rushed forward, loading and firing as they came. The Southern force seemed to be nothing but a hopeless mass of fugitives.

Anyone save Jackson would have despaired even of saving his army. But he dreamed yet of victory. He galloped back for a strong detachment of Virginians who had not yet come upon the field, but could not get them up in time to strike a heavy blow.

It was apparent even to Harry and all the other young lieutenants that the battle was lost. He must have shed tears then, because afterward he found furrows in the mud and burned gunpowder on his face. The combat now was not for victory, but for existence. The Southerners fought to preserve the semblance of an army, and it was well for them that they were valiant Virginians led by a great genius, and dauntless officers.

Stonewall Jackson, in this the only defeat he ever sustained in independent command, never lost his head for a moment. By gigantic exertions he formed a new line at last. The fresher troops covered the shattered regiments. The retreating artillery was posted anew.

Jackson galloped back and forth on Little Sorrel. Everywhere his courage and presence of mind brought the men back from despair to hope. Once anew was proved the truth of Napoleon's famous maxim that men are nothing, a man everything. The soldiers on the Northern side were as brave as those on the Southern but they were not led by one of those flashing spirits of war which emerge but seldom in the ages, men who in all the turmoil and confusion of battle can see what ought to be done and who do it.

The beaten Southern army, but a few thousands, now was formed anew for a last stand. A portion of them seized a stone fence, and others took position in thick timber. The cavalry of Turner Ashby raged back and forth, seeking to protect the flanks, and in the east, coming shadows showed that the twilight might yet protect the South from the last blow.

Harry, in the thick of furious battle, had become separated from his commander. He was still on foot and his sword had been broken at the hilt by a bullet, but he did not yet know it. Chance threw him once more among the Invincibles. He plunged through the smoke almost into the arms of Langdon.

"And here is our Harry again!" shouted the irrepressible South Carolinian. "Stonewall Jackson has lost a battle, but he hasn't lost an army. Night and our courage will save us! Here, take this rifle!"

He picked up a loaded rifle which some falling soldier had dropped and thrust it into Harry's hand.

The boy took the rifle and began mechanically to fire and load and fire again at the advancing blue masses. He resolved himself for a minute into a private soldier, and shouted and fired with the rest. The twilight deepened and darkened in the east, but the battle did not cease. The Northern leaders, grim and determined men, seeing their victory sought to press it to the utmost, and always hurried forward infantry, cavalry and artillery. Had the Southern army been commanded by any other than Jackson it would have been destroyed utterly.

Jackson, resourceful and unconquerable, never ceased his exertions. Wherever he appeared he infused new courage into his men. Harry had seized a riderless horse and was once more in the saddle, following his leader, taking orders and helping him whenever he could. The Virginians who had seized the stone fence and the wood held fast. The eye of Jackson was on them, and they could do nothing else. An Ohio and a Virginia regiment on either side lost and retook their colors six times each. One of the flags had sixty bullets through it. An Indiana regiment gave way, but reinforced by another from the state rallied and returned anew to the attack. A Virginia regiment also retreated but was brought back by its colonel, and fought with fresh courage.

The numerous Northern cavalry forced its way around the Southern flanks, and cut in on the rear, taking many prisoners. Then the horsemen appeared in a great mass on the Southern left, and had not time and chance intervened at the last moment Stonewall Jackson might have passed into obscurity.

The increasing twilight was now just merging into night, and a wood stretched between the Northern cavalry and the Southern flank. The Northern horsemen hesitated, not wishing to become entangled among trees and brush in the dark, and in a few minutes the Southern infantry, falling back swiftly after beating off the attacks on their front, passed out of the trap. Sherburne and Funsten, two of Ashby's most valiant cavalry leaders, came up with their squadrons, and covered the retreat, fighting off the Northern horsemen as Jackson and his army disappeared in the woods, and night came over the lost field.

The Southern army retired, beaten, but sullen and defiant. It did not go far, but stopped at a point where the supply train had been placed. Fires were built and some of the men ate, but others were so much exhausted that without waiting for food they threw themselves upon the ground, and in an instant were fast asleep.

Harry, for the moment, a prey to black despair, followed his general. Only one other officer, a major, was with him. Harry watched him closely, but he did not see him show any emotion. Little Sorrel like his master, although he had been under fire a hundred times, had passed through the battle without a scratch. Now he walked forward slowly, the reins lying loose upon his neck.

Harry was not conscious of weariness. He had made immense exertions, but his system was keyed so high by excitement that the tension held firmly yet a little longer. The night had come on heavy and dark. Behind him he could hear the fitful sounds of the Northern and Southern cavalry still skirmishing with each other. Before him he saw dimly the Southern regiments, retreating in ragged lines. It was almost more than he could stand, and his feelings suddenly found vent in an angry cry.

General Jackson heard him and understood.

"Don't be grieved, my boy," he said quietly. "This is only the first battle."

The calm, unboastful courage strengthened Harry anew. If he should grieve how much more should the general who had led in the lost battle, and upon whom everybody would hasten to put the blame! He felt once more that flow of courage and fire from Jackson to himself, and he felt also his splendid fortune in being associated with a man whose acts showed all the marks of greatness. Like so many other young officers, mere boys, he was fast maturing in the furnace of a vast war.

The general ceased to follow the troops, but turned aside into what seemed to be a thin stretch of forest. But Harry saw that the trees grew in rows and he exclaimed:

"An orchard!"

It seemed to strike Jackson's fancy.

"Well," he said, "an orchard is a good place to sleep in. Can't we make a fire here? I fear that we shall have to burn some fence rails tonight."

Harry and the major—Hawks was his name—hitched the horses, and gathered a heap of dry fence rails. The major set fire to splinters with matches and, in a few minutes a fine fire was crackling and blazing, taking away the sharp chill of the March night.

Harry saw other fires spring up in the orchard, and he went over to one of them, where some soldiers were cooking food.

"Give me a piece of meat and bread," he said to a long Virginian.

"Set, Sonny, an' eat with us!"

"I don't want it for myself."

"Then who in nation are you beggin' fur?"

"For General Jackson. He's sitting over there."

"Thunderation! The gen'ral himself! Here, boy!"

Bearing a big piece of meat in one hand and a big piece of bread in the other Harry returned to Jackson, who had not yet tasted food that day. The general ate heartily, but almost unconsciously. He seemed to be in a deep study. Harry surmised that his thoughts were on the morrow. He had learned already that Stonewall Jackson always looked forward.

Harry foraged and obtained more food for himself, and other officers of the staff who were coming up, some bearing slight wounds that they concealed. He also secured the general's cloak, which was strapped to his saddle and insisted upon his putting it on.

The fire was surrounded presently by officers. Major Hawks had laid together and as evenly as possible a number of fence rails upon which Jackson was to sleep, but as yet no one was disposed to slumber. They had finished eating, but they remained in a silent and somber circle about the fire.

Jackson stood up presently and his figure, wrapped in the long cloak was all dark. The light did not fall upon his face. All the others looked at him. Among them was one of Ashby's young troopers, a bold and reckless spirit. It was a time, too, when the distinction between officers and privates in the great citizen armies was not yet sharply defined. And this young trooper, some spirit of mockery urging him on, stood up and said to his general:

"The Yankees didn't seem to be in any hurry to leave Winchester, did they, general?"

Harry drew a quick, sharp breath, and there was a murmur among the officers, but Stonewall Jackson merely turned a tranquil look upon the presumptuous youth. Then he turned it back to the bed of coals and said in even tones:

"Winchester is a pleasant town to stay in, sir."

The young cavalryman, not abashed at all, continued:

"We heard the Yankees were retreating, but I guess they're retreating after us."

Harry half rose and so did several of the older officers, but Jackson replied quietly:

"I think I may tell you, young sir, that I am satisfied with the result."

The audacity of the youthful trooper could not carry him further. He caught threatening looks from the officers and slipped away in the darkness. Silence fell anew around the fire, and Jackson still stood, gazing into the coals. Soon, he turned abruptly, strode away into the darkness, but came back after a while, lay down on the fence rails and slept soundly.

Harry put four or five rails side by side to protect his body from the cold ground, lay down upon them and threw a cloak over himself. Now he relaxed or rather collapsed completely. The tension that had kept him up so long was gone, and he felt that he could not have risen from the rails had he wished. He saw wavering fires and dusky figures beside them, but sleep came in a few minutes to soothe and heal.

Bye and bye all the army, save the sentinels, slept and the victorious Northern army only two or three miles away also slept, feeling that it had done enough for one day.

Shields that night was sending messages to the North announcing his victory, but he was cherishing no illusions. He told how fierce had been the attack, and with what difficulty it had been beaten off, and in Washington, reading well between the lines they felt that another attack and yet others might come from the same source.

Harry sleeping on his bed of fence rails did not dream of the extraordinary things that the little army of Jackson, beaten at Kernstown was yet to do. McClellan was just ready to start his great army by sea for the attack on Richmond, when suddenly the forgotten or negligible Jackson sprang out of the dark and fixed himself on his flank.

The capital, despite victory, was filled with alarm and the President shared it. The veteran Shields knew this man who had led the attack, and he did not seek to hide the danger. The figure of Stonewall Jackson, gigantic and menacing, showed suddenly through the mists. If McClellan went on to Richmond with the full Northern strength he might launch himself on Washington.

The great scheme of invasion was put out of joint. Shields, although victorious for the time, could not believe that Jackson would attack with so small an army unless he expected reinforcements, and he sent swift expresses to bring back a division of 8,000 men which was marching to cover Washington. Banks, his superior officer, on the way to Washington, too, heard the news at Harper's Ferry and halted there, and Lincoln, detaching a whole corps of nearly 40,000 men from McClellan's army, ordered them to remain at Manassas to protect the capital against Jackson. A dispatch was sent to Banks ordering him to push the valley campaign with his whole strength.

But when Harry rose the next morning from his fence rails he knew nothing of these things. Nor did anyone else in the Southern army, unless it was Stonewall Jackson who perhaps half-divined them. Harry thought afterward that he had foreseen much when he said to the impudent cavalryman that he was satisfied with the result at Kernstown.

They lingered there a little and then began a retreat, unharrassed by pursuit. Scouts of the enemy were seen by Ashby's cavalry, who hung like a curtain between them and the army, but no force strong enough to do any harm came in sight. Harry had secured another horse and most of his duty was at the rear, where he was often sent by the general to get the latest news from Ashby.

He quickly met Sherburne over whose dress difficulties had triumphed at last. His fine cloak, rent in many places, was stained with mud and there was one large dark spot made by his own blood. His face was lined deeply by exhaustion and deep disappointment.

"They were too much for us this time, Harry," he said bitterly. "We can't beat two to one all the time. How does the general take it?"

"As if it were nothing. He'll be ready to fight again in a few days, and we must have struck a hard blow anyhow. The enemy are not pursuing."

"That's true," said Sherburne more cheerfully. "Your argument is a good one."

The army came to a ridge called Rude's Hill and stopped there. Harry was already soldier enough to see that it was a strong position. Before it flowed a creek which the melting snows in the mountains had swollen to a depth of eight or ten feet, and on another side was a fork of the Shenandoah, also swollen. Here the soldiers began to fortify and prepare for a longer stay while Jackson sent for aid.

Harry was not among the messengers for help. Jackson had learned his great ability as a scout, and now he often sent him on missions of observation, particularly with Captain Sherburne, to whom St. Clair and Langdon were also loaned by Colonel Talbot.

Thus the three were together when they rode with Sherburne and a hundred men a few days after their arrival at the ridge.

They were well wrapped in great coats, because the weather, after deceiving for a while with the appearance of spring, had turned cold again. The enemy's scouts and spies were keeping back, where they could blow on their cold fingers or walk a while to restore the circulation to their half frozen legs.

Sherburne was his neat and orderly self again and St. Clair was fully his equal. Langdon openly boasted that he was going to have a dressing contest between them for large stakes as soon as the war was over. But all the young Southerners were in good spirits now. They had learned of the alarm caused in the North by Kernstown, and that a third of McClellan's army had been detached to guard against them. Nor had Banks and Shields yet dared to attack them.

"There's what troubles Banks," said Sherburne, pointing with his saber to a towering mass of mountains which rose somber and dark in the very center of the Shenandoah Valley. "He doesn't know which side of the Massanuttons to take."

Harry looked up at these peaks and ridges, famous now in the minds of all Virginians, towering a half mile in the air, clothed from base to summit with dense forest of oak and pine, although today the crests were wrapped in snowy mists. They cut the Shenandoah valley into two smaller valleys, the wider and more nearly level one on the west. Only a single road by which troops could pass crossed the Massanuttons, and that road was held by the cavalry of Ashby.

"If Banks comes one way and he proves too strong for us we can cross over to the other," said Sherburne. "If he divides his force, marching into both valleys, we may beat one part of his army, then pass the mountain and beat the other."

Sherburne had divined aright. It was the mighty mass of the Massanuttons that weighed upon Banks. As he looked up at the dark ridges and misty crests his mind was torn by doubts. His own forces, great in number though they were, were scattered. Fremont to his right on the slopes of the Alleghanies had 25,000 men; there were other strong detachments under Milroy and Schenck, and he had 17,000 men under his own eye. So he was hesitating while the days were passing and Jackson growing stronger.

"I suppose the nature of the country helps us a lot," said Harry as he looked up at the Massanuttons, following Sherburne's pointing saber.

"It does, and we need help," said Sherburne. "Even as it is they would have been pushing upon us if it hadn't been for the cavalry and the artillery. Every time a detachment advanced we'd open up on it with a masked battery from the woods, and if pickets showed their noses too close horsemen were after them in a second. We've had them worried to death for days and days, and when they do come in force Old Jack will have something up his sleeve."

"I wonder," said Harry.

CHAPTER VII.
ON THE RIDGES

As they rode in the shadow of the Massanuttons Harry continued to wonder. The whole campaign in the valley had become to him an interminable maze. Stonewall Jackson might know what he intended to do, but he was not telling. Meanwhile they marched back and forth. There was incessant skirmishing between cavalry and pickets, but it did not seem to signify anything. Banks, sure of his overwhelming numbers, pressed forward, but always cautiously and slowly. He did not march into any trap. And Harry surmised that Jackson, much too weak to attack, was playing for time.

Sherburne and his troop paused at the very base of the Massanuttons and Harry, who happened to be with them, looked up again at the lofty summits standing out so boldly and majestically in the middle of the valley. The oaks and maples along their slopes were now blossoming into a green that matched the tint of the pines, but far up on the crests there was still a line of snow, and white mists beyond.

"Why not climb the highest summit?" he said to Sherburne. "You have powerful glasses and we could get a good view of what is going on up the valley."

"Most of those slopes are not slopes at all. They're perpendicular like the side of a house. The horses could never get up."

"But they can certainly go part of the way, and some of us can climb the rest on foot."

Sherburne's eyes sparkled. The spirit of adventure was strong within him. Moreover the task, if done, was worth while.

"Good for you, Harry," he exclaimed. "We'll try it! What do you say, St. Clair, you and Langdon?"

"I follow where you lead, and I hope that you lead to the top of the mountain," replied St. Clair.

"Likely it's cold up there," said Langdon, "but there are higher and colder mountains and I choose this one."

They had learned promptness and decision from Stonewall Jackson, and Sherburne at once gave the order to ascend. Several men in his troop were natives of that part of the valley, and they knew the Massanuttons well. They led and the whole troop composed of youths followed eagerly. Bye and bye they dismounted and led their horses over the trails which grew slippery with wet and snow as they rose higher.

When they paused at times to rest they would all look northward over the great valley, where a magnificent panorama had gradually risen into view. They saw a vast stretch of fields turning green, neat villages, dark belts of forest, the gleam of brooks and creeks, and now and then, the glitter from a Northern bayonet.

At length the chief guide, a youth named Wallace, announced that the horses could go no farther. Even in summer when the snow was all gone and the earth was dry they could not find a footing. Now it was certain death for them to try the icy steeps.

Sherburne ordered the main body of the troop to halt in a forested and sheltered glen in the side of the mountain, and, choosing Harry, St. Clair, Langdon, the guide Wallace, and six others, he advanced with them on foot. It was difficult climbing, and more than once they were bruised by falls, but they learned to regard such accidents as trifles, and ardent of spirit they pressed forward.

"I think we'll get a good view," said Sherburne. "See how brilliantly the sun is shining in the valley."

"Yes, and the mists on the crests are clearing away," said Harry.

"Then with the aid of the glasses we can get a sweep up the valley for many miles. Now boys, here we go! up! up!"

If it had not been for the bushes they could never have made the ascent, as they were now in the region of snow and ice and the slopes were like glass. Often they were compelled to crawl, and it was necessary, too, to exercise a good deal of care in crawling.

St. Clair groaned as he rose after climbing a rock, and brushed the knees of his fine gray trousers.

"Cheer up, Arthur," said Langdon, "it could have been worse. The sharp stones there might have cut holes through them."

But in spite of every difficulty and danger they went steadily toward the summit, and streamers of mist yet floating about the mountain often enclosed them in a damp shroud. Obviously, however, the clouds and vapors were thinning, and soon the last shred would float away.

"It ain't more'n a hundred feet more to the top," said Wallace, "an' it's shore that the sun will be shinin' there."

"Shining for us, of course," said Langdon. "It's a good omen."

"I wish I could always look for the best as you do, Tom," said St. Clair.

"I'm glad I can. Gay hearts are better than riches. As sure as I climb, Arthur, I see the top."

"Yes, there it is, the nice snowy bump above us."

They dragged themselves upon the loftiest crest, and, panting, stood there for a few minutes in several inches of snow. Then the wind caught up the last shreds and tatters of mist, and whipped them away southward. Every one of them drew a deep, sharp breath, as the great panorama of the valley to the northward and far below was unrolled before them.

The brilliant sunshine of early spring played over everything, but far down in the valley they seemed to see by contrast the true summer of the sunny south, which is often far from sunny. But seen from the top of the mountain the valley was full of golden rays. Now the roofs of the villages showed plainly and they saw with distinctness the long silver lines that marked the flowing of the rivers and creeks. To the east and to the west further than the eye could reach rose the long line of dim blue mountains that enclosed the valley.

But it was the glitter of the bayonets in the valley that caused the hearts of the Virginians to beat most fiercely. Banners and guidons, clusters of white tents, and dark swarms of men marked where the foot of the invading stranger trod their soil. The Virginians loved the great valley. Enclosed between the blue mountains it was the richest and most beautiful part of all their state. It hurt them terribly to see the overwhelming forces of the North occupying its towns and villages and encamped in its fields.

Harry, not a Virginian himself, but a brother by association, understood and shared their feeling. He saw Sherburne's lips moving and he knew that he was saying hard words between his teeth. But Sherburne's eyes were at the glasses, and he looked a long time, moving them slowly from side to side. After a while he handed them to Harry.

The boy raised the glasses and the great panorama of the valley sprang up to his eyes. It seemed to him that he could almost count the soldiers in the camps. There was a troop of cavalry riding to the southward, and further to the left was another. Directly to the north was their battlefield of Kernstown, and not far beyond it lay Winchester. He saw such masses of the enemy's troops and so many signs of activity among them that he felt some movement must be impending.

"What do you think of it, Harry?" said Sherburne.

"Banks must be getting ready to move forward."

"I think so, too. I wish we had his numbers."

"More men are coming for us. We'll have Ewell's corps soon, and General Jackson himself is worth ten thousand men."

"That's so, Harry, but ten thousand men are far too few. McDowell's whole corps is available, and with it the Yankees can now turn more than seventy thousand men into the valley."

"And they can fight, too, as we saw at Kernstown," said St. Clair.

"That's so, and I'm thinking they'll get their stomachs full of it pretty soon," said Langdon. "Yesterday about dusk I went out in some bushes after firewood, and I saw a man kneeling. It struck me as curious, and I went up closer. What do you think? It was Old Jack praying. Not any mock prayer, but praying to his Lord with all his heart and soul. I'm not much on praying myself, but I felt pretty solemn then, and I slid away from there as quick and quiet as you please. And I tell you, fellows, that when Stonewall Jackson prays it's time for the Yankees to weep."

"You're probably right, Langdon," said Captain Sherburne, "but it's time for us to be going back, and we'll tell what we've seen to General Jackson."

As they turned away a crunching in the snow on the other slope caused them to stop. The faces of men and then their figures appeared through the bushes. They were eight or ten in number and all wore blue uniforms. Harry saw the leader, and instantly he recognized

Shepard. It came to him, too, in a flash of prescience, that Shepard was just the man whom he would meet there.

Sherburne, who had seen the blue uniforms, raised a pistol and fired. Two shots were fired by the Union men at the same instant, and then both parties dropped back from the crest, each on its own side.

Sherburne's men were untouched and Harry was confident that Shepard's had been equally lucky — the shots had been too hasty — but it was nervous and uncomfortable work, lying there in the snow, and waiting for the head of an enemy to appear over the crest.

Harry was near Captain Sherburne, and he whispered to him:

"I know the man whose face appeared first through the bushes."

"Who is he?"

"His name is Shepard. He's a spy and scout for the North, and he is brave and dangerous. He was in Montgomery when President Davis was inaugurated. I saw him in Washington when I was there as a spy myself. I saw him again in Winchester just before the battle of Kernstown, and now here he is once more."

"Must be a Wandering Jew sort of a fellow."

"He wanders with purpose. He has certainly come up here to spy us out."

"In which he is no more guilty than we are."

"That's true, but what are we going to do about it, captain?"

"Blessed if I know. Wait till I take a look."

Captain Sherburne raised himself a little, in order to peep over the crest of the ridge. A rifle cracked on the other side, a bullet clipped the top of his cap, and he dropped back in the snow, unhurt but startled.

"This man, Shepard, is fully as dangerous as you claim him to be," he said to Harry.

"Can you see anything of them?" asked St. Clair.

"Not a thing," said Harry.

"If we show they shoot, and if they show we shoot," said Langdon. "Seems to me it's about the most beautiful case of checkmate that I've known."

"Perhaps we can stalk them," said St. Clair.

"And perhaps they can stalk us," said Langdon. "But I think both sides are afraid to try it."

"You're right, Langdon," said Captain Sherburne, "It's a case of checkmate. I confess that I don't know what to do."

"We could wait here while they waited too, and if we waited long enough it would get so dark we couldn't see each other. But captain, you are a kind-hearted and sympathetic man, do you see any fun in sitting in the snow on top of a mountain, waiting to kill men whom you don't want to kill or to be killed by men who don't want to kill you?"

"No, Tom, I don't," replied Captain Sherburne with a laugh, "and you're talking mighty sound sense. This is not like a regular battle. We've nothing to gain by shooting those men, and they've nothing to gain by shooting us. The Massanuttons extend a long distance and there's nothing to keep scouts and spies from climbing them at other places. We'll go away from here."

He gave the order. They rose and crept as softly as they could through the snow and bushes down the side of the mountain. Harry looked back occasionally, but he saw no faces appear on the crest. Soon he heard Langdon who was beside him laughing softly to himself.

"What's the matter, Tom?" he asked.

"Harry, if I could take my pistol and shoot straight through this mountain the bullet when it came out on the other side would hit a soldier in blue clothes, going at the same rate of speed down the mountain."

"More than likely you're right, Tom, if they're sensible, and that man Shepard certainly is."

Further down they met some of their own men climbing up. The troop had heard the shots and was on the way to rescue, if rescue were needed. Captain Sherburne explained briefly and they continued the descent, leading their horses all the way, and breathing deep relief, when they stood at last in the plain.

"I'll remember that climb," said Langdon to Harry as he sprang into the saddle, "and I won't do it again when there's snow up there, unless General Jackson himself forces me up with the point of a bayonet."

"The view was fine."

"So it was, but the shooting was bad. Not a Yank, not a Reb fell, and I'm not unhappy over it. A curious thing has happened to me, Harry. While I'm ready to fight the Yankee at the drop of the hat I don't seem to hate 'em as much as I did when the war began."

"Same here. The war ought not to have happened, but we're in it, and to my way of thinking we're going to be in it mighty deep and long."

Langdon was silent for a little while, but nothing could depress him long. He was soon chattering away as merrily as ever while the troop rode back to General Jackson. Harry regarded him with some envy. A temperament that could rejoice under any circumstances was truly worth having.

Sherburne reported to Ashby who in return sent him to the commander, Harry going with him to resume his place on the staff. Jackson heard the report without comment and his face expressed nothing. Harry could not see that he had changed much since he had come to join him. A little thinner, a little more worn, perhaps, but he was the same quiet, self-contained man, whose blue eyes often looked over and beyond the one to whom he was talking, as if he were maturing plans far ahead.

Harry occupied a tent for the time with two or three other young officers, and being permitted a few hours off duty he visited his friends of the Invincibles, Colonel Leonidas Talbot and Lieutenant-Colonel Hector St. Hilaire. The two old comrades already had heard the results of the scout from St. Clair and Langdon, but they gave Harry a welcome because they liked him. They also gave him a camp stool, no small luxury in an army that marches and fights hard, using more gunpowder than anything else.

Harry put the stool against a tree, sat on it and leaned back against the trunk, feeling a great sense of luxury. The two men regarded him with a benevolent eye. They, too, were enjoying luxuries, cigars which a cavalry detail had captured from the enemy. It struck Harry at the moment that although one was of British descent and the other of French they were very much alike. South Carolina had bred them and then West Point had cast them in her unbreakable mold. Neat, precise, they sat rigidly erect, and smoked their cigars.

"Do you like it on the staff of General Jackson, Harry," asked Colonel Talbot.

"I felt regrets at leaving the Invincibles," replied Harry truthfully, "but I like it. I think it a privilege to be so near to General Jackson."

"A leader who has fought only one battle in independent command and who lost that," said Lieutenant-Colonel Hector St. Hilaire, thoughtfully—he knew that Harry would repeat nothing, "and who nevertheless has the utmost confidence of his men. He does not joke with them as the young Napoleon did with his soldiers. He has none of the quality that we call magnetic charm, and yet his troops are eager to follow him anywhere. He has won no victories, but his men believe him capable of many. He takes none of his officers into his confidence, but all have it. Incredible, but true. Why is it?"

He put his cigar back in his mouth and puffed meditatively. Colonel Leonidas Talbot, who also had been puffing meditatively while Lieutenant-Colonel Hector St. Hilaire was speaking, now took his cigar from his mouth, blew away the delicate rings of smoke, and said in an equally thoughtful tone:

"It occurs to me, Hector, that it is the power of intellect. Stonewall Jackson has impressed the whole army down to the last and least little drummer with a sense of his mental force. I tell you, sir, that he is a thinker, and thinkers are rare, much more rare than people generally believe. There is only one man out of ten thousand who does not act wholly according to precedent and experience. Habit is so powerful that when we think we are thinking we are not thinking at all, we are merely recalling the experiences of ourselves or somebody else. And of the rare individuals who leave the well-trod paths of thought to think new thoughts, only a minutely small percentage think right. This minutely small fraction represents genius, the one man in a million or rather ten million, or, to be more accurate, the one man in a hundred million."

Colonel Leonidas Talbot put the cigar back in his mouth and puffed with regularity and smoothness. Lieutenant-Colonel Hector St. Hilaire, in his turn, took his cigar from his mouth once more, blew away the fine white rings of smoke and said:

"Leonidas, it appears to me that you have hit upon the truth, or as our legal friends would say, the truth, the whole truth and nothing but the truth. I am in the middle of life and I realize suddenly that in all the years I have lived I have met but few thinkers, certainly not more than half a dozen, perhaps not more than three or four."

He put his cigar back in his mouth and the two puffed simultaneously and with precision, blowing out the fine, delicate rings of smoke at exactly the same time. Gentlemen of the old school they were, even then, but Harry recognized, too, that Colonel Leonidas Talbot had spoken the weighty truth. Stonewall Jackson was a thinker, and thinkers are never numerous in the world. He resolved to think more for himself if he could, and he sat there trying to think, while he absently regarded the two colonels.

Colonel Leonidas Talbot, after two minutes perhaps, took the cigar from his mouth once more and said to Lieutenant-Colonel Hector St. Hilaire:

"Fine cigars the Yankees make, Hector."

"Quite true, Leonidas. One of the best I have ever smoked."

"Not more than a dozen left."

"Then we must get more."

"But how?"

"Stonewall Jackson will think of a way."

Harry, despite his respect for them, was compelled to laugh. But the two colonels laughed with him.

"The words of my friend Leonidas have been proved true within a few minutes," said Lieutenant-Colonel Hector St. Hilaire. "In doubt we turned at once and with involuntary impulse to Stonewall Jackson to think of a way. He has impressed us, as he has impressed the privates, with his intellectual power."

Harry sat with them nearly an hour. He had not only respect but affection also for them. Old-fashioned they might be in some ways, but they were able military men, thoroughly alert, and he knew that he could learn much from them. When he left them he returned to General Jackson and a few more days of waiting followed.

Winter was now wholly gone and spring, treacherous at first, was becoming real and reliable. Reports heavy and ominous were coming from McClellan. He would disembark and march up the peninsula on Richmond with a vast and irresistible force. Jackson might be drawn off from the valley to help Johnston in the defense of the capital. But Banks with his great army would then march down it as if on parade.

Harry heard one morning that a new man was put in command of the Southern forces in Northern Virginia. Robert Edward Lee was his name, and it was a good name, too. He was the son of that famous Light Horse Harry Lee who was a favorite of Washington in the Revolution. Already an elderly man, he was sober and quiet, but the old West Pointers passed the word through Jackson's army that he was full of courage and daring.

Harry felt the stimulus almost at once. A fresh wind seemed to be blowing down the Valley of Virginia. Lee had sent word to Jackson that he might do what he could, and that he might draw to his help also a large division under Ewell. The news spread through the army and there was a great buzzing. Young Virginia was eager to march against any odds, and Harry was with them, heart and soul.

Nor were they kept waiting now. The news had scarcely spread through the army when they heard the crack of carbines in their front. The cavalry of Ashby, increased by many recruits, was already skirmishing with the vanguard of Banks. It was the last day of April and Harry, sent to the front, saw Ashby drive in all the Northern cavalry. When he returned with the news Jackson instantly lifted up his whole division and marched by the flank through the hills, leaving Ewell with his men to occupy Banks in front. The mind of the "thinker" was working, and Harry knew it as he rode behind him. He did not know what this movement meant, but he had full confidence in the man who led them.

Yet the marching, like all the other marching they had done, was of the hardest. The ground, torn by hoofs, cannon wheels and the feet of marching men, was a continuous quagmire. Ponds made newly by the rains stood everywhere. Often it required many horses and men to drag a cannon out of the mud. The junior officers, and finally those of the highest rank, leaped from their horses and gave aid. Jackson himself carried boughs and stones to help make a road.

Despite the utmost possible exertions the army could make only five miles in a single day and at the approach of night it flung itself upon the ground exhausted.

"I call this the Great Muddy Army," said St. Clair, ruefully to Harry, as he surveyed his fine uniform, now smeared over with brown liquid paste.

"It might have been worse," said Langdon. "Suppose we had fallen in a quicksand and had been swallowed up utterly. 'Tis better to live muddy than not to live at all."

"It would be better to call it the Great Tired Army just now," said Harry. "To keep on pulling your feet all day long out of mud half a yard deep is the most exhausting thing I know or ever heard of."

"Where are we going?" asked St. Clair.

"Blessed if I know," replied Harry, "nor does anybody else save one. It's all hid under General Jackson's hat."

"I guess it's Staunton," said Langdon. "That's a fine town, as good as Winchester. I've got kinsfolk there. I came up once from South Carolina and made them a visit."

But it was not Staunton, although Staunton, hearing of the march, had been joyfully expecting Jackson's men. The fine morning came, warm and brilliant with sunshine, raising the spirits of the troops. The roads began to dry out fast and marching would be much easier. But Jackson, leading somberly on Little Sorrel, turned his back on Staunton.

The Virginians stared in amazement when the heads of columns turned away from that trim and hospitable little city, which they knew was so fervently attached to their cause. Before them rose the long line of the Blue Ridge and they were marching straight toward it.

They marched a while in silence, and then a groan ran through the ranks. It was such a compound of dismay and grief that it made Harry shiver. The Virginians were leaving their beloved and beautiful valley, leaving it all to the invader, leaving the pretty little places, Winchester and Staunton and Harrisonburg and Strasburg and Front Royal, and all the towns and villages in which their families and relatives lived. Every one of the Virginians had blood kin everywhere through the valley.

The men began to whisper to one another, but the order of silence was passed sternly along the line. They marched on, sullen and gloomy, but after a while their natural courage and their confidence in their commander returned. Their spirits did not desert them, even when they left the valley behind them and began to climb the Blue Ridge.

Up, up, they went through dense forests. Harry remembered their ascent of the Massanuttons, but the snows were gone now. They pressed on until they reached the crest of the ridges and there the whole army paused, high up in the air, while they looked with eager interest at the rolling Virginia country stretching toward the east until it sank under the horizon.

Harry saw smoke that marked the passing of trains, and he believed that they were now on their way to Richmond to help defend the capital against McClellan. He glanced at Jackson, but the commander was as tight-lipped as ever. Whatever was under that hat remained the secret of its owner.

They descended the mountains and came to a railway station, where many cars were waiting. Troops were hurried aboard expecting to start for Richmond, and then a sudden roar burst from them. The trains did not move toward Richmond, but back, through defiles that would lead them again into their beloved valley. Cheers one after another rolled through the trains, and Harry, who was in a forward car with the Invincibles, joined in as joyfully as the best Virginian of them all.

The boy was so much exhausted that he fell into a doze on a seat. But afterward he dimly remembered that he heard the two colonels talking. They were trying to probe into the depths of Jackson's mind. They surmised that this march over the mountains had been made partly to delude Banks. They were right, at least as far as the delusion of Banks went. He had been telegraphing that the army of Jackson was gone, on its way to Richmond, and that there was nothing in front of him save a few skirmishers.

The Virginians left their trains in the valley again, waited for their wagons and artillery, and then marched on to Staunton, that neat little city that was so dear to so many of them. But the mystery of what was under Jackson's hat remained a mystery. They passed through Staunton, amid the cheering people, women and children waving hats, scarfs and handkerchiefs to their champions. But the terrible Stonewall gave them no chance to dally in that pleasant place. Staunton was left far behind and they never stopped until they went into camp on the side of another range of mountains.

Here in a great forest they built a few fires, more not being allowed, and after a hasty supper most of the men lay down in their blankets to rest. But the young officers did not sleep. A small tent for Jackson had been raised by the side of the Invincibles, and Harry, sitting on a log, talked in low tones with Langdon and St. Clair. The three were of the opinion that some blow was about to be struck, but what it was they did not know.

"The Yankees must have lost us entirely," said Langdon. "To tell you the truth, boys, I've lost myself. I've been marching about so much that I don't know east from west and north from south. I'm sure that this is the Southern army about us, but whether we're still in Virginia or not is beyond me. What do you say, Arthur?"

"It's Virginia still, Tom, but we've undoubtedly done a lot of marching."

"A lot of it! 'Lot' is a feeble word! We've marched a million miles in the last few days. I've checked 'em off by the bunions on the soles of my feet."

"Look out, boys," said St. Clair. "Here comes the general!"

General Jackson was walking toward them. His face had the usual intense, preoccupied look, but he smiled slightly when he saw the three lads.

"Come, young gentlemen," he said, "we're going to take a look at the enemy."

A group of older officers joined him, and the three lads followed modestly. They reached a towering crag and from it Harry saw a deep valley fringed with woods, a river rushing down its center and further on a village. Both banks of the river were thick with troops, men in blue. Over and beyond the valley was a great mass of mountains, ridge on ridge and peak on peak, covered with black forest, and cut by defiles and ravines so narrow that it was always dark within them.

Harry felt a strange, indescribable thrill. The presence of the enemy and the wild setting of the mountains filled him with a kind of awe.

"It's a Northern army under Milroy," whispered St. Clair, who now heard Jackson talking to the older officers.

"Then there's going to be a battle," said Harry.

CHAPTER VIII.
THE MOUNTAIN BATTLE

General Jackson and several of his senior officers were examining the valley with glasses, but Harry, with eyes trained to the open air and long distances, could see clearly nearly all that was going on below. He saw movement among the masses of men in blue, and he saw officers on horseback, galloping along the banks of the river. Then he saw cannon in trenches with their muzzles elevated toward the heights, and he knew that the Union troops must have had warning of Jackson's coming. And he saw, too, that the officers below also had glasses through which they were looking.

There was a sudden blaze from the mouth of one of the cannon. A shell shot upward, whistling and shrieking, and burst far above their heads. Harry heard pieces of falling metal striking on the rocks behind them. The mountains sent back the cannon's roar in a sinister echo.

A second gun flashed and again the shell curved over their heads. But Jackson paid no heed. He was still watching intently through his glasses.

"The enemy is up and alert," whispered St. Clair to Harry. "I judge that these are Western men used to sleeping with their eyes open."

"Like as not a lot of them are mountain West Virginians," said Harry. "They are strong for the North, and it's likely, too, that they're the men who have discovered Jackson's advance."

"And they mean to make it warm for us. Listen to those guns! It's hard shooting aiming at men on heights, but it shows what they could do on level ground."

Jackson presently retired with his officers, and Harry, parting from his friends of the Invincibles, went with him. Back among the ridges all the troops were under arms, the weary ones having risen from their blankets which were now tied in rolls on their backs. They had not yet been able to bring the artillery up the steeps. Harry saw that the faces of all were eager as they heard the thunder of the guns in the valley below. Among the most eager was a regiment of Georgians arrived but recently with the reinforcements.

Many of the men, speaking from the obscurity of the crowded ranks, did not scorn to hurl questions at their officers.

"Are we goin' to fight the Yankees at last?"

"I'd rather take my chances with the bullets than march any more."

"Lead us down an' give us a chance at 'em."

Colonel Leonidas Talbot and Lieutenant-Colonel Hector St. Hilaire were among the officers who had gone with Jackson to the verge of the cliff, and now when they heard the impertinent but eager questions from the massed ranks they looked at each other and smiled. It was not according to West Point, but these were recruits and here was enthusiasm which was a pearl beyond price.

General Jackson beckoned to Harry and three other young staff officers.

"Take glasses," he said, "go back to the verge of the cliff, and watch for movements on the part of the enemy. If any is made be sure that you see it, and report it to me at once."

The words were abrupt, sharp, admitting of no question or delay, and the four fairly ran. Harry and his comrades lay down at the edge of the cliff and swept the valley with their glasses. The great guns were still firing at intervals of about a minute. The gunners could not see the Southern troops drawn back behind the ridges, but Harry believed that they might be guided by signals from men on opposite slopes. But if signalmen were there they were hidden by the forest even from his glasses.

The smoke from the cannon was gathering heavily in the narrow valley, so heavily that it began to obscure what was passing there in the Northern army. But the four, remembering the injunction of Jackson, a man who must be obeyed to the last and minutest detail, still sought to pierce through the smoke both with the naked eye and with glasses. As a rift appeared Harry saw a moving mass of men in blue. It was a great body of troops and the sun shining through the rift glittered over bayonets and rifle barrels. They were marching straight toward a slope which led at a rather easy grade up the side of the mountain.

"They're not waiting to be attacked! They're attacking!" cried Harry, springing to his feet and running to the point where he knew Jackson stood. Jackson received his news, looked for himself, and then began to push on the troops. A shout arose as the army pressed forward to meet the enemy who were coming so boldly.

"We ought to beat 'em, as we have the advantage of the heights," exclaimed Sherburne, who was now on foot.

But the advantage was the other way. Those were staunch troops who were advancing, men of Ohio and West Virginia, and while they were yet on the lower slopes their cannon, firing over their heads, swept the crest with shot and shell. The eager Southern youths, as invariably happens with those firing downward, shot too high. The Northern regiments now opening with their rifles and taking better aim came on in splendid order.

"What a magnificent charge!" Harry heard Sherburne exclaim.

The rifles by thousands were at work, and the unceasing crash sent echoes far through the mountains. The Southerners at the edge of the cliff were cut down by the fire of their enemy from below. Their loss was now far greater than that of the North, and their officers sought to draw them back from the verge, to a ridge where they could receive the charge, just as it reached the crest and pour into them their full fire. The eager young regiment from Georgia refused to obey.

"Have we come all these hundreds of miles from Georgia to run before Yankees?" they cried, and stood there pulling trigger at the enemy, while their own men fell fast before the bitter Northern hail.

Harry, too, was forced to admire the great resolution and courage with which the Northern troops came upward, but he turned away to be ready for any command that Jackson might give him. The general stood by a rock attentively watching the fierce battle that was going on, but not yet giving any order. But Harry fancied that he saw his eyes glisten as he beheld the ardor of his troops.

A detachment of Virginians, posted in the rear, seeing a break in the first line, rushed forward without orders, filled the gap and came face to face with the men in blue. Harry thought he saw Jackson's eyes glisten again, but he was not sure.

The crash of the battle increased fast. The Southern troops had no artillery, but as the Northern charge came nearer the crest their bullets ceased to fly over the heads of their enemies, but struck now in the ranks. The ridges were enveloped in fire and smoke. A fresh Southern regiment was thrown in and the valiant Northern charge broke. The brave men of Ohio and West Virginia, although they fought desperately and encouraged one another to stand fast, were forced slowly back down the slope.

Harry and a half dozen others beside him heard Jackson say, apparently to himself, "The battle will soon be over." Harry knew instinctively that it was true. He had got into the habit of believing every thing Jackson said. The end came in fifteen minutes more, and with it came the night.

The soldiers in their ardor had not noticed that the long shadows were creeping over the mountains. The sun had already sunk in a blood-red blur behind the ridges, and as the men in blue slowly yielded the last slope darkness which was already heavy in the defiles and ravines swept down over the valley.

Jackson had won, but his men had suffered heavily and moreover he had stood on the defense. He could not descend into the valley in the face of the Northern resistance which was sure to be fierce and enduring. The Northern cannon were beginning to send curving shells again over the cliffs, sinister warnings of what the Virginians might expect if they came down to attack. Harry and the other staff officers peering over the crest saw many fires burning along the banks of the river. Milroy seemed to be still bidding Jackson defiance.

Harry saw no preparations for a return assault. Jackson was inspecting the ground, but his men were going over the field gathering up the wounded and burying the dead. The Georgians had suffered terribly — most of all — for their rash bravery, and the whole army was subdued. There was less of exuberant youth, and more of grim and silent resolve.

Harry worked far into the night carrying orders here and there. The moon came out and clothed the strange and weird battlefield in a robe of silver. The heavens were sown with starshine, but it all seemed mystic and unreal to the excited nerves of the boy. The mountains rose to two, three times their real height, and the valley in which the Northern fires burned became a mighty chasm.

It was one o'clock in the morning before Jackson himself left the field and went to his headquarters at a little farmhouse on the plateau. His faithful colored servant was waiting for him with food. He had not touched any the whole day, but he declined it saying that he needed nothing but sleep. He flung himself booted and clothed upon a bed and was sound asleep in five minutes.

There was a little porch on one side of the house, and here Harry, who had received no instructions from his general, camped. He rolled himself in his cavalry cloak, lay down on the hard floor which was not hard to him, and slept like a little child.

He was awakened at dawn as one often is by a presence, even though that presence be noiseless. He felt a great unwillingness to get up. That was a good floor on which he slept, and the cavalry cloak wrapped around him was the finest and warmest that he had ever felt. He did not wish to abandon either. But will triumphed. He opened his eyes and sprang quickly to his feet.

Stonewall Jackson was standing beside him looking intently toward the valley. The edge of a blazing sun barely showed in the east, and in the west all the peaks and ridges were yet in the dusk. Morning was coming in silence. There was no sound of battle or of the voices of men.

"I beg your pardon. I fear that I have overslept myself!" exclaimed Harry.

"Not at all," said Jackson with a slight smile. "The others of the staff are yet asleep. You might have come inside. A little room was left on the floor there."

"I never had a better bed and I never slept better." The general smiled again and gave Harry an approving glance.

"Soldiers, especially boys, learn quickly to endure any kind of hardship," he said. "Come, we'll see if the enemy is still there."

Harry fancied from his tone that he believed Milroy gone, but knowing better than to offer any opinion of his own he followed him toward the edge of the valley. The pickets saluted as the silent figures passed. The sun in the east was rising higher over the valley, and in the west the peaks and ridges were coming out of the dusk.

The general carried his glasses slung over his shoulder, but he did not need them. One glance into the valley and they saw that the army of Milroy was gone. It had disappeared, horse, foot and guns, and Harry now knew that the long row of camp fires in the night had been a show, but only a brave show, after all.

The whole Southern army awoke and poured down the slopes. Yes, Milroy, not believing that he was strong enough for another battle, had gone down the valley. He had fought one good battle, but he would reach Banks before he fought another.

The Southern troops felt that they had won the victory, and Jackson sent a message to Richmond announcing it. Never had news come at a more opportune time. The fortunes of the South seemed to be at the lowest ebb. Richmond had heard of the great battle of Shiloh, the failure to destroy Grant and the death of Albert Sidney Johnston. New Orleans, the largest and richest city in the Confederacy, had been taken by the Northern fleet — the North was always triumphant on the water — and the mighty army of McClellan had landed on the Peninsula of Virginia for the advance on Richmond.

It had seemed that the South was doomed, and the war yet scarcely a year old. But in the mountains the strange professor of mathematics had struck a blow and he might strike another. Both North and South realized anew that no one could ever tell where he was or what he might do. The great force, advancing by land to co-operate with McClellan, hesitated, and drew back.

But Jackson's troops knew nothing then of what was passing in the minds of men at Washington and Richmond. They were following Milroy and that commander, wily as well as brave, was pressing his men to the utmost in order that he might escape the enemy who, he was sure, would pursue with all his power. He knew that he had fought with Stonewall Jackson and he knew the character of the Southern leader.

Sherburne brought his horses through a defile into the valley and his men, now mounted, led the pursuit. Jackson in his eagerness rode with him and Harry was there, too. Behind them came the famous foot cavalry. Thus pursuer and pursued rolled down the valley, and Harry exulted when he looked at the path of the fleeing army. The traces were growing fresher and fresher. Jackson was gaining.

But there were shrewd minds in Milroy's command. The Western men knew many devices of battle and the trail, and Milroy was desperately bent upon saving his force, which he knew would be overwhelmed, if overtaken by Jackson's army. Now he had recourse to a singular device.

Harry, riding with Captain Sherburne, noticed that the trees were dry despite the recent rains. On the slopes of the mountains the water ran off fast, and the thickets were dry also. Then he saw a red light in the forest in front of them. General Jackson saw it at the same time.

"What is that?" he exclaimed.

"It looks like a forest fire, general," replied Sherburne.

"You're right, captain, and it's growing."

As they galloped forward they saw the red light expand rapidly and spread directly across their path. The whole forest was on fire. Great flames rose up the trunks of trees and leaped from bough to bough. Sparks flew in millions and vast clouds of smoke, picked up by the wind, were whirled in their faces.

The troop of cavalry was compelled to pause and General Jackson, brushing the smoke from his eyes, said:

"Clever! very clever! Milroy has put a fiery wall between us."

The device was a complete success. The pursuing men in gray could pass around the fire at points, and wait at other points for it to burn out, but they lost so much time that their cavalry were able only to skirmish with the Northern rear guard. Then when night came on Milroy escaped under cover of the thick and smoky darkness.

Harry slept on the ground that night, but the precious cloak was around him. He slept beyond the dawn as the pursuit was now abandoned, but when he arose smoke was still floating over the valley and the burned forests. He was stiff and sore, but the fierce hunger that assailed him made him forget the aching of his bones. He had eaten nothing for thirty-six hours. He had forgotten until then that there was such a thing as food. But the sight of Langdon holding a piece of frying bacon on a stick afflicted him with a raging desire.

"Give me that bacon, Tom," he cried, "or I'll set the rest of the forest on fire!"

"No need, you old war-horse. I was just bringing it to you. There's plenty more where this came from. The foot cavalry took it at McDowell, and like the wise boys they are brought it on with them. Come and join us. Your general is already riding a bit up the valley, and, as he didn't call you, it follows that he doesn't want you."

Harry followed him gladly. The Invincibles had found a good place, and were cooking a solid breakfast. They had bacon and ham and coffee and bread in abundance, and for a while there was a great eating and drinking.

To youth which had marched and fought without food it was not a breakfast. It was a banquet and a feast. Young frames which recover quickly responded at once. Now and then, the musical clatter of iron spoons and knives on iron cups and plates was broken by deep sighs of satisfaction. But they did not speak for a while. There was lost time to be made up, and they did not know when they would get another such chance—the odds were always against it.

"Enough is enough," said Langdon at last. "It took a lot to make enough, but it's enough. You have to be a soldier, Harry, to appreciate what it is to eat, sleep and rest. I'm willing to wager my uniform against a last winter's snowball that we don't get another such meal in a month. Old Jack won't let us."

"To my mind," said St. Clair, "we're going right into the middle of big things. We've chased the Yankees out of the mountains into the valley, and we'll follow hot on their heels. We've already learned enough of General Jackson to know that he doesn't linger."

"Linger!" exclaimed Langdon indignantly. "Even if there was no fighting to be done he'd march us from one end of the valley to the other just to keep us in practice. Hear that bugle! Off we go! Five minutes to get ready! Or maybe it is only three!"

It was more than five minutes, but not much more, when the whole army was on the march again, but the foot cavalry forgot to grumble when they came again into their beloved valley, across which, and up and down which, they had marched so much.

They threw back their shoulders, their gait became more jaunty and they burst into cheers, at the sight of the rich rolling country, now so beautiful in spring's heavy green. Far off the mountains rose, dark and blue, but they were only the setting for the gem and made it more precious.

"It's ours," said Sherburne proudly to Harry. "We left it to the Yankees for a little while, but we've come back to claim it, and if the unbidden tenant doesn't get out at once we'll put him out. Harry, haven't you got Virginia kinfolks? We want to adopt you and call you a Virginian."

"Lots of them. My great-grandfather, Governor Ware, was born in Maryland, but all the people on my mother's side were of Virginia origin."

"I might have known it. Kentucky is the daughter of Virginia though a large part of Kentucky takes sides with the Yankees. But that's not your fault. Remember, for the time being you're a Virginian, one of us by right of blood and deed."

"Count me among 'em at once," said Harry. He felt a certain pride in this off-hand but none the less real adoption, because he knew that it was a great army with which he marched, and it might immortalize itself.

"What's the news, Harry?" asked Sherburne. "You're always near Old Jack, and if he lets anything come from under that old hat of his, which isn't often, it's because he's willing for it to be known."

"He's said this, and he doesn't mean it to be any secret. Banks is at Strasburg with a big army, but he's fortified himself there and he doesn't know just what to do. He doesn't for the life of him know which way Jackson is coming, nor do I. But I do know that Ewell with his division is going to join us at last and we'll have a sizable army."

"And that means bigger things!" exclaimed Sherburne, joyously. "Between you and me, Harry, Banks won't sleep soundly again for many a night!"

As they marched on the valley people came out joyously to meet them. Even women and girls on horseback, galloping, reined in their horses to tell them where the Union forces lay. Always they had information for Jackson, never any for the North. Here scouts and spies were scarcely needed by the Southern army. Before night Stonewall Jackson knew as much of his enemy as any general needed to know.

They camped at dusk and Langdon, contrary to his prediction, enjoyed another ample meal and plenty of rest. Jackson allowed no tent to be set for himself. The night was warm and beautiful and the songs of birds came from the trees. The general had eaten sparingly, and now he sat on a log in deep thought. Presently he looked up and said:

"Lieutenant Kenton, do you and Lieutenant Dalton ride forward in that direction and meet General Ewell. He is coming, with his staff, to see me. Escort him to the camp."

He pointed out the direction and in an instant Harry and Dalton, also of the staff, were in the camp, following the line of that pointing finger. They had the password and as they passed a little beyond the pickets they saw a half dozen horsemen riding rapidly toward them in the dusk.

"General Ewell, is it not, sir?" said Harry, as he and Dalton gave the salute.

"I'm General Ewell," replied the foremost horseman. "Do you come from General Jackson?"

"Yes, sir. His camp is just before you. You can see the lights now. He has directed us to meet you and escort you."

"Then lead the way."

The two young lieutenants, guiding General Ewell and his staff, were soon inside Jackson's camp, but Harry had time to observe Ewell well. He had already heard of him as a man of great vigor and daring. He had made a name for judgment and dash in the Indian wars on the border. Men spoke of him as a soldier, prompt to obey his superior and ready to take responsibility if his superior were not there. Harry knew that Jackson expected much of him.

He saw a rather slender man with wonderfully bright eyes that smiled much, a prominent and pronounced nose and a strong chin. When he took off his hat at the meeting with Jackson he disclosed a round bald head, which he held on one side when he talked.

Jackson had risen from the log as Ewell rode up and leaped from his magnificent horse—his horses were always of the best—and he advanced, stretching out his hand. Ewell clasped it and the two talked. The staffs of the two generals had withdrawn out of ear shot, but Harry noticed that Ewell did much the greater part of the talking, his head cocked on one side in that queer, striking manner. But Harry knew, too, that the mind and will of Jackson were dominant, and that Ewell readily acknowledged them as so.

The conference did not last long. Then the two generals shook hands again and Ewell sprang upon his horse. Jackson beckoned to Harry.

"Lieutenant Kenton," he said, "ride with General Ewell to his camp. You will then know the way well, and he may wish to send me some quick dispatch."

Harry, nothing loath, was in the saddle in an instant, and at the wish of General Ewell rode by his side.

"You have been with him long?" said Ewell.

"From the beginning of the campaign here, sir."

"Then you were at both Kernstown and McDowell. A great general, young man."

"Yes, sir. He will march anywhere and fight anything."

"That's my own impression. We've heard that his men are the greatest marchers in the world. My own lads under him will acquire the same merit."

"We know, sir, that your men are good marchers already."

General Ewell laughed with satisfaction.

"It's true," he said. "When I told my second in command that we were going to march to join General Jackson he wanted to bring tents. I told him that would load us up with a lot of tent poles and that he must bring only a few, for the sick, perhaps. There must be no baggage, just food and ammunition. I told 'em that when we joined General Jackson we'd have nothing to do but eat and fight."

He seemed now to be speaking to himself rather than to Harry, and the boy said nothing. Ewell, relapsing into silence, urged his horse to a gallop and the staff perforce galloped, too. Such a pace soon brought them to the camp of the second army, and as they rode past the pickets Harry heard the sound of stringed music.

"The Cajuns," said one of the staff, a captain named Morton. Harry did not know what "Cajuns" meant, but he was soon to learn. Meanwhile the sound of the music was pleasant in his ear, and he saw that the camp, despite the lateness of the hour, was vivid with life.

General Ewell gave Harry into Captain Morton's care, and walked away to a small tent, where he was joined by several of his senior officers for a conference. But after they had tethered their horses for the night, Captain Morton took Harry through the camp.

Harry was full of eagerness and curiosity and he asked to see first the strange "Cajuns," those who made the music.

"They are Louisiana French," said Morton, "not the descendants or the original French settlers in that state, but the descendants of the French by the way of Nova Scotia."

"Oh, I see, the Acadians, the exiles."

"Yes, that's it. The name has been corrupted into Cajuns in Louisiana. They are not like the French of New Orleans and Baton Rouge and the other towns. They are rural and primitive. You'll like them. Few of them were ever more than a dozen miles from home before. They love music, and they've got a full regimental band with them. You ought to hear it play. Why, they'd play the heart right out of you."

"I like well enough the guitars and banjos that they're playing now. Seems to me that kind of music is always best at night."

They had now come within the rim of light thrown out by the fires of the Acadians, and Harry stood there looking for the first time at these dark, short people, brought a thousand miles from their homes.

They were wholly unlike Virginians and Kentuckians. They had black eyes and hair, and their naturally dark faces were burned yet darker by the sun of the Gulf. Yet the dark eyes were bright and gay, sparkling with kindliness and the love of pleasure. The guitars and banjos were playing some wailing tune, with a note of sadness in the core of it so keen and penetrating that it made the water come to Harry's eyes. But it changed suddenly to something that had all the sway and lilt of the rosy South. Men sprang to their feet and clasping arms about one another began to sway back and forth in the waltz and the polka.

Harry watched with mingled amazement and pleasure. Most of the South was religious and devout. The Virginians of the valley were nearly all staunch Presbyterians, and Stonewall Jackson, staunchest of them all, never wanted to fight on Sunday. The boy himself had been reared in a stern Methodist faith, and the lightness in this French blood of the South was new to him. But it pleased him to see them sing and dance, and he found no wrong in it, although he could not have done it himself.

Captain Morton noticed Harry's close attention and he read his mind.

"They surprised me, too, at first," he said, "but they're fine soldiers, and they've put cheer into this army many a time when it needed it most. Taylor, their commander, is a West Pointer and he's got them into wonderful trim. They're well clothed and well shod. They never straggle and they're just about the best marchers we have. They'll soon be rated high among Jackson's foot cavalry."

Harry left the Acadians with reluctance, and when he made the round of the camp General Ewell, who had finished the conference, told him that he would have no message to send that night to Jackson. He might go to sleep, but the whole division would march early in the morning. Harry wrapped himself again in his cloak, found a place soft with moss under a tree, and slept with the soft May wind playing over his face and lulling him to deeper slumber.

He rode the next morning with General Ewell and the whole division to join Jackson's army. It was a trim body of men, well clad, fresh and strong, and they marched swiftly along the turnpike, on both sides of which Jackson was encamped further on.

Harry felt a personal pride in being with Ewell when the junction was to be made. He felt that, in a sense, he was leading in this great reinforcement himself, and he looked back with intense satisfaction at the powerful column marching so swiftly along the turnpike.

They came late in the day to Jackson's pickets, and then they saw his army, scattered through the fields on either side of the road.

Harry rejoiced once more in the grand appearance of the new division. Every coat or tunic sat straight. Every shoe-lace was tied, and they marched with the beautiful, even step of soldiers on parade. They were to encamp beyond Jackson's old army, and as they passed along the turnpike it was lined on either side by Jackson's own men, cheering with vigor.

The colonel who was in immediate charge of the encampment, a man who had never seen General Jackson, asked Harry where he might find him. Harry pointed to a man sitting on the top rail of a fence beside the road.

"But I asked for General Jackson," said the colonel.

"That's General Jackson."

The colonel approached and saluted. General Jackson's clothes were soiled and dusty. His feet, encased in cavalry boots that reached beyond the knees, rested upon a lower rail of the fence. A worn cap with a dented visor almost covered his eyes. The rest of his face was concealed by a heavy, dark beard.

"General Jackson, I believe," said the officer, saluting.

"Yes. How far have those men marched?" The voice was kindly and approving.

"We've come twenty-six miles, sir."

"Good. And I see no stragglers."

"We allow no stragglers."

"Better still. I haven't been able to keep my own men from straggling, and you'll have to teach them."

At that moment the Acadian band began to play, and it played the merriest waltz it knew. Jackson gazed at it, took a lemon from his pocket and began to suck the juice from it meditatively. The officer stood before him in some embarrassment.

"Aren't they rather thoughtless for such serious work as war?" asked the Presbyterian general.

"I am confident, sir, that their natural gayety will not impair their value as soldiers."

Jackson put the end of the lemon back in his mouth and drew some juice from it. The colonel bowed and retired. Then Jackson beckoned to Harry, who stood by.

"Follow him and tell him," he said, "that the band can play as much as it likes. I noticed, too, that it plays well."

Jackson smiled and Harry hurried after the officer, who flushed with gratification, when the message was delivered to him.

"I'll tell it to the men," he said, "and they'll fight all the better for it."

That night it was a formidable army that slept in the fields on either side of the turnpike, and in the silence and the dark, Stonewall Jackson was preparing to launch the thunderbolt.

CHAPTER IX.
TURNING ON THE FOE

Harry was awakened at the first shoot of dawn by the sound of trumpets. It was now approaching the last of May and the cold nights had long since passed. A warm sun was fast showing its edge in the east, and, bathing his face at a brook and snatching a little breakfast, he was ready. Stonewall Jackson was already up, and his colored servant was holding Little Sorrel for him.

The army was fast forming into line, the new men of Ewell resolved to become as famous foot cavalry as those who had been with Jackson all along. Ewell himself, full of enthusiasm and already devoted to his chief, was riding among them, and whenever he spoke to one of them he cocked his head on one side in the peculiar manner that was habitual with him. Now and then, as the sun grew warmer, he took off his hat and his bald head gleamed under the yellow rays.

"Which way do you think we're going?" said the young staff officer, George Dalton, to Harry—Dalton was a quiet youth with a good deal of the Puritan about him and Harry liked him.

"I'm not thinking about it at all," replied Harry with a laugh. "I've quit trying to guess what our general is going to do, but I fancy that he means to lead us against the enemy. He has the numbers now."

"I suppose you're right," said Dalton. "I've been trying to guess all along, but I think I'll give it up now and merely follow where the general leads."

The bugles blew, the troops rapidly fell into line and marched northward along the turnpike, the Creole band began to play again one of those lilting waltz tunes, and the speed of the men increased, their feet rising and falling swiftly to the rhythm of the galloping air. Jackson, who was near the head of the column, looked back and

Harry saw a faint smile pass over his grim face. He saw the value of the music.

"I never heard such airs in our Presbyterian church," said Dalton to Harry.

"But this isn't a church."

"No, it isn't, but those Creole tunes suit here. They put fresh life into me."

"Same here. And they help the men, too. Look how gay they are."

Up went the shining sun. The brilliant blue light, shot with gold, spread from horizon to horizon, little white clouds of vapor, tinted at the edges with gold from the sun, floated here and there. It was beautiful May over all the valley. White dust flew from the turnpike under the feet of so many marching men and horses, and the wheels of cannon. Suddenly the Georgia troops that had suffered so severely at McDowell began to sing a verse from the Stars and Bars, and gradually the whole column joined in:

"Now Georgia marches to the front
And close beside her come
Her sisters by the Mexique sea
With pealing trump and drum,
Till answering back from hill and glen
The rallying cry afar,
A nation hoists the Bonnie Blue Flag
That bears a single star."

It was impossible not to feel emotion. The face of the most solemn Presbyterian of them all flushed and his eyes glowed. Now the band, that wonderful band of the Acadians, was playing the tune, and the mighty chorus rolled and swelled across the fields. Harry's heart throbbed hard. He was with the South, his own South, and he was swayed wholly by feeling.

The Acadians were leading the army. Harry saw Jackson whispering something to a staff officer. The officer galloped forward and spoke to Taylor, the commander of the Louisiana troops. Instantly the Acadians turned sharply from the turnpike and walked in a diagonal line through the fields. The whole army followed and they marched steadily northward and eastward.

Harry had another good and close view of the Massanuttons, now one vast mass of dark green foliage, and it caused his thoughts to turn to Shepard. He had no doubt that the wary and astute Northern scout was somewhere near watching the march of Stonewall. He had secured a pair of glasses of his own and he scanned the fields and forests now for a sight of him and his bold horsemen. But he saw no blue uniforms, merely farmers and their wives and children, shouting with joy at the sight of Jackson, eager to give him information, and eager to hide it from Banks.

But Harry was destined to have more than another view of the Massanuttons. Jackson marched steadily for four days, crossing the Massanuttons at the defile, and coming down into the eastern valley. The troops were joyous throughout the journey, although they had not the least idea for what they were destined, and Ewell's men made good their claim to a place of equal honor in the foot cavalry.

They were now in the division of the great valley known as the Luray, and only when they stopped did Harry and his comrades of the staff learn that the Northern army under Kenly was only ten miles away at Front Royal.

The preceding night had been one of great confidence, even of light-heartedness in Washington. The worn and melancholy President felt that a triumphant issue of the war was at hand. The Secretary of War was more than sanguine, and the people in the city joyfully expected speedy news of the fall of Richmond. McClellan was advancing with an overwhelming force on the Southern capital, and the few regiments of Jackson were lost somewhere in the mountains. In the west all things were going well under Grant.

It was only a few who, recognizing that the army of Jackson was lost to Northern eyes, began to ask questions about it. But they were laughed down. Jackson had too few men to do any harm, wherever he might be. Nobody suspected that at dawn Jackson, with a strong force, would be only a little more than three score miles from the Union capital itself. Even Banks himself, who was only half that distance from the Southern army, did not dream that it was coming.

When the sun swung clear that May morning there was a great elation in this army which had been lost to its enemies for days and which the unknowing despised. They ate a good breakfast, and then, as the Creole band began to play its waltzes again, they advanced swiftly on Front Royal.

"We'll be attacking in two hours," said Dalton.

"In less time than that, I'm thinking," said Harry. "Look how the men are speeding it up!"

The band ceased suddenly. Harry surmised that it had been stopped, in order to suppress noise as much as possible, now that they were approaching the enemy. Cheering and loud talking also were stopped, and they heard now the heavy beat of footsteps, horses and men, and the rumble of vehicles, cannon and wagons. The morning was bright and hot. A haze of heat hung over the mountains, and to Harry the valley was more beautiful and picturesque than ever. He had again flitting feelings of melancholy that it should be torn so ruthlessly by war.

If Shepard and other Northern scouts were near, they were lax that morning. Not a soul in the garrison at Front Royal dreamed of Jackson's swift approach. They were soon to have a terrible awakening.

Harry saw Jackson raise the visor of his old cap a little, and he saw the eyes beneath it gleam.

"We must be near Front Royal," he said to Dalton.

"It's just beyond the woods there. It's not more than half a mile away."

The army halted a moment and Jackson sent forward a long line of skirmishers through the wood. Sherburne's cavalry were to ride just behind them, and he dispatched Harry and Dalton with the captain. At the first sound of the firing the whole army would rush upon Front Royal.

The skirmishers, five hundred strong, pressed forward through the wood. They were sun-browned, eager fellows, every one carrying a rifle, and all sharpshooters.

It seemed to Harry that the skirmishers were through the wood in an instant, like a force of Indians bursting from ambush upon an unsuspecting foe. The Northern pickets were driven in like leaves before a whirlwind. The rattle and then the crash of rifles beat upon the ears, and the Southern horsemen were galloping through the streets of the startled village by the time the Northern commander, posted with his main force just behind the town, knew that Jackson had emerged from the wilderness and was upon him. Banks not dreaming of Jackson's nearness, had taken away Kenly's cavalry, and there were only pickets to see.

The Northern commander was brave and capable. He drew up his men rapidly on a ridge and planted his guns in front, but the storm was too heavy and swift.

Harry saw the front of the Southern army burst into fire, and then a deadly sleet of shell and bullets was poured upon the Northern force. He and Dalton did not have time to rejoin Jackson, but they kept with Sherburne's force as the group of wild horsemen swung around toward the Northern rear, intending to cut it off.

Harry heard the Southern bugles playing mellow and triumphant tunes, and they inflamed his brain. All the little pulses in his head began to beat heavily. Millions of black specks danced before his eyes, but the air about them was red. He began to shout with the others. The famous rebel yell, which had in it the menacing quality of the Indian war whoop, was already rolling from the half circle of the attacking army, as it rushed forward.

Kenly hung to his ground, fighting with the courage of desperation, and holding off for a little while the gray masses that rushed upon him. But when he heard that the cavalry of Sherburne was already behind him, and was about to gain a position between him and the river, he retreated as swiftly as he could, setting fire to all his tents and stores, and thundering in good order with his remaining force over the bridge.

These Northern men, New Yorkers largely, were good material, like their brethren of Ohio and West Virginia. Despite the surprise and the overwhelming rush of Jackson, they stopped to set fire to the bridge, and they would have closed that avenue of pursuit had not the Acadians rushed forward, heedless of bullets and flames, and put it out. Yet the bridge was damaged and the Southern pursuit could cross but slowly. Kenly, seeing his advantage, and cool and ready, drew up his men on a hill and poured a tremendous fire upon the bridge.

Harry saw the daring deed of the men from the Gulf coast, and he clapped his hands in delight. But he had only a moment's view.

Sherburne was curving away in search of a ford and all his men galloped close behind him.

Near the town the river was deep and swift and the horsemen would be swept away by it, but willing villagers running at the horses' heads led them to fords farther down.

"Into the river, boys!" shouted Sherburne, as he with Harry and Dalton by his side galloped into the stream. It seemed to Harry that the whole river was full of horsemen in an instant, and then he saw Stonewall Jackson himself, riding Little Sorrel into the stream.

Harry's horse stumbled once on the rocky bottom, but recovered his footing, and the boy urged him on toward the bank, bumping on either side against those who were as eager as he. He was covered with water and foam, churned up by so many horses, but he did not notice it. In a minute his horse put his forefeet upon the bank, pulled himself up, and then they were all formed up by Jackson himself for the pursuit.

"They run! They run already!" cried Sherburne.

They were not running, exactly, but Kenly, always alert and cool, had seen the passage of the ford by the Virginians, and unlimbering his guns, was retreating in good order, but swiftly, his rear covered by the New York cavalry.

Now Harry saw all the terrors of war. It was not sufficient for Jackson to defeat the enemy. He must follow and destroy him. More of his army crossed at the fords and more poured over the bridge.

The New York cavalry, despite courage and tenacity, could not withstand the onset of superior numbers. They were compelled to give way, and Kenly ordered his infantry, retreating on the turnpike, to turn and help them. Jackson had not waited for his artillery, but his riflemen poured volley after volley of bullets upon the beaten army, while his cavalry, galloping in the fields, charged it with sabers on either flank.

Harry was scarcely conscious of what he was doing. He was slashing with his sword and shooting with the rest. Sometimes his eyes were filled with dust and smoke and then again they would clear. He heard the voices of officers shouting to both cavalry and infantry to charge, and then there was a confused and terrible melee.

Harry never remembered much of that charge, and he was glad that he did not. He preferred that it should remain a blur in which he could not pick out the details. He was conscious of the shock, when horse met horse and body met body. He saw the flash of rifle and pistol shots, and the gleam of sabers through the smoke, and he heard a continuous shouting kept up by friend and foe.

Then he felt the Northern army, struck with such terrific force, giving way. Kenly had made a heroic stand, but he could no longer support the attacks from all sides. One of his cannon was taken and then all. He himself fell wounded terribly. His senior officers also fell, as they tried to rally their men, who were giving way at all points.

Sherburne wheeled his troop away again and charged at the Northern cavalry, which was still in order. Harry had seen Jackson himself give the command to the captain. It was the redoubtable commander who saw all and understood all, who always struck, with his sword directly at the weak point in the enemy's armor. Harry saw that eye glittering as he had never seen it glitter before, and the command was given in words of fire that communicated a like fire to every man in the troop.

The Northern cavalry cut to pieces, Kenly's whole army dissolved. The attack was so terrific, so overwhelming, and was pushed home so hard, that panic ran through the ranks of those brave men. They fled through the orchards and the fields, and Jackson never ceased to urge on the pursuit, taking whole companies here and there, and seizing scattered fugitives.

Ashby, with the chief body of the cavalry, galloped on ahead to a railway station, where Pennsylvania infantry were on guard. They had just got ready a telegraphic message to Banks for help, but his men rushed the station before it could be sent, tore up the railroad tracks, cut the telegraph wires, carried by storm a log house in which the Pennsylvanians had taken refuge, and captured them all.

The Northern army had ceased to exist. Save for some fugitives, it had all fallen or was in the hands of Jackson, and the triumphant cheers of the Southerners rang over the field. Banks, at Strasburg, not far away, did not know that Kenly's force had been destroyed. Three hours after the attack had been made, an orderly covered with dust galloped into his camp and told him that Kenly was pressed hard — he did not know the full truth himself.

Banks, whose own force was cut down by heavy drafts to the eastward, was half incredulous. It was impossible that Jackson could be at Front Royal. He was fifty or sixty miles away, and the attack must be some cavalry raid which would soon be beaten off. He sent a regiment and two guns to see what was the matter. He telegraphed later to the Secretary of War at Washington that a force of several thousand rebels gathered in the mountains was pushing Kenly hard.

Meanwhile the victorious Southerners were spending a few moments in enjoying their triumph. They captured great quantities of food and clothing which Kenly had not found time to destroy, and which they joyously divided among themselves.

Harry found the two colonels and all the rest of the Invincibles lying upon the ground in the fields. Some of them were wounded, but most were unhurt. They were merely panting from exhaustion. Colonel Leonidas Talbot sat up when he saw Harry, and Lieutenant-Colonel Hector St. Hilaire also sat up.

"Good afternoon, Harry," said Colonel Talbot, politely. "It's been a warm day."

"But a victorious one, sir."

"Victorious, yes; but it is not finished. I fancy that in spite of everything we have not yet learned the full capabilities of General Jackson, eh, Hector?"

"No, sir, we haven't," replied Lieutenant-Colonel Hector St. Hilaire, emphatically. "I never saw such an appetite for battle. In Mexico General Winfield Scott would press the enemy hard, but he was not anxious to march twenty miles and fight a battle every day."

Harry found St. Clair and Langdon not far away from their chief officers. St. Clair had brushed the dust off his clothing, but he was regarding ruefully two bullet holes in the sleeve of his fine gray tunic.

"He has neither needle nor thread with which to sew up those holes," said Langdon, with wicked glee, "and he must go into battle again with a tunic more holy than righteous. It's been a bad day for clothes."

"A man doesn't fight any worse because he's particular about his uniform, does he?" asked St. Clair.

"You don't. That's certain, old fellow," said Langdon, clapping him on the back. "And just think how much worse it might have been. Those bullets, instead of merely going through your coat sleeve, might have gone through your arm also, shattering every bone in it. Now, Harry, you ride with Old Jack. Tell us what he means to do. Are we going to rest on our rich and numerous laurels, or is it up and after the Yanks hot-foot?"

"He's not telling me anything," replied Harry, "but I think it's safe to predict that we won't take any long and luxurious rest. Nor will we ever take any long and luxurious rest while we're led by Stonewall Jackson."

Jackson marched some distance farther toward Strasburg, where the army of Banks, yet unbelieving, lay, and as the night was coming on thick and black with clouds, went into camp. But among their captured stores they had ample food now, and tents and blankets to protect themselves from the promised rain.

The Acadians, who were wonderful cooks, showed great culinary skill as well as martial courage. They were becoming general favorites, and they prepared all sorts of appetizing dishes, which they shared freely with the Virginians, the Georgians and the others. Then the irrepressible band began. In the fire-lighted woods and on the ground yet stained by the red of battle, it played quaint old tunes, waltzes and polkas and roundelays, and once more the stalwart Pierres and Raouls and Luciens and Etiennes, clasping one another in their arms, whirled in wild dances before the fires.

The heavy clouds opened bye and bye, and then all save the sentinels fled to shelter. Harry and Dalton, who had been watching the dancing, went to a small tent which had been erected for themselves and two more. Next to it was a tent yet smaller, occupied by the commander-in-chief, and as they passed by it they heard low but solemn tones lifted in invocation to God. Harry could not keep from taking one fleeting glance. He saw Jackson on his knees, and then he went quickly on.

The other two officers had not yet come, and Dalton and he were alone in the tent. It was too dark inside for Harry to see Dalton's face, but he knew that his comrade, too, had seen and heard.

"It will be hard to beat a general who prays," said Dalton. "Some of our men laugh at Jackson's praying, but I've always heard that the Puritans, whether in England or America, were a stern lot to face."

"The enemy at least won't laugh at him. I've heard that they had great fun deriding a praying professor of mathematics, but I fancy they've quit it. If they haven't they'll do so when they hear of Front Royal."

The tent was pitched on the bare ground, but they had obtained four planks, every one about a foot wide and six feet or so long. They were sufficient to protect them from the rain which would run under the tent and soak into the ground. Harry had long since learned that a tent and a mere strip of plank were a great luxury, and now he appreciated them at their full value.

He wrapped himself in the invaluable cloak, stretched his weary body upon his own particular plank, and was soon asleep. He was awakened in the night by a low droning sound. He did not move on his plank, but lay until his eyes became used partially to the darkness. Then he saw two other figures also wrapped in their cloaks and stretched on their planks, dusky and motionless. But the fourth figure was kneeling on his plank and Harry saw that it was Dalton, praying even as Stonewall Jackson had prayed.

Then Harry shut his eyes. He was not devout himself, but in the darkness of the night, with the rain beating a tattoo on the canvas walls of the tent, he felt very solemn. This was war, red war, and he was in the midst of it. War meant destruction, wounds, agony and death. He might never again see Pendleton and his father and his aunt and his cousin, Dick Mason, and Dr. Russell and all his boyhood and school friends. It was no wonder that George Dalton prayed. He ought to be praying himself, and lying there and not stirring he said under his breath a simple prayer that his mother had taught him when he was yet a little child.

Then he fell asleep again, and awoke no more until the dawn. But while Harry slept the full dangers of his situation became known to Banks far after midnight at Strasburg. The regiment and the two guns that he had sent down the turnpike to relieve Kenly had been fired upon so incessantly by Southern pickets and riflemen that they were compelled to turn back. Everywhere the Northern scouts and skirmishers were driven in. Despite the darkness and rain they found a wary foe whom they could not pass.

It was nearly two o'clock in the morning when Banks was aroused by a staff officer who said that a man insisted upon seeing him. The man, the officer said, claimed to have news that meant life or death, and he carried on his person a letter from President Lincoln, empowering him to go where he pleased. He had shown that letter, and his manner indicated the most intense and overpowering anxiety.

Banks was surprised, and he ordered that the stranger be shown in at once. A tall man, wrapped in a long coat of yellow oilcloth, dripping rain, was brought into the room. He held a faded blue cap in his hand, and the general noticed that the hand was sinewy and powerful. The front of the coat was open a little at the top, disclosing a dingy blue coat. His high boots were spattered to the tops with mud.

There was something in the man's stern demeanor and his intense, burning gaze that daunted Banks, who was a brave man himself. Moreover, the general was but half dressed and had risen from a warm couch, while the man before him had come in on the storm, evidently from some great danger, and his demeanor showed that he was ready for other and instant dangers. For the moment the advantage was with the stranger, despite the difference in rank.

"Who are you?" asked the general.

"My name, sir, is Shepard, William J. Shepard. I am a spy or a scout in the Union service. I have concealed upon me a letter from President Lincoln, empowering me to act in such a capacity and to go where I please. Do you wish to see it, sir?"

Shepard spoke with deference, but there was no touch of servility in his tone.

"Show me the letter," said Banks.

Shepard thrust a hand into his waistcoat and withdrew a document which he handed to the general. Banks glanced through it rapidly.

"It's from Lincoln," he said; "I know that handwriting, but it would not be well for you to be captured with that upon you."

"If I were about to be captured I should destroy it."

"Why have you come here? What message do you bring?"

"The worst possible message, sir. Stonewall Jackson and an army of twenty thousand men will be upon you in the morning."

"What! What is this you say! It was only a cavalry raid at Front Royal!"

"It was no cavalry raid at Front Royal, sir! It was Jackson and his whole army! I ought to have known, sir! I should have got there and have warned Kenly in time, but I could not! My horse was killed by a rebel sharpshooter in the woods as I was approaching! I could not get up in time, but I saw what happened!"

"Kenly! Kenly, where is he?"

"Mortally wounded or dead, and his army is destroyed! They made a brave stand, even after they were defeated at the village. They might have got away had anybody but Jackson been pursuing. But he gave them no chance. They were enveloped by cavalry and infantry, and only a few escaped."

"Good God!" exclaimed Banks, aghast.

"Nor is that all, sir. They are close at hand! They will attack you at dawn! They are in full force! Ewell's army has joined Jackson and Jackson leads them all! We must leave Strasburg at once or we are lost!"

Shepard's manner admitted of no doubt. Banks hurried forth and sent officers to question the pickets. All the news they brought was confirmatory. Even in the darkness and rain shots had been fired at them by the Southern skirmishers. Banks sent for all of his important officers, the troops were gathered together, and leaving a strong rear-guard, they began a rapid march toward Winchester, which Jackson had loved so well.

Swiftness and decision now on the other side had saved the Northern army from destruction. Banks did not realize until later, despite the urgent words of Shepard, how formidable was the danger that threatened him. Jackson, despite all the disadvantages of the darkness and the rain, wished to get his army up before daylight, but the deep mud formed by the pouring rain enabled Banks to slip away from the trap.

The Southern troops, moreover, were worn to the bone. They had come ninety miles in five days over rough roads, across streams without bridges, and over a high mountain, besides fighting a battle of uncommon fierceness. There were limits even to the endurance of Jackson's foot cavalry.

Harry was first awake in the little tent. He sat up and looked at the other three on their planks who were sleeping as if they would never wake any more. A faint tint of dawn was appearing at the open flap of the door. The four had lain down dressed fully, and Harry, as he sprang from his board, cried:

"Up, boys, up! The army is about to move!"

The three also sprang to their feet, and went outside. Although the dawn was as yet faint, the army was awakening rapidly, or rather was being awakened. The general himself appeared a moment later, dressed fully, the end of a lemon in his mouth, his face worn and haggard by incredible hardships, but his eyes full of the strength that comes from an unconquerable will.

He nodded to Harry, Dalton and the others.

"Five minutes for breakfast, gentlemen," he said, "and then join me on horseback, ready for the pursuit of the enemy!"

The few words were like the effects of a galvanic battery on Harry. Peculiarly susceptible to mental power, Jackson was always a stimulus to him. Close contact revealed to him the fiery soul that lay underneath the sober and silent exterior, and, in his own turn, he caught fire from it. Youthful, impressionable and extremely sensitive to great minds and great deeds, Stonewall Jackson had become his hero, who could do no wrong.

Five minutes for the hasty breakfast and they were in the saddle just behind Jackson. The rain had ceased, the sun was rising in a clear sky, the country was beautiful once more, and down a long line the Southern bugles were merrily singing the advance. Very soon scattered shots all along their front showed that they were in touch with the enemy.

The infantry and cavalry left by Banks as a curtain between himself and Jackson did their duty nobly that morning. The pursuit now led into a country covered with forest, and using every advantage of such shelter, the Northern companies checked the Southern advance as much as was humanly possible. Many of them were good riflemen, particularly those from Ohio, and the cavalry of Ashby, Funsten and Sherburne found the woods very warm for them. Horses were falling continually, and often their riders fell with them to stay.

Harry, in the center with the commander, heard the heavy firing to both right and left, and he glanced often at Jackson. He saw his lips move as if he were talking to himself, and he knew that he was disappointed at this strong resistance. Troops could move but slowly through woods in the face of a heavy rifle fire, and meanwhile Banks with his main body was escaping to Winchester.

"Mr. Kenton," said Jackson sharply, "ride to General Ashby and tell him to push the enemy harder! We must crush at least a portion of this army! It is vital!"

Harry was off as soon as the last words left the general's lips. He spurred his horse from the turnpike, leaped a low rail fence, and galloped across a field toward a forest, where Ashby's cavalry were advancing and the rifles were cracking fast.

Bullets from the Northern skirmishers flew over him and beside him, as he flew about the field, but he thought little of them. He was growing so thoroughly inured to war that he seldom realized the dangers until they were passed.

Neither he nor his horse was hurt—their very speed, perhaps, saved them and they entered the wood, where the Southern cavalry were riding.

"General Ashby!" he cried to the first man he saw. "Where is he? I've a message from General Jackson!"

The soldier pointed to a figure on horseback but a short distance away, and Harry galloped up.

"General Jackson asks you to press the enemy harder!" he said to Ashby. "He wishes him to be driven in rapidly!"

A faint flush came into the brown cheeks of Ashby.

"He shall be obeyed," he replied. "We're about to charge in full force! Hold, young man! You can't go back now! You must charge with us!"

He put his hand on Harry's rein as he spoke, and the boy saw that a strong force of Northern cavalry had now appeared in the fields directly between him and his general. Ashby turned the next instant to a bugler at his elbow and exclaimed fiercely:

"Blow! Blow with all your might!"

The piercing notes of the charge rang forth again and again. Ashby, shouting loudly and continuously and waving his sword above his head, galloped forward. His whole cavalry force galloped with him and swept down upon the defenders.

Nor did Ashby lack support. The Acadians led by Taylor swung forward on a run, and a battery, coming at the double quick, unlimbered and opened fire. Jackson had directed all, he had brought up the converging lines, and the whole Northern rear guard, two thousand cavalry, some infantry and a battery, were caught. Just before them lay the little village of Middletown, and in an instant they were driven into its streets, where they were raked by shot and shell from the cannon, while the rifles of the cavalry and of the Louisiana troops swept them with bullets.

Again the Northern soldiers, brave and tenacious though they might be, could make no stand against the terrible rush of Jackson's victorious and superior numbers. They had no such leading as their foes. The man, the praying professor, was proving himself everything.

As at Front Royal, the Northern force was crushed. It burst from the village in fragments, and fled in many directions. But Jackson urged on the pursuit. Ashby's cavalry charged again and again, taking prisoners everywhere.

The people of Middletown, as red-hot for the South as were those of Front Royal, rushed from their houses and guided the victors along the right roads. They pointed where two batteries and a train of wagons were fleeing toward Winchester, and Ashby, with his cavalry, Harry still at his elbow, raced in pursuit.

CHAPTER X.
WINCHESTER

Ashby's troopers put the armed guard of the wagons to flight in an instant, and then they seized the rich pillage in these wagons. They were not yet used to the stern discipline of regular armies and Ashby strove in vain to bring most of them back to the pursuit of the flying enemy. Harry also sought to help, but they laughed at him, and he had not yet come to the point where he could cut down a disobedient soldier. Nor had the soldiers reached the point where they would suffer such treatment from an officer. Had Harry tried such a thing it is more than likely that he would have been cut down in his turn.

But the delay and similar delays elsewhere helped the retreating Northern army. Banks, feeling that the pursuit was not now so fierce, sent back a strong force with artillery under a capable officer, Gordon, to help the rear. The scattered and flying detachments also gathered around Gordon and threw themselves across the turnpike.

Harry felt the resistance harden and he saw the pursuit of the Southern army slow up. The day, too, was waning. Shadows were already appearing in the east and if Jackson would destroy Banks' army utterly he must strike quick and hard. Harry at that moment caught sight of the general on the turnpike, on Little Sorrel, the reins lying loose on the horse's neck, his master sitting erect, and gazing at the darkening battlefield which was spread out before him.

Harry galloped up and saluted.

"I could not come back at once, sir," he said, "because the enemy was crowded in between Ashby and yourself."

"But you've come at last. I was afraid you had fallen."

Harry's face flushed gratefully. He knew now that Stonewall Jackson would have missed him.

"If the night were only a little further away," continued Jackson, "we could get them all! But the twilight is fighting for them! And they fight for themselves also! Look, how those men retreat! They do well for troops who were surprised and routed not so long ago!"

He spoke in a general way to his staff, but his tone expressed decided admiration. Harry felt again that the core of the Northern resistance was growing harder and harder. The hostile cannon blazed down the road, and the men as they slowly retired sent sheets of rifle bullets at their pursuers. Detachments of their flying cavalry were stopped, reformed on the flanks, and had the temerity to charge the victors more than once.

Harry did not notice now that the twilight was gone and the sun had sunk behind the western mountains. The road between pursuer and pursued was lighted up by the constant flashes of cannon and rifles, and at times he fancied that he could see the vengeful and threatening faces of those whom he followed, but it was only fancy, fancy bred by battle and its excitement.

The pursued crossed a broad marshy creek, the Opequon, and suddenly formed in line of battle behind it with the cavalry on their flanks. The infantry poured in heavier volleys than before and their horsemen, charging suddenly upon a Virginia regiment that was trying to cross, sent it back in rapid retreat.

After the great volleys it was dark for a moment or two and then Harry saw that General Jackson and his staff were sitting alone on their horses on the turnpike. The Northern rifles flashed again on the edge of the creek, and from a long stone fence, behind which they had also taken refuge for a last stand.

Harry and his comrades urged Jackson off the turnpike, where he was a fair target for the rifles whenever there was light, and into the bushes beside it. They were just in time, as the night was illuminated an instant later by cannon flashes and then a shower of bullets swept the road where Jackson and his staff had been.

Harry thought that they would stop now, but he did not yet know fully his Stonewall Jackson. He ordered up another Virginia regiment, which, reckless of death, charged straight in front, crossed the creek and drove the men in blue out of their position.

Yet the Northern troops, men from Massachusetts, refused to be routed. They fell back in good order, carrying their guns with them, and stopping at intervals to fire with cannon and rifles at their pursuers. Jackson and his staff spurred through the Opequon. Water and mud flew in Harry's face, but he did not notice them. He was eager to be up with the first, because Jackson was still urging on the pursuit, even far into the night. Banks with his main force had escaped him for the time, but he did not mean that the Northern commander should make his retreat at leisure.

Harry had never passed through such a night. It contained nothing but continuous hours of pursuit and battle. The famous foot cavalry had marched nearly twenty miles that day, they had fought a hard combat that afternoon, and they were still fighting. But Jackson allowed not a moment's delay. He was continually sending messengers to regiments and companies to hurry up, always to hurry up, faster, and faster and yet faster.

Harry carried many such messages. In the darkness and the confusion his clothing was half torn off him by briars and bushes. His horse fell twice, stumbling into gulleys, but fortunately neither he nor his rider was injured. Often he was compelled to rein up suddenly lest he ride over the Southern lads themselves. All around him he heard the panting of men pushed to the last ounce of their strength, and often there was swearing, too. Once in the darkness he heard the voice of a boy cry out:

"Oh, Lord, have mercy on me and let me go to Hades! The Devil will have mercy on me, but Stonewall Jackson never will!"

Harry did not laugh, nor did he hear anyone else laugh. He had expressed the opinion that many of them held at that moment. Stonewall Jackson was driving them on in the darkness and the light that he furnished them was a flaming sword. It was worse to shirk and face him, than it was to go on and face the cannon and rifles of the enemy.

They called upon their reserves of strength for yet another ounce, and it came. The pursuit thundered on, through the woods and bushes and across the hills and valleys, but the men in blue, in spite of everything, retained their ranks on the turnpike, retreated in order, and facing at intervals, sent volley after volley against the foe. It was impossible for the Southern army to ride them down or destroy them with cannon and rifle.

Harry came back about midnight from one of his messages, to Jackson, who was again riding on the turnpike. Most of his staff were gone on like errands, but General Taylor who led the Acadians was now with him. Off in front the rifles were flashing, and again and again, bullets whistled near them. Harry said nothing but fell in behind Jackson and close to him to await some new commission.

They heard the thunder of a horse's hoofs behind them, and a man galloped up, he as well as his horse breathing hard.

He was the chief quartermaster of the army, and Jackson recognized him at once, despite the dark.

"Where are the wagon trains?" exclaimed Jackson, shouting forth his words.

"They're far behind. They were held up by a bad road in the Luray valley. We did our best, sir," replied the officer, his voice trembling with weariness and nervousness.

"And the ammunition wagons, where are they?"

The voice was stern, even accusing, but the officer met Jackson's gaze firmly.

"They are all right, sir," he replied. "I sacrificed the other wagons for them, though. They're at hand."

"You have done well, sir," said Jackson, and Harry thought he saw him smile. No food for his veterans, but plenty of powder. It was exactly what would appeal to Stonewall Jackson.

"Supply more powder and bullets to the men," said Jackson presently. "Keep on pushing the enemy! Never stop for a moment."

Harry mechanically put his hand in his pocket, why he did not know, but he felt a piece of bread and meat that he had put there in the morning. He fingered the foreign substance a moment, and it occurred to him that it was good to eat. It occurred to him next that he had not eaten anything since morning, and this body of his, which for the time being seemed to be dissevered from mind, might be hungry.

He took out the food and looked at it. It was certainly good to the eyes, and the body was not so completely dissevered after all, as it began to signal the mind that it was, in very truth, hungry. He was about to raise the food to his lips and then he remembered.

Spurring forward a little he held out the bread and meat to Jackson.

"It's cold and hard, sir," he said, "but you'll find it good."

"It's thoughtful of you," said Jackson. "I'll take half and see that you eat the rest. Give none of it to this hungry horde around me. They're able to forage for themselves."

Jackson ate his half and Harry his. That reminded most of the officers that they had food also, and producing it they divided it and fell to with an appetite. As they ate, a shell from one of the retreating Northern batteries burst almost over their heads and fragments of hot metal struck upon the hard road. They ate on complacently. When Jackson had finished his portion he took out one of his mysterious lemons and began to suck the end of it.

Midnight was now far behind and the pursuit never halted. One of the officers remarked jokingly that he had accepted an invitation to take breakfast on the Yankee stores in Winchester the next morning. Jackson made no comment. Harry a few minutes later uttered a little cry.

"What is it?" asked Jackson.

"We're coming upon our old battlefield of Kernstown. I know those hills even in the dark."

"So we are. You have good eyes, boy. It's been a long march, but here we are almost back in Winchester."

"The enemy are massing in front, sir," said Dalton. "It looks as if they meant to make another stand."

The Massachusetts troops, their hearts bitter at the need to retreat, were forming again on a ridge behind Kernstown, and the Pennsylvanians and others were joining them. Their batteries opened heavily on their pursuers, and the night was lighted again with the flame of many cannon and rifles.

But their efforts were vain against the resistless advance of Jackson. The peal of the Southern trumpets was heard above cannon and rifles, always calling upon the men to advance, and, summoning their strength anew, they hurled themselves upon the Northern position.

Fighting hard, but unable to turn the charge, the men in blue were driven on again, leaving more prisoners and more spoil in the hands of their pursuers. The battle at three o'clock in the morning lasted but a short time.

The sound of the retreating column, the footsteps, the hoof-beats and the roll of the cannon, died away down the turnpike. But the sound of the army marching in pursuit died, also. Jackson's men could call up no further ounce of strength. The last ounce had gone long ago. Many of them, though still marching and at times firing, were in a mere daze. The roads swam past them in a dark blur and more than one babbled of things at home.

It would soon be day and there was Winchester, where the kin of so many of them lived, that Winchester they had left once, but to which they were now coming back as conquerors, conquerors whose like had not been seen since the young Napoleon led his republican troops to the conquest of Italy. No, those French men were not as good as they. They could not march so long and over such roads. They could not march all day and all night, too, fighting and driving armies of brave men before them as they fought. Yes, the Yankees were brave men! They were liars who said they wouldn't fight! If you didn't believe it, all you had to do was to follow Stonewall Jackson and see!

Such thoughts ran in many a young head in that army and Harry's, too, was not free from them, although it was no new thing to him to admit that the Yankees could and would fight just as well as the men of his South. The difference in the last few days lay in the fact that the Southern army was led by a man while the Northern army was led by mere men.

The command to halt suddenly ran along the lines of Jackson's troops, and, before it ceased to be repeated, thousands were lying prostrate in the woods or on the grass. They flung themselves down just as they were, reckless of horses or wagons or anything else. Why should they care? They were Jackson's men. They had come a hundred miles, whipping armies as they came, and they were going to whip more. But now they meant to rest and sleep a little while, and they would resume the whipping after sunrise.

It was but a little while until dawn and they lay still. Harry, who had kept his eyes open, felt sorry for them as they lay motionless in the chill of the dawn, like so many dead men.

Jackson himself took neither sleep nor rest. Without even a cloak to keep off the cold of dawn, he walked up and down, looking at the silent ranks stretched upon the ground, or going forward a little to gaze in the direction of Winchester. Nothing escaped his eye, and he heard everything. Dalton, too, had refused to lie down and he stood with Harry. The two gazed at the sober figure walking slowly to and fro.

"He begins to frighten me," whispered Dalton. "He now seems to me at times, Harry, not to be human, or rather more than human. It has been more than a day and night now since he has taken a second of rest, and he appears to need none."

"He is human like the rest of us, but the flame in him burns stronger. He gets cold and hungry and tired just as we do, but his will carries him on all the same."

"I'm thankful that I fight with him and not against him," said Dalton earnestly.

"Yes, and you're going to march again with him in five minutes. See the gray blur in the east, George. It's the dawn and Jackson never waits on the morning."

Jackson was already giving the order for the men to awake and march forth to battle. It seemed to most of them that they had closed their eyes but a minute before. They rose, half awake, without food, cold, and stiff from the frightful exertions of the day and night before, and advanced mechanically in line.

The sun again was yellow and bright in a clear blue sky, and soon the day would be warm. As they heard the sound of the trumpets they shook sleep wholly from their eyes, and, as they moved, much of the soreness went from their bones. Not far before them was Winchester.

Banks was in Winchester with his army. The fierce pursuit of the night before had filled him with dismay, but with the morning he recalled his courage and resolved to make a victorious stand with the valiant troops that he led. Many of his officers told him how these men had fought Jackson all through the night, and he found abundant cause for courage.

Harry and Dalton sprang into the saddle again, and, as they rode with Jackson, they saw that the whole Southern army was at hand. Ewell was there and the cavalry and the Acadians, their band saluting the morning with a brave battle march. It sent the blood dancing through Harry's veins. He forgot his immense exertions, dangers and hardships and that he had had no sleep in twenty-four hours.

Before him lay the enemy. It was no longer Jackson who retreated before overwhelming numbers. He had the larger force now, at least where the battle was fought, and although the Northern troops in the valley exceeded him three or four to one, he was with his single army destroying their detached forces in detail.

General Jackson, General Taylor and several other high officers were just in front of the first Southern line, and Harry and Dalton sat on their horses a few yards in the rear. The two generals were examining the Northern position minutely through their glasses, and the chief, turning presently to Harry, said:

"You have young and strong eyes. Tell me what you can see."

Harry raised the splendid pair of glasses that he had captured in one of the engagements and took a long, careful look.

"I can see west of the turnpike," he said, "at least four or five regiments and a battery of eight big guns. I think, too, that there is a force of cavalry behind them. On the right, sir, I see stone fences and the windings of the creeks with large masses of infantry posted behind them."

He spoke modestly, but with confidence.

"Your eyesight agrees with mine," said Jackson. "We outnumber them, but they have the advantage of the defense. But it shall not avail them."

He spoke to himself rather than to the others, but Harry heard every word he said, and he already felt the glow of the victory that Jackson had promised. He now considered it impossible for Jackson to promise in vain.

The sun was rising on another brilliant morning, and the two armies that had been fighting all through the dark now stood face to face in full force in the light. Behind the Northern army was Winchester in all the throes of anxiety or sanguine hope.

The people had heard two or three days before that Jackson was fighting his way back toward the north, winning wherever he fought. They had heard in the night the thunder of his guns coming, always nearer, and the torrents of fugitives in the dark had told them that the Northern army was pushed hard. Now in the morning they were looking eagerly southward, hoping to see Jackson's gray legions driving the enemy before him. But it was yet scarcely full dawn, and for a while they heard nothing.

Jackson waited a little and scanned the field again. The morning had now come in the west as well as in the east, and he saw the strong Northern artillery posted on both sides of the turnpike, threatening the Southern advance.

"We must open with the cannon," he said, and he dispatched Harry and Dalton to order up the guns.

The Southern batteries were pushed forward, and opened with a terrific crash on their enemy, telling the waiting people in Winchester that the battle had begun. The infantry and cavalry on either side, eager despite their immense exertions and loss of rest and lack of food, were held back by their officers, while the artillery combat went on.

Jackson, anxious to see the result, rode a little further forward, and the group of staff officers, of course, went with him. Some keen-eyed Northern gunner picked them out, and a shell fell near. Then came another yet nearer, and when it burst it threw dirt all over them.

"A life worth so much as General Jackson's should not be risked this way," whispered Dalton to Harry, "but I don't dare say anything to him."

"Nor do I, and if we did dare he'd pay no attention to us. Our gunners don't seem to be driving their gunners away. Do you notice that, George?"

"Yes, I do and so does General Jackson. I can see him frowning."

The Northern batteries, nearly always of high quality, were doing valiant service that morning. The three batteries on the left of the turnpike and another of eight heavy rifled guns on the right, swept the whole of Jackson's front with solid shot, grape and shell. The Southern guns, although more numerous, were unable to crush them. The batteries of the South were suffering the more. One of them was driven back with the loss of half its men and horses. At another every officer was killed.

"They outshoot us," said Dalton to Harry, "and they make a splendid stand for men who have been kept on the run for two days and nights."

"So they do," said Harry, "but sooner or later they'll have to give way. I heard General Jackson say that we would win a victory."

Dalton glanced at him.

"So you feel that way, too," he said very seriously. "I got the belief some time ago. If he says we'll win we'll win. His prediction settles it in my mind."

"There's a fog rising from the creek," said Harry, "and it's growing heavier. I think Ewell was to march that way with his infantry and it will hold him back. Chance is against us."

"His guns have been out of action, but there they come again! I can't see them, but I can hear them through the mist."

"And here goes the main force on our left. Stonewall is about to strike."

Harry had discovered the movement the moment it was begun. The whole Stonewall brigade, the Acadians and other regiments making a formidable force, moved to the left and charged. Gordon, Banks' able assistant, threw in fresh troops to meet the Southern rush, and they fired almost point blank in the faces of the men in gray. Harry, riding forward with the eager Jackson, saw many fall, but the Southern charge was not checked for a moment. The men, firing their rifles, leaped the stone fences and charged home with the bayonet. The Northern regiments were driven back in disorder and their cavalry sweeping down to protect them, were met by such a sleet of bullets that they, too, were driven back.

Now all the Southern regiments came up. Infantry, cavalry and artillery crossed the creek and the ridges and formed in a solid line which nothing could resist. The enemy, carrying away what cannon he could, was driven swiftly before them. The rebel yell, wild and triumphant, swelled from ten thousand throats as Jackson's army rushed forward, pursuing the enemy into Winchester.

Harry was shouting with the rest. He couldn't help it. The sober Dalton had snatched off his cap, and he, too, was shouting. Then

Harry saw Jackson himself giving way to exultation, for the first time. He was back at Winchester which he loved so well, he had defeated the enemy before it, and now he was about to chase him through its streets. He spurred his horse at full speed down a rocky hill, snatched off his cap, whirled it around his head and cried at the top of his voice again and again:

"Chase them to the Potomac! Chase them to the Potomac!"

Harry and Dalton, hearing the cry, took it up and shouted it, too. Before them was a vast bank of smoke and dust, shot with fire, and the battle thundered as it rolled swiftly into Winchester. The Northern officers, still strove to prevent a rout. They performed prodigies of valor. Many of them fell, but the others, undaunted, still cried to the men to turn and beat off the foe.

Winchester suddenly shot up from the dust and smoke. The battle went on in the town more fiercely than ever. Torrents of shell and bullets swept the narrow streets, but many of the women did not hesitate to appear at the windows and shout amid all the turmoil and roar of battle cheers and praise for those whom they considered their deliverers. Over all rose the roar and flame of a vast conflagration where Banks had set his storehouses on fire, but the women cheered all the more when they saw it.

Harry did his best to keep up with his general, but Jackson still seemed to be aflame with excitement. He was in the very front of the attack and he cried to his men incessantly to push on. It was not enough to take Winchester. They must follow the beaten army to the Potomac.

Harry had a vision of flame-swept streets, of the whizzing of bullets and shell, of men crowded thick between the houses, and of the faces of women at windows, handkerchiefs and veils in their hands. Before him was a red mist sown with sparks, but every minute or two the mist was rent open by the blast of a cannon, and then the fragments of shell whistled again about his ears. He kept his eyes on Jackson, endeavoring to follow him as closely as possible.

He heard suddenly a cry behind him. He saw Dalton's horse falling, and then Dalton and the horse disappeared. He felt a catch at the heart, but it was not a time to remember long. The Southern troops were still pouring forward driving hard on the Northern resistance.

He heard a moment or two later a voice by his side and there was Dalton again mounted.

"I thought you were gone!" Harry shouted.

"I was gone for a minute but it was only my horse that stayed. He was shot through the heart but I caught another—plenty of riderless ones are galloping about—and here I am."

The houses and the narrow streets offered some support to the defense of Banks, but he was gradually driven through the town and out into the fields beyond. Then the women, careless of bullets, came out of the houses and weeping and cheering urged on the pursuit. It always seemed to Harry that the women of this section hated the North more than the men did, and now it was in very fact and deed the fierce women of the South cheering on their men.

He came in the fields into contact with the Invincibles. St. Clair was on foot, his horse killed, but Langdon was still riding, although there was a faint trickle of blood from his shoulder. Some grim demon seized him as he saw Harry.

"We said we were coming back to Winchester," he shouted in his comrade's ear, "and we have come, but we don't stay. Harry, how long does Old Jack expect us to march and fight without stopping?"

"Until you get through."

Then the Invincibles, curving a little to the right, were lost in the flame and smoke, and the pursuit, Jackson continually urging it, swept on. He seemed to Harry to be all fire. He shouted again and again. "We must follow them to the Potomac! To the Potomac! To the Potomac!" He sent his staff flying to every regimental commander with orders. He had the horses cut from the artillery and men mounted on them to continue the pursuit. He inquired continually for the cavalry. Harry, after returning from his second errand with orders, was sent on a third to Ashby. There was no time to write any letter. He was to tell him to come up with cavalry and attack the Federal rear with all his might.

Harry found Ashby far away on the right, and with but fifty men. The rest had been scattered. He galloped back to his general and reported. He saw Jackson bite his lip in annoyance, but he said nothing. Harry remained by his side and the chase went on through the fields. Winchester was left out of sight behind, but the crashing of the rifles and the shouts of the troopers did not cease.

The Northern army had not yet dissolved. Although many commands were shattered and others destroyed, the core of it remained, and, as it retreated, it never ceased to strike back. Harry saw why Jackson was so anxious to bring up his cavalry. A strong charge by them and the fighting half of the Northern force would be split asunder. Then nothing would be left but to sweep up the fragments.

But Jackson's men had reached the limit of human endurance. They were not made of steel as their leader was, and the tremendous exultation of spirit that had kept them up through battle and pursuit began to die. Their strength, once its departure started, ebbed fast. Their knees crumpled under them and the weakest fell unwounded in the fields. The gaps between them and the Northern rear-guard widened, and gradually the flying army of Banks disappeared among the hills and woods.

Banks, deeming himself lucky to have saved a part of his troops, did not stop until he reached Martinsburg, twenty-two miles north of Winchester. There he rested a while and resumed his flight, other flying detachments joining him as he went. He reached the Potomac at midnight with less than half of his army, and boats carried the wearied troops over the broad river behind which they found refuge.

Most of the victors meanwhile lay asleep in the fields north of Winchester, but others had gone back to the town and were making an equitable division of the Northern stores among the different regiments. Harry and Dalton were sent with those who went to the town. On their way Harry saw St. Clair and Langdon lying under an apple tree, still and white. He thought at first they were dead, but stopping a moment he saw their chests rising and falling with regular motion, and he knew that they were only sleeping. The whiteness of their faces was due to exhaustion.

Feeling great relief he rode on and entered the exultant town. He marked many of the places that he had known before, the manse where the good minister lived, the churches and the colonnaded houses, in more than one of which he had passed a pleasant hour.

Here Harry saw people that he knew. They could not do enough for him. They wanted to overwhelm him with food, with clothes, with anything he wanted. They wanted him to tell over and over again of that wonderful march of theirs, how they had issued suddenly from the mountains in the wake of the flying Milroy, how they had marched down the valley winning battle after battle, marching and fighting without ceasing, both by day and by night.

He was compelled to decline all offers of hospitality save food, which he held in his hands and ate as he went about his work. When he finished he went back to his general, and being told that he was wanted no more for the night, wrapped himself in his cloak and lay down under an apple tree.

He felt then that mother-earth was truly receiving him into her kindly lap. He had not closed his eyes for nearly two days – it seemed a month – and looking back at all through which he had passed it seemed incredible. Human beings could not endure so much. They marched through fire, where Stonewall Jackson led, and they never ceased to march. He saw just beyond the apple tree a dusky figure walking up and down. It was Jackson. Would he never rest? Was he not something rather more than normal after all? Harry was very young and he rode with his hero, seeing him do his mighty deeds.

But nature had given all that it had to yield, and soon he slept, lying motionless and white like St. Clair and Langdon. But all through the night the news of Jackson's great blow was traveling over the wires. He had struck other fierce blows, but this was the most terrible of them all. Alarm spread through the whole North. Lincoln and his Cabinet saw a great army of rebels marching on Washington. A New York newspaper which had appeared in the morning with the headline, "Fall of Richmond," appeared at night with the headline "Defeat of General Banks." McDowell's army, which, marching by land, was to co-operate with McClellan in the taking of Richmond, was recalled to meet Jackson. The governors of the loyal states issued urgent appeals for more troops.

Harry learned afterward how terribly effective had been the blow. The whole Northern campaign had been upset by the meteoric appearance of Jackson and the speed with which he marched and fought. McDowell's army of 40,000 men and a hundred guns had been scattered, and it would take him much time to get it all together again. McClellan, advancing on Richmond, was without the support on his right which McDowell was to furnish and was compelled to hesitate.

But Jackson's foot cavalry were soon to find that they were not to rest on their brilliant exploits. As eager as ever, their general was making them ready for another great advance further into the North.

CHAPTER XI.
THE NIGHT RIDE

Harry was back with the general in a few hours, but now he was allowed a little time for himself. It seemed to occur suddenly to Jackson that the members of his staff, especially the more youthful ones, could not march and fight more than two or three days without food and rest.

"You've done well, Harry," he said—he was beginning to call the boy by his first name.

The words of praise were brief, and they were spoken in a dry tone, but they set Harry's blood aflame. He had been praised by Stonewall Jackson, the man who considered an ordinary human being's best not more than third rate. Harry, like all the others in the valley army, saw that Jackson was setting a new standard in warfare.

Tremendously elated he started in search of his friends. He found the Invincibles, that is, all who were left alive, stretched flat upon their sides or backs in the orchard. It seemed to him that St. Clair and Langdon had not moved a hair's breadth since he had seen them there before. But their faces were not so white now. Color was coming back.

He put the toe of his boot against Langdon's side and shoved gently but firmly. Langdon awoke and sat up indignantly.

"How dare you, Harry Kenton, disturb a gentleman who is occupied with his much-needed slumbers?" he asked.

"General Jackson wants you."

"Old Jack wants me! Now, what under the sun can he want with me?"

"He wants you to take some cavalry, gallop to Washington, go all around the city, inspect all its earthworks and report back here by nightfall."

"You're making that up, Harry; but for God's sake don't make that suggestion to Old Jack. He'd send me on that trip sure, and then have me hanged as an example in front of the whole army, when I failed."

"I won't say anything about it."

"You're a bright boy, Harry, and you're learning fast. But things could be a lot worse. We could have been licked instead of licking the enemy. I could be dead instead of lying here on the grass, tired but alive. But, Harry, I'm growing old fast."

"How old are you, Tom?"

"Last week I was nineteen, to-day I'm ninety-nine, and if this sort of thing keeps up I'll be a hundred and ninety-nine next week."

St. Clair also awoke and sat up. In some miraculous manner he had restored his uniform to order and he was as neat and precise as usual.

"You two talk too much," he said. "I was in the middle of a beautiful dream, when I heard you chattering away."

"What was your dream, Arthur?" asked Harry.

"I was in St. Andrew's Hall in Charleston, dancing with the most beautiful girl you ever saw. I don't know who she was, I didn't identify her in my dream. There were lots of other beautiful girls there dancing with fellows like myself, and the roses were everywhere, and the music rose and fell like the song of angels, and I was so happy and—I awoke to find myself here on a hillside with a ragged army that's been marching and fighting for days and weeks, and which, for all I know, will keep it up for years and years longer."

"I've a piece of advice for you, Arthur," said Langdon.

"What is it?"

"Quit dreaming. It's a bad habit, especially when you're in war. The dream is sure to be better than the real thing. You won't be dancing again in Charleston for a long time, nor will I. All those beautiful girls you were dreaming about but couldn't name will be without partners until we're a lot older than we are now."

Langdon spoke with a seriousness very uncommon in him, and lay back again on the ground, where he began to chew a grass stem meditatively.

"Go back to sleep, boys, you'll need it," said Harry lightly. "Our next march is to be a thousand miles, and we're to have a battle at every milestone."

"You mean that as a joke, but it wouldn't surprise me at all if it came true," said Langdon, as he closed his eyes again.

Harry went on and found the two colonels sitting in the shadow of a stone fence. One of them had his arm in a sling, but he assured Harry the wound was slight. They gave him a glad and paternal welcome.

"In the kind of campaign we're waging," said Colonel Leonidas Talbot, "I assume that anybody is dead until I see him alive. Am I not right, eh, Hector?"

"Assuredly you're right, Leonidas," replied Lieutenant-Colonel Hector St. Hilaire. "Our young men don't get frightened because they don't have time to think about it. Before we can get excited over the battle in which we are engaged we've begun the next one. It is also a matter of personal pride to me that one of the best bodies of troops in the service of General Jackson is of French descent like myself."

"The Acadians, colonel," said Harry. "Grand troops they are."

"It is the French fighting blood," said Lieutenant-Colonel Hector St. Hilaire, with a little trace of the grandiloquent in his tone. "Slurs have been cast at the race from which I sprang since the rout and flight at Waterloo, but how undeserved they are! The French have burned more gunpowder and have won more great battles without the help of allies than any other nation in Europe. And their descendants in North America have shown their valor all the way from Quebec to New Orleans, although we are widely separated now, and scarcely know the speech of one another."

"It's true, Hector," said Colonel Leonidas Talbot. "I think I've heard you say as much before, but it will bear repeating. Do you think, Hector, that you happen to have about you a cigarette that has survived the campaign?"

"Several of them, Leonidas. Here, help yourself. Harry, I would offer one to you, but I do not recommend the cigarette to the young. You don't smoke! So much the better. It's a bad habit, permissible only to the old. Leonidas, do you happen to have a match?"

"Yes, Hector, I made sure about that before I asked you for the cigarettes. Be careful when you light it. There is only one match for the cigarettes of both."

"I'll bring you a coal from one of the campfires," said Harry, springing up.

But Lieutenant-Colonel Hector St. Hilaire waved him down courteously, though rather reprovingly.

"You would never fire a cannon shot to kill a butterfly," he said, "and neither will I ever light a delicate cigarette with a huge, shapeless coal from a campfire. It would be an insult to the cigarette, and after such an outrage I could never draw a particle of flavor from it. No, Harry, we thank you, you mean well, but we can do it better."

Harry sat down again. The two colonels, who had been through days of continuous marching and fighting, knelt in the lee of the fence, and Lieutenant-Colonel Hector St. Hilaire also shaded the operation with his hat as an additional protection. Colonel Leonidas Talbot carefully struck the match. The flame sputtered up and his friend brought his hat closer to protect it. Then both lighted their cigarettes, settled back against the fence, and a deep peace appeared upon their two faces.

"Hector," said Colonel Talbot, "only we old soldiers know how little it takes to make a man happy."

"You speak truly, Leonidas. In the last analysis it's a mere matter of food, clothes and shelter, with perhaps a cigarette or two. In Mexico, when we advanced from Vera Cruz to the capital, it was often very cold on the mountains. I can remember coming in from some battle, aching with weariness and cold, but after I had eaten good food and basked half an hour before a fire I would feel as if I owned the earth. Physical comfort, carried to the very highest degree, produces mental comfort also."

"Sound words, Hector. The starved, the cold and the shelterless can never be happy. God knows that I am no advocate of war, although it is my trade. It is a terrible thing for people to kill one another, but it does grind you down to the essentials. Because it is war you and I have an acute sense of luxury, lying here against a stone fence, smoking a couple of cigarettes."

"That is, Leonidas, we are happy when we have attained what we have needed a long time, and which we have been a long time without. It has occurred to me that the cave-man, in all his primitive nakedness, must have had some thrilling moments, moments of pleasures of the body, the mind and the imagination allied, which we modern beings cannot feel."

"To what moments do you allude, Hector?"

"Suppose that he has just eluded a monstrous saber-toothed tiger, and has slipped into his cave by the opening, entirely too small for any great beast of prey. He is in his home. A warm fire is burning on a flat stone. His wife—beautiful to him—is cooking savory meats for him. Around the walls are his arms and their supplies. They eat placidly while the huge tiger from which he has escaped by a foot or less roars and glowers without. The contrast between the danger and that house, which is the equivalent to a modern palace, comes home to him with a thrill more keen and penetrating than anything we can ever feel.

"The man and his wife eat their evening meal, and retire to their bed of dry leaves in the corner. They fall asleep while the frenzied and ferocious tiger is still snarling and growling. They know he cannot get at them, and his gnashings and roarings are merely a lullaby, soothing them to the sweetest of slumbers. You could not duplicate that in the age in which we live, Leonidas."

"No, Hector, we couldn't. But, as for me, I can spare such thrills. It seems to me that we have plenty of danger of our own just now. I must say, however, that you put these matters in a fine, poetic way. Have you ever written verses, Hector?"

"A few, but never for print, Leonidas. I am happy to think that a few sonnets and triolets of mine are cherished by middle-aged but yet handsome women of Charleston that we both know."

Harry left them still talking in rounded sentences and always in perfect agreement. He thought theirs a beautiful friendship, and he hoped that he should have friendships like it, when he was as old as they.

But he and all the other prophets were right. The restless Jackson soon took up the northward march again. He was drawing farther and farther away from McClellan and the Southern army before

Richmond, and the great storm that was gathering there. The army of Banks was not yet wholly destroyed, and there were other Northern and undestroyed armies in the valley. His task there was not yet finished. Jackson pushed on toward Harper's Ferry on the Potomac. He was now, though to the westward, further north than Washington itself, and with other armies in his rear he was taking daring risks. But as usual, he kept his counsels to himself. All was hidden under that battered cap to become later an old slouch hat, and the men who followed him were content to go wherever he led.

The old Stonewall Brigade was in the van and Jackson and his staff were with it. The foot cavalry refreshed by a good rest were marching again at a great rate.

Harry was detached shortly after the start, and was sent to General Winder with orders for him to hurry forward with the fine troops under his command. Before he could leave Winder he ran into a strong Northern force at Charleston, and the Southern division attacked at once with all the dash and vigor that Jackson had imparted to his men. They had, too, the confidence bred by continuous victory, while the men in blue were depressed by unbroken defeats.

The Northern force was routed in fifteen or twenty minutes and fled toward the river, leaving behind it all its baggage and stores. Harry carried the news to Jackson and saw the general press his thin lips together more closely than ever. He knew that the hope of destroying Banks utterly was once more strong in the breast of their leader. The members of the staff were all sent flying again with messages to the regiments to hurry.

The whole army swung forward at increased pace. Jackson did not know what new troops had come for Banks, but soon he saw the heights south of Harper's Ferry, and the same glance told him that they were crowded with soldiers. General Saxton with seven thousand men and eighteen guns had undertaken to hold the place against his formidable opponent.

General Jackson held a brief council, and, when it was over, summoned Harry and Dalton to him.

"You are both well mounted and have had experience," he said. "You understand that the army before us is not by any means the only one that the Yankees have. Shields, Ord and Fremont are all leading armies against us. We can defeat Saxton's force, but we must not be caught in any trap. Say not a word of this to anybody, but ride in the direction I'm pointing and see if you can find the army of Shields. Other scouts are riding east and west, but you must do your best, nevertheless. Perhaps both of you will not come back, but one of you must. Take food in your saddle bags and don't neglect your arms."

He turned instantly to give orders to others and Harry and Dalton mounted and rode, proud of their trust, and resolved to fulfill it. Evening was coming as they left the army, and disappeared among the woods. They had only the vague direction given by Jackson, derived probably from reports, brought in by other scouts, but it was their mission to secure definite and exact information.

"You know this country, George, don't you?" asked Harry.

"I've ridden over all of it. They say that Shields with a large part of McDowell's army is approaching the valley through Manassas Gap. It's a long ride from here, Harry, but I think we'd better make for it. This horse of mine is one of the best ever bred in the valley. He could carry me a hundred miles by noon to-morrow."

"Mine's not exactly a plough horse," said Harry, as he stroked the mane of his own splendid bay, one especially detailed for him on this errand. "If yours can go a hundred miles by noon to-morrow so can mine."

"Suppose, then, we go a little faster."

"Suits me."

The riders spoke a word or two. The two grand horses stretched out their necks, and they sped away southward. For a while they rode over the road by which they had come. It was yet early twilight and they saw many marks of their passage, a broken-down wagon, a dead horse, an exploded caisson, and now and then something from which they quickly turned away their eyes.

Dalton knew the roads well, and at nightfall they bore in toward the right. They had already come a long distance, and in the darkness they went more slowly.

"I think there's a farmhouse not much further on," said Dalton, "and we'll ask there for information. It's safe to do so because all the people through here are on our side. There, you can see the house now."

The moonlight disclosed a farmhouse, surrounded by a lawn that was well sprinkled with big trees, but as they approached Harry and Dalton simultaneously reined their horses back into the wood. They had seen a dozen troopers on the lawn, and the light was good enough to show that their uniforms were or had been blue. A woman was standing in the open door of the house, and one of the men, who seemed to be the leader, was talking to her.

"Yankee scouts," whispered Harry.

"Undoubtedly. The Yankee generals are waking up — Jackson has made 'em do it, but I didn't expect to find their scouts so far in the valley."

"Nor I. Suppose we wait here, George, until they leave."

"It's the thing to do."

They rode a little further into the woods where they were safe from observation, and yet could watch what was passing at the house. But they did not have to wait long. The troopers evidently got little satisfaction from the woman to whom they were talking and turned their horses. Harry saw her disappear inside, and he fairly heard the door slam when it closed. The men galloped southward down the road.

Harry heard a chuckle beside him and he turned in astonishment.

"I'm laughing," said Dalton, "because I've got a right to laugh. Here in the valley we are all kin to one another just as you people in Kentucky are all related. The woman who stood in the doorway is Cousin Eliza Pomeroy. She's about my seventh cousin, but she's my cousin just the same, and if we could have heard it we would have enjoyed what she was saying to those Yankees."

"Oughtn't we to stop also and get news, if we can?"

"Of course. We must have a talk with Cousin Eliza."

They emerged from the woods, opened the gate and rode upon the lawn. Not a ray of light came from the house anywhere. Every door and shutter was fast.

"Knock on the door with the hilt of your sword, Harry," said Dalton. "It will bring Cousin Eliza. She can't have gone to sleep yet."

Harry dismounted and holding the reins of his horse over his arm, knocked loudly. There was no reply.

"Beat harder, Harry. She's sure to hear."

Harry beat upon that door until he bruised the hilt of his sword. At last it was thrown open violently, and a powerful woman of middle years appeared.

"I thought you Yankees had gone forever!" she exclaimed. "You'd better hurry or Stonewall Jackson will get you before morning!"

"We're not Yankees, ma'am," said Harry, politely. "We're Southerners, Stonewall Jackson's own men, scouts from his army, here looking for news of the enemy."

"A fine tale, young man. You're trying to fool me with your gray uniform. Stonewall Jackson's men are fifteen miles north of here, chasing the Yankees by thousands into the Potomac. They say he does it just as well by night as by day, and that he never sleeps or rests."

"What my comrade tells you is true. Good evening, Cousin Eliza!" said a gentle voice beyond Harry.

The woman started and then stepped out of the door. Dalton rode forward a little where the full moonlight fell upon him.

"You remember that summer six years ago when you spanked me for stealing the big yellow apples in the orchard."

"George! Little George Dalton!" she cried, and as Dalton got off his horse she enclosed him in a powerful embrace, although he was little no longer.

"And have you come from Stonewall Jackson?" she asked breathless with eagerness.

"Straight from him. I'm on his staff and so is my friend here. This is Harry Kenton of Kentucky, Mrs. Pomeroy, and he's been through all the battles with us. We were watching from the woods and we saw those Yankees at your door. They didn't get any information, I know that, but I'm thinking that we will."

Cousin Eliza Pomeroy laughed a low, deep laugh of pride and satisfaction.

"Come into the house," she exclaimed. "I'm here with four children. Jim, my husband, is with Johnston's army before Richmond, but we've been able to take care of ourselves thus far, and I reckon we'll keep on being able. I can get hot coffee and good corn cakes ready for you inside of fifteen minutes."

"It's not food we want, Cousin Eliza," said Dalton. "We want something far better, what those Yankees came for—news. So I think we'd better stay outside and run no risk of surprise. The Yankees might come back."

"That's so. You'll grow up into a man with a heap of sense, George. I've got real news, and I was waiting for a chance to send it through to Stonewall Jackson. Billy! Billy!"

A small boy, not more than twelve, but clothed fully, darted from the inside of the house. He was well set up for his age, and his face was keen and eager.

"This is Billy Pomeroy, my oldest son," said Cousin Eliza Pomeroy, with a swelling of maternal pride. "I made him get in bed and cover himself up, boots and all, when the Yankees came. Billy has been riding to-day. He ain't very old, and he ain't very big, but put him on a horse and he's mighty nigh a man."

The small, eager face was shining.

"What did you see, Billy, when you rode so far?" asked Dalton.

"Yankees! Yankees, Cousin George, and lots of 'em, toward Manassas Gap! I saw some of their cavalry this side of the Gap, and I heard at the store that there was a big army on the other side, marching hard to come through it, and get in behind our Stonewall."

Harry looked at Dalton.

"That confirms the rumors we heard," he said.

"You can believe anything that Billy tells you," said Mrs. Pomeroy.

"I know it," said Dalton, "but we've got to go on and see these men for ourselves. Stonewall Jackson is a terrible man, Cousin Eliza. If we tell him that the Yankees are coming through Manassas Gap and closing in on his rear, he'll ask us how we know it, and when we reply that a boy told us he'll break us as unfit to be on his staff."

"And I reckon Stonewall Jackson will be about right!" said Cousin Eliza Pomeroy, who was evidently a woman of strong mind. "Billy, you lead these boys straight to Manassas Gap."

"Oh, no, Cousin Eliza!" exclaimed Dalton. "Billy's been riding hard all day, and we can find the way."

"What do you think Billy's made out of?" asked his mother contemptuously. "Ain't he a valley boy? Ain't he Jim Pomeroy's son and mine? I want you to understand that Billy can ride anything, and he can ride it all day long and all night long, too!"

"Make 'em let me go, ma!" exclaimed Billy, eagerly. "I can save time. I can show 'em the shortest way!"

Harry and George glanced at each other. Young Billy Pomeroy might be of great value to them. Moreover, the choice was already made for them, because Billy was now running to the stable for his horse.

"He goes with us, or rather he leads us, Cousin Eliza," said Dalton.

Billy appeared the next instant, with his horse saddled and bridled, and his own proud young self in the saddle.

"Billy, take 'em straight," said his Spartan mother, as she drew him down in the saddle and kissed him, and Billy, more swollen with pride than ever, promised that he would. But the mother's voice broke a little when she said to Dalton:

"He's to guide you wherever you want to go, but you must bring him back to me unhurt."

"We will, Cousin Eliza," said Dalton earnestly.

Then they galloped away in the dark with Billy leading and riding like a Comanche. He had taken a fresh horse from the stall and it was almost as powerful as those ridden by Harry and Dalton.

"See the mountains," said Billy, pointing eastward to a long dark line dimly visible in the moonlight. "That's the Blue Ridge, and further south is the Gap, but you can't see it at night until you come right close to it."

"Do you know any path through the woods, Billy?" asked Harry. "We don't want to run the risk of capture."

"I was just about to lead you into it," replied the boy, still rejoicing in the importance of his role. "Here it is."

He turned off from the road into a path leading into thick forest, wide enough for only one horse at a time. Billy, of course, led, Harry followed, and Dalton brought up the rear. The path, evidently a short cut used by farmers, was enclosed by great oaks, beeches and elms, now in full leaf, and it was dark there. Only a slit of moonlight showed from above, and the figures of the three riders grew shadowy.

"They'll never find us here, will they, Billy?" said Harry.

"Not one chance in a thousand. Them Yankees don't know a thing about the country. Anyway, if they should come into the path at the other end, we'd hear them long before they heard us."

"You're right, Billy, and as we ride on we'll all three listen with six good ears."

"Yes, sir," said Billy.

Harry, although only a boy himself, was so much older than Billy, who addressed him as "sir," that he felt himself quite a veteran.

"Billy," he said, "how did it happen that you were riding down this way, so far from home, to-day?"

"'Cause we heard there was Yanks in the Gap. Ma won't let me go an' fight with Stonewall Jackson. She says I ain't old enough an' big enough, but she told me herself to get on the horse an' ride down this way, an' see if what we heard was true. I saw 'em in little bunches, an' then that gang come to our house to-night, less 'n ten minutes after I come back. We'll be at a creek, sir, in less than five minutes. It runs down from the mountains, an' it's pretty deep with all them big spring rains. I guess we'll have to swim, sir. We could go lower down, where there's always a ford, but that's where the Yankees would be crossing."

"We'll swim, if necessary, Billy."

"When even the women and little children fight for us, the South will be hard to conquer," was Harry's thought, but he said no more until they reached the creek, which was indeed swollen by the heavy rains, and was running swiftly, a full ten feet in depth.

"Hold on, Billy, I'll lead the way," said Harry.

But Billy was already in the stream, his short legs drawn up, and his horse swimming strongly. Harry and Dalton followed without a word, and the three emerged safely on the eastern side.

"You're a brave swimmer, Billy," said Harry admiringly.

"'Tain't nothin, sir. I didn't swim. It was my horse. I guess he'd take me across the Mississippi itself. I wouldn't have anything to do but stick on his back. Look up, sir, an' you can see the mountains close by."

Harry and Dalton looked up through the rift in the trees, and saw almost over them the lofty outline of the Blue Ridge, the eastern rampart of the valley, heavy with forest from base to top.

"We must be near the Gap," said Dalton.

"We are," said Billy. "We've been coming fast. It's nigh on to fifteen miles from here to home."

"And must be a full thirty to Harper's Ferry," said Dalton.

"Does this path lead to some point overlooking the Gap," asked Harry, "where we can see the enemy if he's there, and he can't see us?"

"Yes, sir. We can ride on a slope not more than two miles from here and look right down into the Gap."

"And if troops are there we'll be sure to see their fires," said Dalton. "Lead on, Billy."

Billy led with boldness and certainty. It was the greatest night of his life, and he meant to fulfill to the utmost what he deemed to be his duty. The narrow path still wound among mighty trees, the branches of which met now and then over their heads, shutting out the moonlight entirely. It led at this point toward the north and they were rapidly ascending a shoulder of the mountain, leaving the Gap on their right.

Harry, riding on such an errand, felt to the full the weird quality of mountains and forest, over which darkness and silence brooded. The foliage was very heavy, and it rustled now and then as the stray winds wandered along the slopes of the Blue Ridge. But for that and the hoofbeats of their own horses, there was no sound save once, when they heard a scuttling on the bark of a tree. They saw nothing, but Billy pronounced it a wildcat, alarmed by their passage.

The three at length came out on a level place or tiny plateau. Billy, who rode in advance, stopped and the others stopped with him.

"Look," said the boy, pointing to the bottom of the valley, about five hundred feet below.

A fire burned there and they could discern men around it, with horses in the background.

"Yankees," said Billy. "Look at 'em through the glasses."

Harry raised his glasses and took a long look. They had the full moonlight where they stood and the fire in the valley below was also a help. He saw that the camp was made by a strong cavalry force. Many of them were asleep in their blankets, but the others sat by the fire and seemed to be talking.

Then he passed the glasses to Dalton, who also, after looking long and well, passed them to Billy, as a right belonging to one who had been their real leader, and who shared equally with them their hardships and dangers.

"How large would you say that force is, George?" asked Harry.

"Three or four hundred men at least. There's a great bunch of horses. I should judge, too, from the careless way they've camped, that they've no fear of being attacked. How many do you think they are, Billy?"

"Just about what you said, Cousin George. Are you going to attack them?"

Harry and Dalton laughed.

"No, Billy," replied Dalton. "You see we're only three, and there must be at least three hundred down there."

"But we've been hearin' that Stonewall Jackson's men never mind a hundred to one," said Billy, in an aggrieved tone. "We hear that's just about what they like."

"No, Billy, my boy. We don't fight a hundred to one. Nobody does, unless it's like Thermopylae and the Alamo."

"Then what are we going to do?" continued Billy in his disappointed tone.

"I think, Billy, that Harry and I are going to dismount, slip down the mountainside, see what we can see, hear what we can hear, and that you'll stay here, holding and guarding the horses until we come back."

"I won't!" exclaimed Billy in violent indignation. "I won't, Cousin George. I'm going down the mountain with you an' Mr. Kenton."

"Now, Billy," said Dalton soothingly, "you've got a most important job here. You're the reserve, and you also hold the means of flight. Suppose we're pursued hotly, we couldn't get away without the horses that you'll hold for us. Suppose we should be taken. Then it's for you to gallop back with the news that Shields' whole army will be in the pass in the morning, and under such circumstances, your mother would send you on to General Jackson with a message of such immense importance."

"That's so," said Billy with conviction, in the face of so much eloquence and logic, "but I don't want you fellows to be captured."

Dalton and Harry dismounting, gave the reins of their horses into the hands of Billy, and the small fingers clutched them tightly.

"Stay exactly where you are, Billy," said Harry. "We want to find you without trouble when we come back."

"I'll be here," said Billy proudly.

Harry and Dalton began the descent through the bushes and trees. They had not the slightest doubt that this was the vanguard of the Northern army which they heard was ten thousand strong, and that this force was merely a vanguard for McDowell, who had nearly forty thousand men. But they knew too well to go back to Stonewall Jackson with mere surmise, however plausible.

"We've got to find out some way or other whether their army is certainly at hand," whispered Dalton.

Harry nodded, and said:

"We must manage to overhear some of their talk, though it's risky business."

"But that's what we're here for. They don't seem to be very watchful, and as the woods and bushes are thick about 'em we may get a chance."

They continued their slow and careful descent. Harry glanced back once through an opening in the bushes and saw little Billy, holding the reins of the three horses and gazing intently after them. He knew that among all the soldiers of Jackson's army, no matter how full of valor and zeal they might be, there was not one who surpassed Billy in eagerness to serve.

They reached the bottom of the slope, and lay for a few minutes hidden among dense bushes. Both had been familiar with country life, they had hunted the 'possum and the coon many a dark night, and now their forest lore stood them in good stead. They made no sound as they passed among the bushes and trailing vines, and they knew that they were quite secure in their covert, although they lay within a hundred yards of one of the fires.

Harry judged that most of the men whom they saw were city bred. It was an advantage that the South had over the North in a mighty war, waged in a country covered then mostly with forest and cut by innumerable rivers and creeks, that her sons were familiar with such conditions, while many of those of the North, used to life in the cities, were at a loss, when the great campaigns took them into the wilderness.

Both he and Dalton, relying upon this knowledge, crept a little closer, but they stopped and lay very close, when they saw a man advancing to a hillock, carrying under his arm a bundle which they took to be rockets.

"Signals," whispered Dalton. "You just watch, Harry, and you'll see 'em answered from the eastward."

The officer on the summit of the hillock sent up three rockets, which curved beautifully against the blue heavens, then sank and died. Far to the eastward they saw three similar lights flame and die.

"How far away would you say those answering rockets were?" whispered Harry.

"It's hard to say about distances in the moonlight, but they may be three or four miles. I take it, Harry, that they are sent up by the Northern main force."

"So do I, but we've got to get actual evidence in words, or we've got to see this army. I'm afraid to go back to General Jackson with anything less. Now, we won't have time to go through the Gap, see the army and get back to the general before things begin to happen, so we've got to stick it out here, until we get what we want."

"True words, Harry, and we must risk going a little nearer. See that line of bushes running along there in the dark? It will cover us, and we're bound to take the chance. We must agree, too, Harry, that if we're discovered, neither must stop in an attempt to save the other. If one reaches Jackson it will be all right."

"Of course, George. We'll run for it with all our might, and if it's only one it's to be the better runner."

They lay almost flat on their stomachs, and passing through the grass, reached the line of bushes. Here they could rise from such an uncomfortable position, and stooping they came within fifty yards of the first fire, where they saw very clearly the men who were not asleep, and who yet moved about. Most of them were not yet sunburned, and Harry judged at once that they had come from the mills and workshops of New York or New England. As far as he could see they had no pickets, and he inferred their belief that no enemy was nearer than Jackson's army, at least thirty miles away. Perhaps the little band of horsemen who had knocked at Mrs. Pomeroy's door had brought them the information.

They lay there nearly an hour, not thinking of the danger, but consumed with impatience. Officers passed near them talking, but they could catch only scraps, not enough for their purpose. A set of signals was sent up again and was answered duly from the same point to the east of the Gap. But after long waiting, they were rewarded. Few of the officers or men ever went far from the fires. They seemed to be at a loss in the dark and silent wilderness which was absolute confirmation to Harry that they were city dwellers.

Two officers, captains or majors, stopped within twenty feet of the crouching scouts, and gazed for a long time through the Gap toward the west into the valley, at the northern end of which Jackson and his army lay.

"I tell you, Curtis," one of them said at last, "that if we get through the Gap to-morrow and Fremont and the others also come up, Jackson can't possibly get away. We'll have him and his whole force in a trap and with three or four to one in our favor, it will be all over."

"It's true, if it comes out as you say, Penfield," said the other, "but there are several 'ifs,' and as we have reason to know, it's hard to put your hand on Jackson. Why, when we thought he was lost in the mountains he came out of them like an avalanche, and some of our best troops were buried under that avalanche."

"You're too much of a pessimist, Curtis. We've learned a lot in the last few days. As sure as you and I stand here the fox will be trapped. Why, he's trapped already. We'll be through the Gap here with ten thousand men in the morning, squarely in Jackson's rear. To-morrow we'll have fifty or sixty thousand good troops between him and Richmond and Johnston. His army will be taken or destroyed, and the Confederacy will be split asunder. McClellan will be in

Richmond with an overwhelming force, and within a month the war will be practically over."

"There's no doubt of that, if we catch Jackson, and it certainly looks as if the trap were closing down upon him. In defeating Banks and then following him to the Potomac he has ruined himself and his cause."

Harry felt a deadly fear gripping at his heart. What these men were saying was probably true. Every fact supported their claim. The tough and enduring North, ready to sustain any number of defeats and yet win, was pouring forward her troops with a devotion that would have wrung tears from a stone. And she was destined to do it again and again through dark and weary years.

The two men walked further away, still talking, but Harry and Dalton could no longer hear what they were saying. The rockets soared again in the pass, and were answered in the east, but now nearer, and the two knew that it was not worth while to linger any longer. They knew the vital fact that ten thousand men were advancing through the pass, and that all the rest was superfluity. And time had a value beyond price to their cause.

CHAPTER XII.
THE CLOSING CIRCLE

"George," said Harry, "we must chance it now and get back to the horses. We've got to reach General Jackson before the Northern army is through the pass."

"You lead," said Dalton. "I don't think we'll have any danger except when we are in that strip of grass between these bushes and the woods."

Harry started, and when he reached the grass threw himself almost flat on his face again, crawling forward with extreme caution. Dalton, close behind him, imitated his comrade. The high grass merely rippled as they passed and the anxious Northern officers walking back and forth were not well enough versed in woodcraft to read from any sign that an enemy was near.

Once Dalton struck his knee against a small bush and caused its leaves to rustle. A wary and experienced scout would have noticed the slight, though new noise, and Harry and Dalton, stopping, lay perfectly still. But the officers walked to and fro, undisturbed, and the two boys resumed their creeping flight.

When they reached the forest, they rose gladly from their knees, and ran up the slope, still bearing in mind that time was now the most pressing of all things. They whistled softly as they neared the little plateau, and Billy's low answering whistle came back. They hurried up the last reach of the slope, and there he was, the eyes shining in his eager face, the three bridles clutched tightly in his small right hand.

"Did you get what you wanted?" he asked in a whisper.

"We did, Billy," answered Harry.

"I saw 'em sendin' up shootin' stars an' other shootin' stars way off to the east answerin', an' I didn't know what it meant."

"It was their vanguard in the Gap, talking to their army several miles to the eastward. But we lay in the bushes, Billy, and we heard what their officers said. All that you heard was true. Ten thousand Yankees will be through the pass in the morning, and Stonewall Jackson will have great cause to be grateful to William Pomeroy, aged twelve."

The boy's eyes fairly glowed, but he was a man of action.

"Then I guess that we've got to jump on our horses and ride lickety split down the valley to give warnin' to General Jackson," he said.

Harry knew what was passing in the boy's mind, that he would go with them all the way to Jackson, and he did not have the heart to say anything to the contrary just then. But Dalton replied:

"Right you are, Billy. We ride now as if the woods were burning behind us."

Billy was first in the saddle and led the way. The horses had gained a good rest, while Harry and Dalton were stalking the troopers in the valley, and, after they had made the descent of the slope, they swung into a long easy gallop across the level.

The little lad still kept his place in front. Neither of the others would have deprived him of this honor which he deserved so well. He sat erect, swinging with his horse, and he showed no sign of weariress. They took no precautions now to evade a possible meeting with the enemy. What they needed was haste, haste, always haste. They must risk everything to carry the news to Jackson. A mere half hour might mean the difference between salvation and destruction.

Harry felt the great tension of the moment. The words of the Northern officers had made him understand what he already suspected. The whole fate of the Confederacy would waver in the balance on the morrow. If Jackson were surrounded and overpowered, the South would lose its right arm. Then the armies that engulfed him would join McClellan and pour forward in an overwhelming host on Richmond.

Their hoofbeats rang in a steady beat on the road, as they went forward on that long easy gallop which made the miles drop swiftly behind them. The skies brightened, and the great stars danced in a solid sheet of blue. They were in the gently rolling country, and occasionally they passed a farmhouse. Now and then, a watchful dog barked at them, but they soon left him and his bark behind.

Harry noticed that Billy's figure was beginning to waver slightly, and he knew that weariness and the lack of sleep were at last gaining the mastery over his daring young spirit. It gave him relief, as it solved a problem that had been worrying him. He rode up by the side of Billy, but he said nothing. The boy's eyelids were heavy and the youthful figure was wavering, but it was in no danger of falling. Billy could have ridden his horse sound asleep.

Harry presently saw the roof of Mrs. Pomeroy's house showing among the trees.

"It's less than half a mile to your house, Billy," he said.

"But I'm not going to stop there. I'm goin' on with you to General Jackson, an' I'm goin' to help him fight the Yankees."

Harry was silent, but when they galloped up to the Pomeroy house, Billy was nearly asleep.

The door sprang open as they approached, and the figure of the stalwart woman appeared. Harry knew that she had been watching there every minute since they left. He was touched by the dramatic spirit of the moment, and he said:

"Mrs. Pomeroy, we bring back to you the most gallant soldier in Stonewall Jackson's army of the Valley of Virginia. He led us straight to the Gap where we were able to learn the enemy's movements, a knowledge which may save the Confederacy from speedy destruction. We bring him back to you, safe and unharmed, and sleeping soundly in his saddle."

He lifted Billy from the saddle and put him in his mother's arms.

"Billy's a hero, Cousin Eliza," said Dalton. "Few full-grown men have done as important deeds in their whole lives as he has done to-night. When he awakens he'll be angry because he didn't go with us, but you tell him we'll see that he's a duly enrolled member of General Jackson's army. Stonewall Jackson never forgets such deeds as his."

"It's a proud woman I am to-night," said Mrs. Pomeroy. "Good-bye, Cousin George, and you, too, Mr. Kenton. I can see that you're in a hurry to be off, and you ought to be. I want to see both of you in my house again in better days."

She went inside, carrying the exhausted and sleeping boy in her arms, and Harry and Dalton galloped away side by side.

"How's your horse, Harry?" asked Dalton.

"Fine. Smooth as silk! How's yours?"

"The machinery moves without a jar. I may be stiff and sore myself, but I'm so anxious to get to General Jackson that I haven't time to think about it."

"Same here. Suppose we speed 'em up a little more."

They came into the turnpike, and now the horses lengthened out their stride as they fled northward. It was yet some time until dawn, but the two young riders took the cold food from their knapsacks and ate as they galloped on. It was well that they had good horses, staunch and true, as they were pushing them hard now.

Harry looked toward the west, where the dark slope of Little North Mountain closed in the valley from that side, and he felt a shiver which he knew did not come from the night air. He knew that a powerful Northern force was off there somewhere, and he wondered what it was doing. But he and Dalton had done their duty. They had uncovered one hostile force, and doubtless other men who rode in the night for Jackson would attend to the rest.

Both Harry and Dalton had been continuously in the saddle for many hours now, but they did not notice their weariness. They were still upborne by a great anxiety and a great exaltation, too. Feeling to the full the imminence and immensity of the crisis, they were bending themselves heart and soul to prevent it, and no thought of weariness could enter their minds. Each was another Billy, only on a larger and older scale.

Later on, the moon and all the stars slipped away, and it became very dark. Harry felt that it was merely a preliminary to the dawn, and he asked Dalton if he did not think so, too.

"It's too dark for me to see the face of my watch," said Dalton, "but I know you're right, Harry. I can just feel the coming of the dawn. It's some quality in the air. I think it grows a little colder than it has been in the other hours of the night."

"I can feel the wind freshening on my face. It nips a bit for a May morning."

They slackened speed a little, wishing to save their horses for a final burst, and stopped once or twice for a second or two to listen for the sound of other hoofbeats than their own. But they heard none.

"If the Yankee armies are already on the turnpike they're not near us. That's sure," said Dalton.

"Do you know how many men they have?"

"Some of the spies brought in what the general believed to be pretty straight reports. The rumors said that Shields was advancing to Manassas Gap with ten thousand men, and from what we heard we know that is true. A second detachment, also ten thousand strong, from McDowell's army is coming toward Front Royal, and McDowell has twenty thousand men east of the Blue Ridge. What the forces to the west are I don't know but the enemy in face of the general himself on the Potomac must now number at least ten thousand."

Harry whistled.

"And at the best we can't muster more than fifteen thousand fit to carry arms!" he exclaimed.

Dalton leaned over in the dark, and touched his comrade on the shoulder.

"Harry," he said, "don't forget Old Jack. Where Little Sorrel leads there is always an army of forty thousand men. I'm not setting myself up to be very religious, but it's safe to say that he was praying to-night, and when Old Jack prays, look out."

"Yes, if anybody can lead us out of this trap it will be Old Jack," said Harry. "Look, there's the dawn coming over the Blue Ridge, George."

A faint tint of gray was appearing on the loftiest crests of the Blue Ridge. It could scarcely be called light yet, but it was a sign to the two that the darkness there would soon melt away. Gradually the gray shredded off and then the ridges were tipped with silver which soon turned to gold. Dawn rushed down over the valley and the pleasant forests and fields sprang into light.

Then they heard hoofbeats behind them coming fast. The experienced ears of both told them that it was only a single horseman who came, and, drawing their pistols, they turned their horses across the road. When the rider saw the two threatening figures he stopped, but in a moment he rode on again. They were in gray and so was he.

"Why, it's Chris Aubrey of the general's own staff!" exclaimed Dalton. "Don't you know him, Harry?"

"Of course I do. Aubrey, we're friends. It's Dalton and Kenton."

Aubrey dashed his hands across his eyes, as if he were clearing a mist from them. He was worn and weary, and his look bore a singular resemblance to that of despair.

"What is it, Chris?" asked Dalton with sympathy.

"I was sent down the Luray Valley to learn what I could and I discovered that Ord was advancing with ten thousand men on Front Royal, where General Jackson left only a small garrison. I'm going as fast as my horse can take me to tell him."

"We're on the same kind of a mission, Chris," said Harry. "We've seen the vanguard of Shields, ten thousand strong coming through Manassas Gap, and we also are going as fast as our horses can take us to tell General Jackson."

"My God! Does it mean that we are about to be surrounded?"

"It looks like it," said Harry, "but sometimes you catch things that you can't hold. George and I never give up faith in Old Jack."

"Nor do I," said Aubrey. "Come on! We'll ride together! I'm glad I met you boys. You give me courage."

The three now rode abreast and again they galloped. One or two early farmers going phlegmatically to their fields saw them, but they passed on in silence. They had grown too used to soldiers to pay much attention to them. Moreover, these were their own.

The whole valley was now flooded with light. To east and to west loomed the great walls of the mountains, heavy with foliage, cut here and there by invisible gaps through which Harry knew that the Union troops were pouring.

They caught sight of moving heads on a narrow road coming from the west which would soon merge into theirs. They slackened speed for a moment or two, uncertain what to do, and then Aubrey exclaimed:

"It's a detachment of our own cavalry. See their gray uniforms, and that's Sherburne leading them!"

"So it is!" exclaimed Harry, and he rode forward joyfully. Sherburne gave all three of them a warm welcome, but he was far from cheerful. He led a dozen troopers and they, like himself, were covered with dust and were drooping with weariness. It was evident to Harry that they had ridden far and hard, and that they did not bring good news.

"Well, Harry," said Sherburne, still attempting the gay air, "chance has brought us together again, and I should judge from your appearance that you've come a long way, bringing nothing particularly good."

"It's so. George and I have been riding all night. We were in Manassas Gap and we learned definitely that Shields is coming through the pass with ten thousand men."

"Fine," said Sherburne with a dusty smile. "Ten thousand is a good round number."

"And if we'll give him time enough," continued Harry, "McDowell will come with twice as many more."

"Look's likely," said Sherburne.

"We've been riding back toward Jackson as fast as we could," continued Harry, "and a little while ago Aubrey riding the same way overtook us."

"And what have you seen, Aubrey?" asked Sherburne.

"I? Oh, I've seen a lot. I've been down by Front Royal in the night, and I've seen Ord with ten thousand men coming full tilt down the Luray Valley."

"What another ten thousand! It's funny how the Yankees run to even tens of thousands, or multiples of that number."

"I've heard," said Harry, "that the force under Banks and Saxton in front of Jackson was ten thousand also."

"I'm sorry, boys, to break up this continuity," said Sherburne with a troubled laugh, "but it's fifteen thousand that I've got to report. Fremont is coming from the west with that number. We've seen 'em. I've no doubt that at this moment there are nearly fifty thousand Yankees in the valley, with more coming, and all but ten thousand of them are in General Jackson's rear."

It seemed that Sherburne, daring cavalryman, had lost his courage for the moment, but the faith of the stern Presbyterian youth, Dalton, never faltered.

"As I told Harry a little while ago, we have at least fifty thousand men," he said.

"What do you mean?" asked Sherburne.

"I count Stonewall Jackson as forty thousand, and the rest will bring the number well over fifty thousand."

Sherburne struck his gauntleted hand smartly on his thigh.

"You talk sense, Dalton!" he exclaimed. "I was foolish to despair! I forgot how much there was under Stonewall Jackson's hat! They haven't caught the old fox yet!"

They galloped on anew, and now they were riding on the road, over which they had pursued so hotly the defeated army of Banks. They would soon be in Jackson's camp, and as they approached their hearts grew lighter. They would cast off their responsibilities and trust all to the leader who appeared so great to them.

"I see pickets now," said Aubrey. "Only five more minutes, boys, but as soon as I give my news I'll have to drop. The excitement has kept me up, but I can't last any longer."

"Nor I," said Harry, who realized suddenly that he was on the verge of collapse. "Whether our arrival is to be followed by a battle or a retreat I'm afraid I won't be fit for either."

They gave the password, and the pickets pointed to the tent of Jackson. They rode straight to him, and dismounted as he came forth from the tent. They were so stiff and sore from long riding that Dalton and Aubrey fell to their knees when they touched the ground, but they quickly recovered, and although they stood somewhat awkwardly they saluted with the deepest respect. Jackson's glance did not escape their mishap, and he knew the cause, but he merely said:

"Well, gentlemen."

"I have to report, sir," said Sherburne, speaking first as the senior officer, "that General Fremont is coming from the west with fifteen thousand men, ready to fall upon your right flank."

"Very good, and what have you seen, Captain Aubrey?"

"Ord with ten thousand men is in our rear and is approaching Front Royal."

"Very good. You have done faithful work, Captain Aubrey. What have you seen, Lieutenant Kenton and Lieutenant Dalton?"

"General Shields, sir, is in Manassas Gap this morning with ten thousand men, and he and General Ord can certainly meet to-day if they wish. We learned also that General McDowell can come up in a few days with twenty thousand more."

The face of Stonewall Jackson never flinched. It looked worn and weary but not more so than it did before this news.

"I thank all of you, young gentlemen," he said in his quiet level tones. "You have done good service. It may be that you're a little weary. You'd better sleep now. I shall call you when I want you."

The four saluted and General Jackson went back into the tent. Aubrey made a grimace.

"We may be a little tired!" he said. "Why, I haven't been out of the saddle for twenty-four hours, and I felt so anxious that every one of those hours was a day long."

"But it's a lot to get from the general an admission that you may be even a little tired," said Dalton. "Remember the man for whom you ride."

"That's so," said Aubrey, "and I oughtn't to have said what I did. We've got to live up to new standards."

Sherburne, Aubrey and Dalton picked out soft spots on the grass and almost instantly were sound asleep, but Harry lingered a minute or two longer. He saw across the river the glitter of bayonets and the dark muzzles of cannon. He also saw many troops moving on the hills and he knew that he was looking upon the remains of Banks' army reinforced by fresh men, ready to dispute the passage or fight Jackson if he marched northward in any other way, while the great masses of their comrades gathered behind him.

Harry felt again for a moment that terrible sinking of the heart which is such close kin to despair. Enemies to the north of them, enemies to the south of them, and to the east and to the west, enemies everywhere. The ring was closing in. Worse than that, it had closed in already and Stonewall Jackson was only mortal. Neither he nor any one else could lead them through the overwhelming ranks of such a force.

But the feeling passed quickly. It could not linger, because the band of the Acadians was playing, and the dark men of the Gulf were singing. Even with the foe in sight, and a long train of battles and marches behind them, with others yet worse to come, they began to dance, clasped in one another's arms.

Many of the Acadians had already gone to a far land and they would never again on this earth see Antoinette or Celeste or Marie, but the sun of the south was in the others and they sang and danced in the brief rest allowed to them.

Harry liked to look at them. He sat on the grass and leaned his back against a tree. The music raised up the heart and it was wonderfully lulling, too. Why worry? Stonewall Jackson would tell them what to do.

The rhythmic forms grew fainter, and he slept. He was awakened the next instant by Dalton. Harry opened his eyes heavily and looked reproachfully at his friend.

"I've slept less than a minute," he said.

Dalton laughed.

"So it seemed to me, too, when I was awakened," he said, "but you've slept a full two hours just as I did. What do you expect when you're working for Stonewall Jackson. You'll be lucky later on whenever you get a single hour."

Harry brushed the traces of sleep from his eyes and stood up straight.

"What's wanted?" he asked.

"You and I and some others are going to take a little railroad trip, escorted by Stonewall Jackson. That's all I know and that's all anybody knows except the general. Come along and look your little best."

Harry brushed out his wrinkled uniform, straightened his cap, and in a minute he and Dalton were with the group of staff officers about Jackson. There was still a section of railway in the valley held by the South, and Jackson and his aides were soon aboard a small train on their way back to Winchester. Harry, glancing from the window, saw the troops gathering up their ammunition and the teamsters hitching up their horses.

"It's going to be a retreat up the valley," he whispered to Dalton. "But masses more than three to one are gathering about us."

"I tell you again, you just trust Old Jack."

Harry looked toward the far end of the coach where Jackson sat with the older members of his staff. His figure swayed with the train, but he showed no sign of weariness or that his dauntless soul dwelt in a physical body. He was looking out at the window, but it was obvious that he did not see the green landscape flashing past. Harry knew that he was making the most complex calculations, but like Dalton he ceased to wonder about them. He put his faith in Old Jack, and let it go at that.

There was very little talking in the train. Despite every effort, Harry's eyes grew heavy and he began to doze a little. He would waken entirely at times and straighten up with a jerk. Then he would see the fields and forests still rushing past, now and then a flash as they crossed a stream, and always the sober figure of the general, staring, unseeing, through the window.

He suddenly became wide-awake, when he heard sharp comment in the coach. All the older officers were gazing through the windows with the greatest interest. Harry saw a man in Confederate uniform galloping across the fields and waving his hands repeatedly to the train which was already checking speed.

"A staff officer with news," said Dalton.

"Yes," said Harry, "and I'm thinking it will seem bad news to you and me."

The train stopped in a field, and the officer, panting and covered with dust and perspiration, rode alongside. Jackson walked out on the steps, followed by his eager officers.

"What is it?" asked Jackson.

"The Northern army has retaken Front Royal. The Georgia regiment you left in garrison there has been driven out and without support is marching northward. I have here, sir, a dispatch from Colonel Connor, the commander of the Georgians."

He handed the folded paper to the general, who received it but did not open it for a moment. There was something halfway between a sigh and a groan from the officers, but Jackson said nothing. He smiled, but, as Harry saw it, it was a strange and threatening smile. Then he opened the dispatch, read it carefully, tore it into tiny bits and threw them away. Harry saw the fragments picked up by the wind and whirled across the field. Jackson nearly always destroyed his dispatches in this manner.

"Very good," he said to the officer, "you can rejoin Colonel Connor."

He went back to his seat. The train puffed, heaved and started again. Jackson leaned against the back of the seat and closed his eyes. He seemed to be asleep. But the desire for sleep was driven from Harry. The news of the retaking of Front Royal had stirred the whole train. Officers talked of it in low tones, but with excitement. The Northern generals were acting with more than their customary promptness. Already they had struck a blow and Ord with his ten thousand men had undoubtedly passed from the Luray Valley into the main Valley of Virginia to form a junction with Shields and his ten thousand.

What would Jackson do? Older men in the train than Harry and Dalton were asking that question, but he remained silent. He kept his eyes closed for some time, and Harry thought that he must be fast asleep, although it seemed incredible that a man with such responsibilities could sleep at such a time. But he opened his eyes presently and began to talk with a warm personal friend who occupied the other half of the seat.

Harry did not know the tenor of this conversation then, but he heard of it later from the general's friend. Jackson had remarked to the man that he seemed to be surrounded, and the other asked what he would do if the Northern armies cut him off entirely. Jackson replied that he would go back toward the north, invade Maryland and march straight on Baltimore and Washington. Few more daring plans have ever been conceived, but, knowing Jackson as he learned to know him, Harry always believed that he would have tried it.

But the Southern leaders within that mighty and closing ring in the valley were not the only men who had anxious minds. At the

Union capital they did not know what had become of Jackson. They knew that he was somewhere within the ring, but where? He might pounce upon a division, deal another terrible blow and then away! In a week he had drawn the eyes of the world upon him, and his enemies no longer considered anything impossible to him. Many a patriot who was ready to die rather than see the union of the states destroyed murmured: "If he were only on our side!" There was already talk of recalling McClellan's great army to defend Washington.

The object of all this immense anxiety and care was riding peacefully in a train to Winchester, talking with a friend but conscious fully of his great danger. It seemed that the Northern generals with their separate armies were acting in unison at last, and must close down on their prey.

They came again into Winchester, the town torn so often by battle and its anxieties, and saw the Presbyterian minister, his face gray with care, greet Jackson. Then the two walked toward the manse, followed at a respectful distance by the officers of the staff.

Harry soon saw that the whole of Winchester was in gloom. They knew there of the masses in blue converging on Jackson, and few had hope. While Jackson remained at the manse he sat upon the portico within call. There was little sound in Winchester. The town seemed to have passed into an absolute silence. Most of the doors and shutters were closed.

And yet the valley had never seemed more beautiful to Harry. Far off were the dim blue mountains that enclosed it on either side, and the bright skies never bent in a more brilliant curve.

He felt again that overpowering desire to sleep, and he may have dozed a little when he sat there in the sun, but he was wide awake when Jackson called him.

"I want you to go at once to Harper's Ferry with this note," he said, "and give it to the officer in command. He will bring back the troops to Winchester, and you are to come with him. You can go most of the way on the train and then you must take to your horse. The troops will march back by the valley turnpike."

Harry saluted and was off. He soon found that other officers were going to the various commands with orders similar to his, and he no longer had any doubt that the whole force would be consolidated and would withdraw up the valley. He was right. Jackson had abandoned the plan of entering Maryland and marching on Baltimore and Washington, and was now about to try another, fully as daring, but calling for the most sudden and complicated movements. He had arranged it all, as he rode in the train, most of it as he leaned against the back of the seat with his eyes shut.

Harry was soon back in Harper's Ferry, and the troops there immediately began their retreat. Most all of them knew of the great danger that menaced their army, but Harry, a staff officer, understood better than the regimental commanders what was occurring. The Invincibles were in their division and he rode with the two colonels, St. Clair and Happy Tom Langdon. They went at a swift pace and behind them came the steady beat of the marching troops on the turnpike.

"You have been with General Jackson in Winchester, Harry," said Colonel Leonidas Talbot in his precise manner, "and I judge that you must have formed some idea of his intentions. This indicates a general retreat southward, does it not?"

"I think so, sir. General Jackson has said nothing, but I know that orders have been sent to all our detachments to draw in. He must have some plan of cutting his way through toward the south. What do you think, Colonel St. Hilaire?"

"It must be so," replied Lieutenant-Colonel Hector St. Hilaire, "but how he will do it is beyond me. When I look around at all these blue mountains, Leonidas, it seems to me that we're enclosed by living battlements."

"Or that Jackson is like the tiger in the bush, surrounded by the beaters."

"Yes, and sometimes it's woe to the beaters when they come too near."

Harry dropped back with his younger friends who were by no means of sad demeanor. St. Clair had restored his uniform to its usual immaculate neatness or in some manner he had obtained a new one. Tom Langdon was Happy Tom again.

"We've eaten well, and we've slept well," said Langdon, "and Arthur and I are restored completely. He's the finest dandy in the army again, and I'm ready for another week's run with Jackson.

I know I won't get another chance to rest in a long time, but Old Stonewall needn't think I can't march as long as he can."

"You'll get your fill of it," said Harry, "and of fighting, too. Take a look all around you. No, not a half circle, but a complete circle."

"Well, I've twisted my neck until my head nearly falls off. What signifies the performance?"

"There was no time when you were turning around the circle that your eyes didn't look toward Yankees. Nearly fifty thousand of 'em are in the valley. We're in a ring of steel, Happy."

"Well, Old Jack will just take his sword and slash that steel ring apart. And if he should fail I'm here. Lead me to 'em, Harry."

Langdon's spirits were infectious. Even the marching men who heard Happy Tom laugh, laughed with him and were more cheerful. They marched faster, too, and from other points men were coming quickly to Jackson at Winchester. They were even coming into contact with the ring of steel which was closing in on them. Fremont, advancing with his fifteen thousand from the mountains, met a heavy fire from a line of ambushed riflemen. Not knowing where Jackson was or what he was doing, and fearing that the great Confederate commander might be before him with his whole army, he stopped at Cedar Creek and made a camp of defense.

Shields, in the south, moving forward, found a swarm of skirmishers in his front, and presently the Acadians, sent in that direction by Jackson, opened up with a heavy fire on his vanguard. Shields drew back. He, too, feared that Jackson with his entire army was before him and rumor magnified the Southern force. Meanwhile the flying cavalry of Ashby harassed the Northern advance at many points.

All the time the main army of Jackson was retreating toward Winchester, carrying with it the prisoners and a vast convoy of wagons filled with captured ammunition and stores. Jackson had foreseen everything. He had directed the men who were leading these forces to pass around Winchester in case he was compelled to abandon it, circle through the mountains and join him wherever he might be.

But Harry when he returned to Winchester breathed a little more freely. He felt in some manner that the steel ring did not compress so tightly. Jackson, acting on the inside of the circle, had spread consternation. The Northern generals could not communicate with one another because either mountains or Southern troops came between. Prisoners whom the Southern cavalry brought in told strange stories. Rumor in their ranks had magnified Jackson's numbers double or triple. Many believed that a great force was coming from Richmond to help him. Jackson was surrounded, but the beaters were very wary about pressing in on him.

Yet the Union masses in the valley had increased. McDowell himself had now come, and he sent forward cavalry details which, losing the way, were compelled to return. Fremont on the west at last finding the line of riflemen before him withdrawn, pushed forward, and saw the long columns of the Southern army with their wagons moving steadily toward the south. His cavalry attacking were driven off and the Southern division went on.

Harry with the retreating division wondered at these movements and admired their skill. Jackson's army, encumbered as it was with prisoners and stores, was passing directly between the armies of Fremont and Shields, covering its flanks with clouds of skirmishers and cavalry that beat off every attack of the hostile vanguards, and that kept the two Northern armies from getting into touch.

Jackson had not stopped at Winchester. He had left that town once more to the enemy and was still drawing back toward the wider division of the valley west of the Massanuttons. The great mind was working very fast now. The men themselves saw that warlike genius incarnate rode on the back of Little Sorrel. Jackson was slipping through the ring, carrying with him every prisoner and captured wagon.

His lightning strokes to right and to left kept Shields and Fremont dazed and bewildered, and McDowell neither knew what was passing nor could he get his forces together. Harry saw once more and with amazement the dark bulk of the Massanuttons rising on his left and he knew that these great isolated mountains would again divide the Union force, while Jackson passed on in the larger valley.

He felt a thrill, powerful and indescribable. Jackson in very truth had slashed across with his sword that great ring of steel and was passing through the break, leaving behind not a single prisoner, nor a single wagon. Sixty-two thousand men had not only failed to hold sixteen thousand, but their scattered forces had suffered numerous severe defeats from the far smaller army. It was not that the Northern men were inferior to the Southern in courage and tenacity, but the Southern army was led by a genius of the first rank, unmatched as a military leader in modern times, save by Napoleon and Lee.

It was the last day of May and the twilight was at hand. The dark masses of Little North Mountain to the west and of the Massanuttons to the east were growing dim. Harry rode by the side of Dalton a few paces in the rear of Jackson, and he watched the somber, silent man, riding silently on Little Sorrel. There was nothing bright or spectacular about him. The battered gray uniform was more battered than ever. In place of the worn cap an old slouched hat now shaded his forehead and eyes. But Harry knew that their extraordinary achievements had not been due to luck or chance, but were the result of the mighty calculations that had been made in the head under the old slouched hat.

Harry heard behind him the long roll and murmur of the marching army, the wheels of cannon and wagons grating on the turnpike, the occasional neigh of a horse, the rattle of arms and the voices of men talking low. Most of these men had been a year and a half ago citizens untrained for war. They were not mere creatures of drill, but they were intelligent, and they thought for themselves. They knew as well as the officers what Jackson had done and henceforth they looked upon him as something almost superhuman. Confident in his genius they were ready to follow wherever Jackson led, no matter what the odds.

These were exactly the feelings of both Harry and Dalton. They would never question or doubt again. Both of them, with the hero worship of youth felt a mighty swell of pride, that they should ride with so great a leader, and be so near to him.

The army marched on in the darkening hours, leaving behind it sixty thousand men who closed up the ring only to find their game gone.

Harry heard from the older staff officers that they would go on up the valley until they came to the Gaps of the Blue Ridge. There in an impregnable position they could turn and fight pursuit or take the railway to Richmond and join in the defense against McClellan. It all depended on what Jackson thought, and his thoughts were uniformly disclosed by action.

Meanwhile the news was spreading through the North that Jackson had escaped, carrying with him his prisoners and captured stores. Odds had counted for nothing. All the great efforts directed from Washington had been unavailing. All the courage and energy of brave men had been in vain. But the North did not cease her exertions for an instant. Lincoln, a man of much the same character as Jackson, but continually thwarted by mediocre generals, urged the attack anew. Dispatches were sent to all the commanders ordering them to push the pursuit of Jackson and to bring him to battle.

Cut to the quick by their great failure, Fremont, Shields, Ord, Banks, McDowell and all the rest, pushed forward on either side of the Massanuttons, those on the west intending to cross at the gap, join their brethren, and make another concerted attempt at Jackson's destruction.

But Harry ceased to think of armies and battles as he rode on in the dark. He was growing sleepy again and he dozed in his saddle. Half consciously he thought of his father and wondered where he was. He had received only one letter from him after Shiloh, but he believed that he was still with the Confederate army in the west, taking an active part. Much as he loved his father it was the first time that he had been in his thoughts in the last two weeks. How could any one think of anything but the affair of the moment at such a time, when the seconds were ticked off by cannon-shots!

In this vague and pleasant dream he also remembered Dick Mason, his cousin, who was now somewhere there in the west fighting on the other side. He thought of Dick with affection and he liked him none the less because he wore the blue. Then, curiously enough, the last thing that he remembered was his Tacitus, lying in his locked desk in the Pendleton Academy. He would get out that old fellow again some day and finish him. Then he fell sound asleep in his saddle, and the horse went steadily on, safely carrying his sleeping master.

He did not awake until midnight, when Dalton's hand on his shoulder caused him to open his eyes.

"I've been asleep, too, Harry," said Dalton, "but I woke up first. We're going into camp here for the rest of the night."

"I'm glad to stop," said Harry, "but I wonder what the dawn will bring."

"I wonder," said Dalton.

CHAPTER XIII.
THE SULLEN RETREAT

Harry, like the rest of the army, slept soundly through the rest of the night and they rose to a brilliant first day of June. The scouts said that the whole force of Fremont was not far behind, while the army of Shields was marching on a parallel line east of the Massanuttons, and ready at the first chance to form a junction with Fremont.

Youth seeks youth and Harry and Dalton found a little time to talk with St. Clair and Langdon.

"We've broken their ring and passed through," said Langdon, "but as sure as we live we'll all be fighting again in a day. If the Yankees follow too hard Old Jack will turn and fight 'em. Now, why haven't the Yankees got sense enough to let us alone and go home?"

"They'll never do it," said Dalton gravely. "We've got to recognize that fact. I'm never going to say another word about the Yankees not being willing to fight."

"They're too darned willing," said Happy Tom. "That's the trouble."

"I woke up just about the dawn," said Dalton. "Everybody was asleep, but the general, and I saw him praying."

"Then it means fighting and lots of it," said St. Clair. "I'm going to make the best use I can of this little bit of rest, as I don't expect another chance for at least a month. Stonewall Jackson thinks that one hour a day for play keeps Jack from being a dull boy."

"Just look at our colonels, will you?" said Happy Tom. "They're believers in what Arthur says."

Colonel Leonidas Talbot and Lieutenant-Colonel Hector St. Hilaire were sitting in a corner of a rail fence opposite each other, and their bent gray heads nearly touched. But their eyes were on a small board between them and now and then they moved carved figures back and forth.

"They're playing chess," whispered Happy Tom. "They found the board and set of men in the captured baggage, and this is their first chance to use them."

"They can't possibly finish a game," said Harry.

"No," said Tom, "they can't, and it's just as well. Why anybody wants to play chess is more than I can understand. I'd rather watch a four-mile race between two turtles. It's a lot swifter and more thrilling."

"It takes intelligence to play chess, Happy," said St. Clair.

"And time, too," rejoined Happy. "If a thing consumes a lifetime anyway, what's the use of intelligence?"

A bugle sounded. The two colonels raised their gray heads and gave the chess men and the board to an orderly. The four boys returned to their horses, and in a few minutes Jackson's army was once more on the march, the Acadian band near the head of the column playing as joyously as if it had never lost a member in battle. The mountains and the valley between were bathed in light once more. The heavy dark green foliage on the slopes of the Massanuttons rested the eye and the green fields of the valley were cheering.

"I don't believe I'd ever forget this valley if I lived to be a thousand," said Harry. "I've marched up and down it so much and every second of the time was so full of excitement."

"Here's one day of peace, or at least it looks so," said Dalton.

But Jackson beckoned to Harry, bade him ride to the rear and report if there was any sign of the enemy. They had learned to obey quickly and Harry galloped back by the side of the marching army. Even now the men were irrepressible and he was saluted with the old familiar cries:

"Hey, Johnny Reb, come back! You're going toward the Yankees, not away from 'em."

"Let him go ahead, Bill. He's goin' to tell the Yankees to stop or he'll hurt 'em."

"That ain't the way to ride a hoss, bub. Don't set up so straight in the saddle."

Harry paid no attention to this disregard of his dignity as an officer. He had long since become used to it, and, if they enjoyed it, he was glad to furnish the excuse. He reached the rear guard of scouts and skirmishers, and, turning his horse, kept with them for a while, but they saw nothing. Sherburne, with a detachment of the cavalry was there, and Ashby, who commanded all the horse, often appeared.

"Fremont's army is not many miles behind," said Sherburne. "If we were to ride a mile or two toward it we could see its dust. But the Yanks are tired and they can't march fast. I wish I knew how far up the Luray Shields and his army are. We've got to look out for that junction of Shields and Fremont."

"We'll pass the Gap before they can make the junction," said Harry confidently.

"How's Old Jack looking?"

"Same as ever."

"That is, like a human sphinx. Well, you can never tell from his face what he's thinking, but you can be sure that he's thinking something worth while."

"You think then I can report to him that the pursuit will not catch up to-day?"

"I'm sure of it. I've talked with Ashby also about it and he says they're yet too far back. Harry, what day is this?"

Harry smiled at the sudden question, but he understood how Sherburne, amid almost continuous battle, had lost sight of time.

"I heard someone say it was the first of June," he replied.

"No later than that? Why, it seemed to me that it must be nearly autumn. Do you know, Harry, that on this very day, two years ago, I was up there in those mountains to the west with a jolly camping party. I was just a boy then, and now here I am an old man."

"About twenty-three, I should say."

"A good guess, but anyway I've been through enough to make me feel sixty. I promise you, Harry, that if ever I get through this war alive I'll shoot the man who tries to start another. Look at the fields! How fine and green they are! Think of all that good land being torn up by the hoofs of cavalry and the wheels of cannon!"

"If you are going to be sentimental I'll leave you," said Harry, and the action followed the word. He rode away, because he was afraid he would grow sentimental himself.

The army continued its peaceful march up the valley and most of the night that followed. Harry was allowed to obtain a few hours sleep in the latter part of the night in one of the captured wagons. It was a covered wagon and he selected it because he noticed that the night, even if it was the first of June, was growing chill. But he had no time to be particular about the rest. He did not undress—he had not undressed in days—but lying between two sacks of meal with his head on a third sack he sank into a profound slumber.

When Harry awoke he felt that the wagon was moving. He also heard the patter of rain on his canvas roof. It was dusky in there, but he saw in front of him the broad back of the teamster who sat on the cross seat and drove.

"Hello!" exclaimed Harry, sitting up. "What's happened?"

A broad red face was turned to him, and a voice issuing from a slit almost all the way across its breadth replied:

"Well, if little old Rip Van Winkle hasn't waked up at last! Why, you've slept nigh on to four hours, and nobody in Stonewall Jackson's army is ever expected to sleep more'n three and that's gospel truth, as shore's my name is Sam Martin."

"But, Sam, you don't tell me what's happened!"

"It's as simple as A, B, C. We're movin' ag'in, and that fine June day yestiddy that we liked so much is gone forever. The second o' June ain't one little bit like the first o' June. It's cold and it's wet. Can't you hear the rain peltin' on the canvas? Besides, the Yanks are comin' up, too. I done heard the boomin' o' cannon off there toward the rear."

"Oh, why wasn't I called! Here I am sleeping away, and the enemy is already in touch with us!"

"Don't you worry any 'bout that, sonny. Don't you be so anxious to git into a fight, 'cause you'll have plenty of chances when you can't keep out o' it. 'Sides, Gin'ral Jackson ain't been expectin' you. We're up near the head o' the line an' 'bout an hour ago when we was startin' a whiskered man on a little sorrel hoss rid up an' said: 'Which o' my staff have you got in there? I remember 'signin' one to you last night.' I bows very low an' I says: 'Gin'ral Jackson, I don't know his name. He was too sleepy to give it, but he's a real young fellow, nice an' quiet. He ain't give no trouble at all. He's been sleepin' so hard I think he has pounded his ear clean through one o' them bags o' meal.' Gin'ral Jackson laughs low an' just a little, and then he takes a peek into the wagon. 'Why, it's young Harry Kenton!' he says. 'Let him sleep on till he wakes. He deserves it!' Then he lets fall the canvas an' he ups an' rides away. An' if I was in your place, young Mr. Kenton, I'd feel mighty proud to have Stonewall Jackson say that I deserved more rest."

"I am proud, but I've got to go now. I don't know where I'll find my horse."

"I know, an' what's more I'll tell. An orderly came back with him saddled an' bridled an' he's hitched to this here wagon o' mine. Goodbye, Mr. Kenton, I'm sorry you're goin' 'cause you've been a nice, pleasant boarder, sayin' nothin' an' givin' no trouble."

Harry thanked him, and then in an instant was out of the wagon and on his horse. It required only a few minutes to overtake Jackson and his staff, who were riding soberly along in the rain. He noticed with relief that he was not the last to join the chief. Two or three others came up later. Jackson nodded pleasantly to them all as they came.

But the morning was gloomy in the extreme. Harry was glad to shelter himself with the heavy cavalry cloak from the cold rain. All the skies were covered with sullen clouds, and the troops trudged silently on in deep mud. Now and then a wind off the mountains threshed the rain sharply into their faces. From the rear came the deep, sullen mutter which Harry so readily recognized as the sound of the big guns. Sam Martin was right. The enemy was most decidedly "in touch."

Dalton handed Harry some cold food and he ate it in the saddle. Jackson rode on saying nothing, his head bowed a little, his gaze far away. The officers of his staff were also silent. Jackson after a while reined his horse out of the road, and his staff, of course, followed. The troops filed past and Jackson said:

"We will soon pass the Gap in the Massanuttons, and Shields cannot come out there ahead of us. That danger is left behind."

"What of the junction between Shields and Fremont, General?" asked one of the older officers.

Jackson cast one glance at the somber heavens.

"Providence favors us," he said. "The south fork of the Shenandoah flows between Fremont and Shields. It is swollen already by the rains and the rushing torrents from the mountains, and if I read the skies right we're going to have other long and heavy rains. They can't ford the Shenandoah and they can't stop to bridge it. It will be a long time before they can bring a united force against us."

But while he spoke the mutter of the guns grew louder. Jackson listened attentively a long time, and then sent several of his staff officers to the rear with orders to the cavalry, the Invincibles under Talbot, and one other regiment to hold the enemy off at all costs. As Harry galloped back the mutter of the cannon grew into thunder. There was also the sharper crash of rifle fire. Presently he saw the flash of the firing and numerous spires of smoke rising.

His own message was to the Invincibles and he delivered the brief note to Colonel Talbot, who read it quickly and then tore it up.

"Stay with us a while, Harry," he said, "and you can then report more fully to the general what is going on. They crowd us hard. Look how their sharpshooters are swarming in the woods and fields yonder."

An orchard to the left of the road and only a short distance away was filled with the Union riflemen. Running from tree to tree and along the fences they sent bullets straight into the ranks of the Invincibles. Four guns were turned and swept the orchard with shell, but the wary sharpshooters darted to another point, and again came the hail of bullets. Colonel Talbot bade his weary men turn, but at the moment, Sherburne, with a troop of cavalry, swept down on the riflemen and sent them flying. Harry saw Colonel Talbot's lips moving, and he knew that he was murmuring thanks because Sherburne had come so opportunely.

"We're not having an easy time," he said to Harry. "They press us hard. We drive them back for a time, and they come again. They have field guns, too, and they are handled with great skill. If I do not mistake greatly, they are under the charge of Carrington, who, you remember, fought us at that fort in the valley before Bull Run, John Carrington, old John Carrington, my classmate at West Point, a man who wouldn't hurt a fly, but who is the most deadly artillery officer in the world."

Harry remembered that famous duel of the guns in the hills and Colonel Talbot's admiration of his opponent, Carrington. Now he could see it shining in his eyes as strongly as ever.

"Why are you so sure, colonel, that it's Carrington?" he asked.

"Because nobody else could handle those field guns as he does. He brings 'em up, sends the shot and shell upon us, then hitches up like lightning, is away before we can charge, and in a minute or two is firing into our line elsewhere. Trust Carrington for such work, and I'm glad he hasn't been killed. John's the dearest soul in the world, as gentle as a woman. Down! Down! all of you! There are the muzzles of his guns in the bushes again!"

Colonel Talbot's order was so sharp and convincing that most of the Invincibles mechanically threw themselves upon their faces, just as four field pieces crashed and the shell and shrapnel flew over their heads. That rapid order had saved them, but the officers on horseback were not so lucky. A captain was killed, Lieutenant-Colonel St. Hilaire was grazed on the shoulder, and the horse of Colonel Talbot was killed under him.

But Colonel Talbot, alert and agile, despite his years, sprang clear of the falling horse and said emphatically to his second in command, Lieutenant-Colonel Hector St. Hilaire:

"The last doubt is gone! It's Carrington as sure as we live!"

Then he gave a quick order to his men to rise and fire with the rifles, but the woods protected the gunners, and, when Sherburne with his cavalry charged into the forest, Carrington and his guns were gone.

Colonel Talbot procured another horse, and the Invincibles, sore of body and mind, resumed their slow and sullen retreat. Harry left them and rode further along the front of the rear guard. Under the somber skies and in the dripping rain there was a long line of flashing rifles and the flaming of big guns at intervals.

Fremont was pushing the pursuit and pushing it hard. Harry recognized anew the surpassing skill of Jackson in keeping his enemies separated by mountains and streams, while his own concentrated force marched on. He felt that Fremont would hold Jackson in battle if he could until the other Northern armies came up, and he felt also that Jackson would lead Fremont beyond a junction with the others and then turn. Yet these Northern men were certainly annoying. They did not seem to mind defeats. Here they were fighting as hard as ever, pursuing and not pursued.

Harry, turning to the left, saw a numerous body of cavalry under Ashby, supported by guns also, and he joined them. Ashby on his famous white horse was riding here and there, exposing himself again and again to the fire of the enemy, who was pressing close. He nodded to Harry, whom he knew.

"You can report to General Jackson," he said, "that the enemy is continually attacking, but that we are continually beating him off."

Just as he spoke a trumpet sounded loud and clear in the edge of a wood only three or four hundred yards away. There was a tremendous shout from many men, and then the thunder of hoofs. A cavalry detachment, more than a thousand strong, rushed down upon them, and to right and left of the horse, regiments of infantry, supported by field batteries, charged also.

The movement was so sudden, so violent and so well-conceived that Ashby's troops were swept away, despite every effort of the leader, who galloped back and forth on his white horse begging them to stand. So powerful was the rush that the cavalry were finally driven in retreat and with them the Invincibles.

Some of the troops, worn by battles and marches until the will weakened with the body, broke and ran up the road. Harry heard behind him the triumphant shouts of their pursuers and he saw the Northern bayonets gleaming as they came on in masses. Ashby was imploring his men to stand but they would not. The columns pressing upon them were too heavy and they scarcely had strength enough left to fight.

More and yet more troops came into battle. The Northern success for the time was undoubted. The men in blue were driving in the Southern rear guard, and Ashby was unable to hold the road.

But the two colonels at last succeeded in drawing the Invincibles across the turnpike, where they knelt in good order and sent volley after volley into the pursuing ranks. Fremont's men wavered and then stopped, and Ashby, upbraiding his horsemen and calling their attention to the resolute stand of the infantry, brought them into action again. Infantry and cavalry then uniting, drove back the

Northern vanguard, and, for the time being, the Southern rear guard was safe once more.

But the Invincibles and the cavalry were almost exhausted. Harry found St. Clair wounded, not badly, but with enough loss of blood for Colonel Talbot to send him to one of the wagons. He insisted that he was still fit to help hold the road, but Colonel Talbot ordered two of the soldiers to put him in the wagon and he was compelled to submit.

"We can't let you die now from loss of blood, you young fire-eater," said Colonel Talbot severely, "because you may be able to serve us better by getting killed later on."

St. Clair smiled wanly and with his formal South Carolina politeness said:

"Thanks, sir, it helps a lot when you're able to put it in such a satisfactory way."

Harry, who was unhurt, gave St. Clair a strong squeeze of the hand.

"You'll be up and with us again soon, Arthur," he said consolingly, and then he rode away to Ashby.

"You may tell General Jackson that we can hold them back," said the cavalry leader grimly. "You have just seen for yourself."

"I have, sir," replied Harry, and he galloped away from the rear. But he soon met the general himself, drawn by the uncommonly heavy firing. Harry told him what had happened, but the expression of Jackson's face did not change.

"A rather severe encounter," he said, "but Ashby can hold them."

All that day, nearly all that night and all the following day Harry passed between Jackson and Ashby or with them. It was well for the Virginians that they were practically born on horseback and were trained to open air and the forests. For thirty-six hours the cavalry were in the saddle almost without a break. And so was Harry. He had forgotten all about food and rest. He was in a strange, excited mood. He seemed to see everything through a red mist. In all the thirty-six hours the crash of rifles or the thud of cannon ceased scarcely for a moment. It went on just the same in day or in night. The Northern troops, although led by no such general as Stonewall Jackson, showed the splendid stuff of which they were made. They were always eager to push hard and yet harder.

The Southern troops burnt the bridges over the creeks as they retreated, but the Northern men waded through the water and followed. The clouds of cavalry were always in touch. A skirmish was invariably proceeding at some point. Toward evening of the second day's pursuit, they came to Mount Jackson, to which they had retreated once before, and there went into camp in a strong place.

But the privates themselves knew that they could not stay there long. They might turn and beat off Fremont's army, but then they would have to reckon with the second army under Shields and the yet heavier masses that McDowell was bringing up. But Jackson himself gave no sign of discouragement. He went cheerfully among the men, and saw that attention, as far as possible at such a time, was given to their needs. Harry hunted up St. Clair and found him with a bandaged shoulder sitting in his wagon. He was sore but cheerful.

"The doctor tells me, Harry, that I can take my place in the line in three more days," he said, "but I intend to make it two. I fancy that we need all the men we can get now, and that I won't be driven back to this wagon."

"If I were as well fixed as you are, Arthur," said Langdon, who appeared at this moment on the other side of the wagon, "I'd stay where I was. But it's so long since I've been hauled that I'm afraid the luxury would overpower me. Think of lying on your back and letting the world float peacefully by! Did I say 'think of it'? I was wrong. It is unthinkable. Now, Harry, what plans has Old Jack got for us?"

"I don't know."

"Well, he'll get us out of this. We're sure of that. But when? That's the question."

The question remained without an answer. Early the next morning they were on the march again under lowering skies. The heavens from horizon to horizon were a sodden gray and began to drip rain. Harry was sent again to the rear-guard, where Ashby's cavalry hung like a curtain, backed by the Invincibles and one or two other skeleton regiments.

Harry joined Sherburne and now the drip of the rain became a steady beat. Chilling winds from the mountains swept over them. He had preserved through thick and thin, through battle and through march that big cavalry cloak, and now he buttoned it tightly around him.

He saw down the road puffs of smoke and heard the lashing fire of rifles, but it did not make his pulses beat any faster now. He had grown so used to it that it seemed to be his normal life. A bullet fired from a rifle of longer range than the others plumped into the mud at the feet of his horse, but he paid no attention to it.

He joined Sherburne, who was using his glasses, watching through the heavy, thick air the Northern advance. The brilliant young cavalryman, while as bold and enduring as ever, had changed greatly in the last two or three weeks. The fine uniform was stained and bedraggled. Sherburne himself had lost more than twenty pounds and his face was lined and anxious far more than the face of a mere boy of twenty-three should have been.

"I think they'll press harder than ever," said Sherburne.

"Why?"

"The Shenandoah river, or rather the north fork of it, isn't far ahead. They'd like to coop us up against it and make us fight, while their army under Shields and all their other armies—God knows how many they have—are coming up."

"The river is bridged, isn't it?"

"Yes, but it takes a good while to get an army such as ours, loaded down with prisoners and spoil, across it, and if they rushed us just when we were starting over it, we'd have to turn and give battle. Jupiter, how it rains! Behold the beauties of war, Harry!"

The wind suddenly veered a little, and with it the rain came hard and fast. It seemed to blow off the mountains in sheets and for a moment or two Harry was blinded. The beat of the storm upon leaves and earth was so hard that the cracking of the rifles was dulled and deadened. Nevertheless the rifle fire went on, and as well as Harry could judge, without any decrease in violence.

"Hear the bugles now!" said Sherburne. "Their scouts are warning them of the approach to the Shenandoah. They'll be coming up in a minute or two in heavier force. Ah, see, Ashby understands, too! He's massing the men to hold them back!"

The rain still poured with all the violence of a deluge, but the Northern force, horse and cannon, pushed forward through the mud and opened with all their might. Ashby's cavalry and the infantry in support replied. There was something grim and awful to Harry in this fight in the raging storm. Now and then, he could not see the flame of the firing for the rain in his eyes. By a singular chance a bullet cut the button of his cloak at the throat and the cloak flew open there. In a minute he was soaked through and through with water, but he did not notice it.

The cavalry, the Invincibles and the other regiments were making a desperate stand in order that the army might cross the bridge of the Shenandoah. Harry was seized with a sort of fury. Why should these men try to keep them from getting across? It was their right to escape. Presently he found himself firing with his pistols into the great pillar of fire and smoke and rain in front of him. Mud splashed up by the horses struck him in the face now and then, and stung like gunpowder, but he began to shout with joy when he saw that Ashby was holding back the Northern vanguard.

Ahead of him the Southern army was already rumbling over the bridge, while the swollen and unfordable waters of the Shenandoah raced beneath it. But the Northern brigades pressed hard. Harry did not know whether the rain helped them or hurt them, but at any rate it was terribly uncomfortable. It poured on them in sheets and sheets and the earth seemed to be a huge quagmire. He wondered how the men were able to keep their ammunition dry enough to fire, but that they did was evident from the crash that went on without ceasing.

"In thinking of war before I really knew it," said Harry, "I never thought much of weather."

"Does sound commonplace, but it cuts a mighty big figure I can tell you. If it hadn't rained so hard just before Waterloo Napoleon would have got up his big guns more easily, winning the battle, and perhaps changing the history of the world. Confound it, look at that crowd pushing forward through the field to take us in the flank!"

"Western men, I think," said Harry. "Here are two of our field guns, Sherburne! Get 'em to throw some grape in there!"

It was lucky that the guns approached at that moment. Their commander, as quick of eye as either Harry or Sherburne, unlimbered and swept back the western men who were seeking to turn their flank. Then Sherburne, with a charge of his cavalry, sent them back further. But at the call of Ashby's trumpet they turned quickly and galloped after Jackson's army, the main part of which had now passed the bridge.

"I suppose we'll burn the bridge after we cross it," said Harry.

"Of course."

"But how on earth can we set fire to it with this Noah's flood coming down?"

"I don't know. They'll manage it somehow. Look, Harry, see the flames bursting from the timbers now. Gallop, men! Gallop! We may get our faces scorched in crossing the bridge, but when we're on the other side it won't be there for the Yankees!"

The Invincibles and the other infantry regiments all were advancing at the double quick, with the cavalry closing up the rear. Behind them many bugles rang and through the dense rain they saw the Northern cavalry leaders swinging their sabers and cheering on their men, and they also saw behind them the heavy masses of infantry coming up.

Harry knew that it was touch-and-go. The bulk of the army was across, and if necessary they must sacrifice Ashby's cavalry, but that sacrifice would be too great. Harry had never seen Ashby and his gallant captains show more courage. They fought off the enemy to the very last and then galloped for the bridge, under a shower of shell and grape and bullets. Ashby's own horse was killed under him, falling headlong in the mud, but in an instant somebody supplied him with a fresh one, upon which he leaped, and then they thundered over the burning bridge, Ashby and Sherburne the last two to begin the crossing.

Harry, who was just ahead of Ashby and Sherburne, felt as if the flames were licking at them. With an involuntary motion he threw up his hands to protect his eyes from the heat, and he also had a horrible sensation lest the bridge, its supporting timbers burned through, should fall, sending them all into the rushing flood.

But the bridge yet held and Harry uttered a gasp of relief as the feet of his horse struck the deep mud on the other side. They galloped on for two or three hundred yards, and then at the command of Ashby turned.

The bridge was a majestic sight, a roaring pyramid that shot forth clouds of smoke and sparks in myriads.

"How under the sun did we cross it?" Harry exclaimed.

"We crossed it, that's sure, because here we are," said Sherburne. "I confess myself that I don't know just how we did it, Harry, but it's quite certain that the enemy will never cross it. The fire's too strong. Besides, they'd have our men to face."

Harry looked about, and saw several thousand men drawn up to dispute the passage, but the Northern troops recognizing its impossibility at that time, made no attempt. Nevertheless their cannon sent shells curving over the stream, and the Southern cannon sent curving shells in reply. But the burning bridge roared louder and the pyramid of flame rose higher. The rain, which had never ceased to pour in a deluge, merely seemed to feed it.

"Ah, she's about to go now," exclaimed Sherburne.

The bridge seemed to Harry to rear up before his eyes like a living thing, and then draw together a mass of burning timbers. The next moment the whole went with a mighty crash into the river, and the blazing fragments floated swiftly away on the flood. The deep and rapid Shenandoah flowed a barrier between the armies of Jackson and Fremont.

"A river can be very beautiful without a bridge, Harry, can't it?" said a voice beside him.

It was St. Clair, a heavy bandage over his left shoulder, but a smoking rifle in his right hand, nevertheless.

"I couldn't stand it any longer, Harry," he said. "I had to get up and join the Invincibles, and you see I'm all right."

Harry was compelled to laugh at the sodden figure, from which the rain ran in streams. But he admired St. Clair's spirit.

"It was by a hair's breadth, Arthur," he said.

"But we won across, just the same, and now I'm going back to that wagon to finish my cure. I fancy that we'll now have a rest of six or eight hours, if General Jackson doesn't think so much time taken from war a mere frivolity."

The Southern army drew off slowly, but as soon as it was out of sight the tenacious Northern troops undertook to follow. They attempted to build a bridge of boats, but the flood was so heavy that they were swept away. Then Fremont set men to work to rebuild the bridge, which they could do in twenty-four hours, but Jackson, meanwhile, was using every one of those precious hours.

CHAPTER XIV.
THE DOUBLE BATTLE

The twenty-four hours were a rest, merely by comparison. There was no pursuit, at least, the enemy was not in sight, but the scouts brought word that the bridge over the Shenandoah would be completed in a day and night, and that Fremont would follow. Jackson's army triumphantly passed the last defile of the Massanuttons and the army of Shields did not appear issuing from it. It was no longer possible for them to be struck in front and on the flank at the same time, and the army breathed a mighty sigh of relief. At night of the next day Harry was sitting by the camp of the Invincibles, having received a brief leave of absence from the staff, and he detailed the news to his eager friends.

"General Jackson is stripping again for battle," he said to Colonel Leonidas Talbot and Lieutenant-Colonel Hector St. Hilaire. "He's sent all the sick and wounded across a ferry to Staunton, and he's dispatched his prisoners and captured stores by another road. So he has nothing left but men fit for battle."

"Which includes me," said St. Clair proudly, showing his left shoulder from which the bandage had been taken, "I'm as well as ever."

"Men get well fast with Stonewall Jackson," said Colonel Talbot. "I'll confess to you lads that I thought it was all up with us there in the lower valley, when we were surrounded by the masses of the enemy, and I don't see yet how we got here."

"But we are here, Leonidas," said Lieutenant-Colonel Hector St. Hilaire, "and that's enough for us to know."

"Right, Hector, old friend. It's enough for us to know. Do you by chance happen to have left two of those delightful cigarettes?"

"Just two, Leonidas, one for you and one for me, and now is a chance to smoke 'em."

The young lieutenants drew to one side while the two old friends smoked and compared notes. They did not smoke, but they compared notes also, as they rested on the turf. The rain had ceased and the grass was dry. They saw through the twilight the dark mass of the Massanuttons, the extreme southern end, and Happy Tom Langdon waved his hand toward the mountain, like one who salutes a friend.

"Good old mountain," he said. "You've been a buffer between us and the enemy more than once, but it took a mind like Stonewall Jackson's to keep moving you around so you would stand between the armies of the enemy and make the Yankees fight, only one army at a time."

"You're right," said Harry, who was enjoying the deep luxury of rest. "I didn't know before that mountains could be put to such good use. Look, you can see lights on the ridge now."

They saw lights, evidently those of powerful lanterns swung to and fro, but they did not understand them, nor did they care much.

"Signals are just trifles to me now," said Happy Tom. "What do I care for lights moving on a mountain four or five miles away, when for a month, day and night without stopping, a million Yankees have been shooting rifle bullets at me, and a thousand of the biggest cannon ever cast have been pouring round shot, long shot, shell, grape, canister and a hundred other kinds of missiles that I can't name upon this innocent and unoffending head of mine."

"They'll be on us tomorrow, Happy," said St. Clair, more gravely. "This picnic of ours can't last more than a day."

"I think so, too," said Harry. "So long, boys, I've got to join Captain Sherburne. The general has detached me for service with him under Ashby, and you know that when you are with them, something is going to happen."

Harry slept well that night, partly in a camp and partly in a saddle, and he found himself the next day with Ashby and Sherburne near a little town called Harrisonburg. They were on a long hill in thick forest, and the scouts reported that the enemy was coming. The Northern armies were uniting now and they were coming up the valley, expecting to crush all opposition.

"Take your glasses, Harry," said Sherburne, "and you'll see a strong force crossing the fields, but it's not strong enough. We've a splendid position here in the forest and you just watch. Ah, here come your friends, the Invincibles. See, Ashby is forming them in the center, while we, of the horse, take the flanks."

The men in blue, catching sight of the Confederate uniforms in the wood, charged with a shout, but they did not know the strength of the force before them. The Invincibles poured in a deadly fire at close range, and then Ashby's cavalry with a yell charged on either flank. The Northern troops, taken by surprise, gave way, and the Southern force followed, firing continuously.

They came within a half mile of Harrisonburg, and the main Northern army of Fremont was at hand. The general who had pursued so long, saw his men retreating, and, filled with chagrin and anger, he hurried forward heavier forces of both cavalry and infantry. Other troops came to the relief of Ashby also, and Harry saw what he thought would be only a heavy skirmish grow into a hot battle of size.

Fremont, resolved that the North should win a battle in the open field, and rejoiced that he had at last brought his enemy to bay, never ceased to hurry his troops to the combat. Formidable lines of the western riflemen rushed on either flank, and before their deadly rifles Ashby's cavalry wavered. Harry saw with consternation that they were about to give way, but Ashby galloped up to the unbroken lines of infantry and ordered them to charge.

The words were scarcely out of his mouth, when his horse, shot through, fell to the ground. Ashby fell with him, but he sprang instantly to his feet, and shouted in a loud voice:

"Charge men, for God's sake! Charge! Charge!" With a rush and roar, the Invincibles and their comrades swept forward, but at the same instant Harry saw Ashby fall again. With a cry of horror he leaped from his horse and ran to him, lifting him in his arms. But he quickly laid him back on the grass. Ashby had been shot through the heart and killed instantly.

Harry gazed around him, struck with grief and dismay, but he saw only the resistless rush of the infantry. The Invincibles and their comrades were avenging the death of Turner Ashby. Tired of retreating and hot for action they struck the Northern division with a mighty impact, shattering it and driving it back rapidly. The Southern cavalry, recovering also, struck it on the flank, and the defeat was complete. Fremont's wish was denied him. After so much hard marching and such a gallant and tenacious pursuit, he had gone the way of the other Northern generals who opposed Jackson, and was beaten.

Although they had driven back the vanguard, winning a smart little victory, and telling to Fremont and Shields that the pursuit of Jackson had now become dangerous, there was gloom in the Southern army. The horsemen did not know until they trotted back and saw Harry kneeling beside his dead body, that the great Ashby was gone. For a while they could not believe it. Their brilliant and daring leader, who had led Jackson's vanguard in victory, and who had hung like a covering curtain in retreat, could not have fallen. It seemed impossible that the man who had led for days and days through continuous showers of bullets could have been slain at last by some stray shot.

But they lifted him up finally and carried him away to a house in the little neighboring village of Port Republic, Sherburne and the other captains, hot from battle, riding with uncovered heads. He was put upon a bed there, and Harry, a staff officer, was selected to ride to Jackson with the news. He would gladly have evaded the errand, but it was obvious that he was the right messenger.

He rode slowly and found Jackson coming up with the main force, Dr. McGuire, his physician, and Colonel Crutchfield, his chief of artillery, riding on either side of him. The general gave one glance at Harry's drooping figure.

"Well," he said, "have we not won the victory? From a hilltop our glasses showed the enemy in flight."

"Yes, general," said Harry, taking off his hat, "we defeated the enemy, but General Ashby is dead."

Jackson and his staff were silent for a moment, and Harry saw the general shrink as if he had received a heavy blow.

"Ashby killed! Impossible!" he exclaimed.

"It's true, sir. I helped to carry his body to a house in Port Republic, where it is now lying."

"Lead us to that house, Mr. Kenton," said Jackson.

Harry rode forward in silence, and the others followed in the same silence. At the house, after they had looked upon the body, Jackson asked to be left alone awhile with all that was left of Turner Ashby. The others withdrew and Harry always believed that Jackson prayed within that room for the soul of his departed comrade.

When he came forth his face had resumed its sternness, but was without other expression, as usual.

"He will not show grief, now," said Sherburne, "but I think that his soul is weeping."

"And a bad time for Fremont and Shields is coming," said Harry.

"It's a risk that we all take in war," said Dalton, who was more of a fatalist than any of the others.

The chief wrote a glowing official tribute to Ashby, saying that his "daring was proverbial, his powers of endurance almost incredible, his character heroic, and his sagacity almost intuitive in divining the purposes and movements of the enemy." Yet deeply as Harry had been affected by Ashby's death, it could not remain in his mind long, because they had passed the Massanuttons now, and Fremont and Shields following up the valley must soon unite.

Harry believed that Jackson intended to strike a blow. The situation of the Confederacy was again critical—it seemed to Harry that it was always critical—and somebody must wield the sword, quick and strong. McClellan with his great and well-trained army was before Richmond. It was only the rapid marches and lightning strokes of Jackson that had kept McDowell with another great army from joining him, but to keep back this force of McDowell until they dealt with McClellan, there must be yet other rapid marches and lightning strokes.

Harry's sleep that night was the longest in two weeks, but he was up at dawn, and he was directed by Jackson to ride forward with Sherburne toward the southern base of the Massanuttons, observe the approach of both Fremont and Shields and report to him.

Harry was glad of his errand. He always liked to ride with Sherburne, who was a fount of cheerfulness, and he was still keyed up to that extraordinary intensity and pitch of excitement that made all things possible. He now understood how the young soldiers of Napoleon in Italy had been able to accomplish so much. It was the man, a leader of inspiration and genius, surcharging them all with electrical fire.

Sherburne's troop was a portion of a strong cavalry force, which divided as it reached the base of the Massanuttons, a half passing on either side. Sherburne and Harry rode to the right in order to see the army of Shields. The day was beautiful, with a glorious June sun and gentle winds, but Harry, feeling something strange about it, realized presently that it was the silence. For more than two weeks cannon had been thundering and rifles crashing in the valley, almost without cessation. Neither night nor storm had caused any interruption.

It seemed strange, almost incredible now, but they heard birds singing as they flew from tree to tree, and peaceful rabbits popped up in the brush. Yet before they went much further they saw the dark masses of the Northern army under Shields moving slowly up the valley, and anxious for the junction with Fremont.

But the Northern generals were again at a loss. Jackson had turned suddenly and defeated Fremont's vanguard with heavy loss, but what had become of him afterward? Fremont and Shields were uncertain of the position of each other, and they were still more uncertain about Jackson's. He might fall suddenly upon either, and they grew very cautious as they drew near to the end of the Massanuttons.

Sherburne and Harry, after examining the Northern army through their glasses, rode back with a dozen men to the south base of the Massanuttons. Most of them were signal officers, and Harry and Sherburne, dismounting, climbed the foot of the mountain with them. When they stood upon the crest and looked to right and left in the clear June air, they beheld a wonderful sight.

To the south along Mill Creek lay Jackson's army. To the west massed in the wider valley was the army of Fremont, which had followed them so tenaciously, and to the east, but just separated from it by the base of the Massanuttons, were the masses of Shields advancing slowly.

Harry through his powerful glasses could see the horsemen in front scouting carefully in advance of either army, and once more he appreciated to the full Jackson's skill in utilizing the mountains and rivers to keep his enemies apart. But what would he do now that they were passing the Massanuttons, and there was no longer anything to separate Shields and Fremont. He dismissed the thought. There was an intellect under the old slouch hat of the man who rode Little Sorrel that could rescue them from anything.

"Quite a spectacle," said Sherburne. "A man can't often sit at ease on a mountaintop and look at three armies. Now, Barron, you are to signal from here to General Jackson every movement of our enemies, but just before either Shields or Fremont reaches the base of the mountain, you're to slip down and join us."

"We'll do it, sir," said Barron, the chief signal officer. "We're not likely to go to sleep up here with armies on three sides of us."

Sherburne, Harry and two other men who were not to stay slowly descended the mountain. Harry enjoyed the breathing space. On the mountainside he was lifted, for a while, above the fierce passions of war. He saw things from afar and they were softened by distance. He drew deep breaths of the air, crisp and cool, on the heights, and Sherburne, who saw the glow on his face, understood. The same glow was on his own face.

"It's a grand panorama, Harry," he said, "and we'll take our fill of it for a few moments." They stood on a great projection of rock and looked once more and for a little while into the valley and its divisions. The two Northern armies were nearer now, and they were still moving. Harry saw the sun flashing over thousands of bayonets. He almost fancied he could hear the crack of the teamsters' whips as the long lines of wagons in the rear creaked along.

They descended rapidly, remounted their horses and galloped back to Jackson.

They buried Ashby that day, all the leading Southern officers following him to his grave, and throughout the afternoon the silence was continued. But the signals on the mountain worked and worked, and the signalmen with Jackson replied. No movement of the two pursuing armies was unknown to the Southern leader.

Harry, with an hour's leave, visited once more his friends of the Invincibles. He had begged a package of fine West Indian cigarettes from Sherburne, and he literally laid them at the feet of the two colonels—he found them sitting together on the grass, lean gray men who seemed to be wholly reduced to bone and muscle.

"This is a great gift, Harry, perhaps greater than you think," said Colonel Leonidas Talbot gravely. "I tried to purchase some from the commissariat, but they had none—it seems that General Stonewall Jackson doesn't consider cigarettes necessary for his troops. Anyhow, the way our Confederate money is going, I fancy a package of cigarettes will soon cost a hundred dollars. Here, Hector, light up. We divide this box, half and half. That's right, isn't it, Harry?"

"Certainly, sir."

Harry passed on to the junior officers and found St. Clair and Happy Tom lying on the grass. Happy pretended to rouse from sleep when Harry came.

"Hello, old omen of war," he said. "What's Old Jack expecting of us now?"

"I told you never to ask me such a question as that again. The general isn't what you'd call a garrulous man. How's your shoulder, Arthur?"

"About well. The muscles were not torn. It was just loss of blood that troubled me for the time."

"I hear," said Langdon, "that the two Yankee armies are to join soon. The Massanuttons won't be between them much longer, and then they'll have only one of the forks of the river to cross before they fall upon each other's breasts and weep with joy. Harry, it seems to me that we're always coming to a fork of the Shenandoah. How many forks does it have anyhow?"

"Only two, but the two forks have forks of their own. That's the reason we're always coming to deep water and by the same token the Yankees are always coming to it, too, which is a good thing for us, as we get there first, when the bridges are there, and when the Yankees come they are gone."

But not one of these boys understood the feeling in the Northern armies. Late the day before a messenger from Shields had got through the Massanuttons to Fremont, and had informed him that an easy triumph was at hand. Jackson and his army, he said, fearing the onset of overwhelming numbers, was retreating in great disorder.

The two generals were now convinced of speedy victory. They had communicated at last, and they could have some concert of movement. Jackson was less than thirty miles away, and his army was now but a confused mass of stragglers which would dissolve under slight impact. Both had defeats and disappointments to avenge, and they pushed forward now with increased speed, Shields in particular showing the greatest energy in pursuit. But the roads were still deep in mud, and his army was forced to toil on all that day and the next, while the signalmen on the top of the Massanuttons told every movement he made to Stonewall Jackson.

The signals the second evening told Jackson that the two Northern armies were advancing fast, and that he would soon have before him an enemy outnumbering him anywhere from two to three to one. He had been talking with Ewell just before the definite news was brought, and Harry, Dalton and other officers of the staff stood near, as their duty bade them.

Harry knew the nature of the information, as it was not a secret from any member of the staff, and now they all stood silently on one side and watched Jackson. Even Ewell offered no suggestion, but kept his eyes fixed anxiously on his chief. Harry felt that another one of those critical moments, perhaps the most dangerous of all, had arrived. They had fought army after army in detail, but now they must fight armies united, or fly. He did not know that the silent general was preparing the most daring and brilliant of all his movements in the valley. In the face of both Shields and Fremont his courage flamed to the highest, and the brain under the old slouch hat grew more powerful and penetrating than ever. And flight never for a moment entered into his scheme.

Jackson at length said a few words to Ewell, who sprang upon his horse and rode away to his division. Then, early in the morning, Jackson led the rest of the army into a strange district, the Grottoes of the Shenandoah. It was a dark region, filled beneath with great caves and covered thickly with heavy forest, through the leaves of which the troops caught views of the Massanuttons to the north or of the great masses of the Blue Ridge to the east, while far to the west lay other mountains, range on range. But all around them the country was wooded heavily.

The army did not make a great amount of noise when it camped in the forest over the caves, and the fires were few. Perhaps some of the men were daunted by the dangers which still surrounded them so thickly after so many days of such fierce fighting. At any rate, they were silent. The Acadians had played no music for a day now, and the band lay upon the ground sunk in deep slumber.

Harry had not been sent on any errand, and he was sitting on a stone, finishing his supper, when Dalton, who had been away with a message, returned.

"What's happened, George?" asked Harry.

"Nothing yet, but a lot will happen soon."

"Where have you been?"

"I've been on the other side of the Shenandoah. You needn't open your eyes. It's so. Moreover, Ewell's whole division is over there, and it will meet the vanguard of Fremont as he advances. I think I begin to see the general's scheme."

"I do, too. Ewell will fight off Fremont, holding him there until Jackson can annihilate Shields. Then he will retreat over the river to Jackson, burning the bridge behind him."

Dalton nodded.

"Looks that way to a man up a tree," he said.

"It's like the general," said Harry. "He could bring his whole army on this side, burn the bridge, and in full force attack Shields, but he prefers to defeat them both."

"Yes; but I wish to Heaven we had more men."

"Sh! Here comes the general," said Harry.

The two were silent as General Jackson and an officer passed. The general spoke a word or two to the boys and went on. They were but ordinary words, but both felt uplifted because he had spoken to them.

Morning found them motionless in the forest, over the caves. They ate a hasty breakfast and waited. But the scouts were all out, and presently Harry and Dalton were sent toward the Shenandoah. Finding nothing there, they crossed over the bridge and came to Ewell's division, where they had plenty of acquaintances.

The sun was now high, and while they were talking with their friends, they heard the faint report of rifle shots far in their front. Presently the scouts came running back, and said that the enemy was only two miles away and was advancing to the attack.

Ewell took off his hat and his bald head glistened in the sun's rays. But, like Jackson, he was always cool, and he calmly moved his troops into position along a low ridge, with heavy woods on either flank. Harry knew the ground, alas, too well. It was among the trees just behind the ridge that Turner Ashby had been slain. Ewell had before him Fremont with two to one, and the rest of the army under Jackson's immediate command was four miles away, facing Shields.

"Do you hear anything behind you, Harry?" asked Dalton.

"No, why do you ask?"

"If we heard the booming of guns, and we'd hear 'em at four miles, we'd know that General Jackson himself was engaged. But as there's no sound, Shields hasn't come up, and we'll wait here a while to see if we can't have something important to report."

"I don't think so," said Harry. "We know that the enemy is about to attack here in full force, and that's enough to know about this side of the river. We ought to gallop back to General Jackson and tell him."

"You're right, Harry," said the Virginian, in whom the sense of duty was strong. "The general may be attacked by the time we get there, and he'll want to know exactly how things are."

They galloped back as fast as they could and found that General Jackson had moved his headquarters to the little village of Port Republic. They found him and told him the news as he was mounting his horse, but at the same time an excited and breathless messenger came galloping up from another direction. The vanguard of Shields had already routed his pickets, and the second Northern army was pressing forward in full force.

As he spoke, the Northern cavalry came in sight, and if those Northern horsemen had known what a prize was almost within their hands, they would have spared no exertion.

"Make for the bridge! Make for the bridge, general!" cried Dalton.

The horsemen in blue were not coming fast. They rode cautiously through the streets. Southern villages were not friendly to them, and this caution saved Stonewall Jackson. He was on his horse in an instant, galloping for the bridge, and Harry and Dalton were hot behind him. They thundered over the bridge with the Northern cavalry just at their heels, and escaped by a hair's breadth. But the chief of artillery and Dr. McGuire and one of the captains, Willis, were captured, and the rest of the staff was dispersed.

"My God!" exclaimed Harry, when the Northern cavalry stopped at the bridge. "What an escape!"

He was thinking of Jackson's escape, not his own, and while he was wondering what the general would do, he saw him ride to the bank of the river and watch the Northern cavalry on the other side. Then Harry and Dalton uttered a shout as they saw a Southern battery push forward from the village and open on the cavalry. An infantry regiment, which had been forming in the town, also came up at full speed, uttering the long, high-pitched rebel yell.

The Northern vanguard, which had come so near to such a high achievement, was driven back with a rush, and a Southern battery appearing on its flank, swept it with shell as it retreated. So heavy was the Southern attack, that the infantry also were driven back and their guns taken. The entire vanguard was routed, and as it received no support, even Harry and Dalton knew that the main army under Shields had not yet come up.

"That was the closest shave I ever saw," said Dalton. "So it was," said Harry. "But just listen to that noise behind you!"

A tremendous roar and crash told them that the battle between Ewell and Fremont had opened. Jackson beckoned to Harry, Dalton and the members of his staff who had reassembled. The three, who were captured, subsequently escaped in the confusion and turmoil and rejoined their general. Setting a powerful force to guard the bridge, Jackson said to his staff:

"While we are waiting for Shields to come up with his army, we'll ride over and see how the affair between Ewell and Fremont is coming on."

The roar and crash told them it was coming on with great violence, but Fremont, so strong in pursuit was not so strong in action. Now that he was face to face with the enemy, he did not attack with all his might. He hesitated, not from personal fear, but from fear on account of his army. The whole force of Jackson might be in front of him, and the apprehensions that he did not feel in pursuit assailed him when he looked at the ridge covered with the enemy.

Harry and Dalton watched with breathless interest. A portion of Fremont's army, but not all of it, just when it was needed most, was sent to the charge. Led by the pickets and skirmishers they came forward gallantly, a long line of glittering bayonets. In the thick woods on their flank lay three Southern regiments, ambushed and not yet stirring. No sunlight penetrated there to show their danger to the soldiers who were breasting the slope.

Harry foresaw all, and he drew a long breath for brave men who were marching to a certain fate.

"Why don't they look! Why don't they look!" he found himself exclaiming.

The next instant the entire wood burst into flame. Picking their aim and firing at short range, the Southern riflemen sent sheet after sheet of bullets into the charging ranks. It was more than human blood and flesh could stand, and the Northern regiments gave way. But it was not a rout. They retreated on their reserves, and stood there recovering themselves, while the Southern riflemen reloaded, but did not pursue. The regiments which had done the deadly work sank back in the woods, and seemingly the battle was over.

Harry had not been under fire. He and Dalton, the rest of Jackson's staff and the general himself merely watched. Nor did Jackson give any further orders to his able lieutenant, Ewell. He allowed him to make the battle his own, and in Harry's opinion he was making it right.

There came a silence that seemed interminably long to Harry. The sunlight blazed down, and the two armies stood looking at each other across a field that was strewn with the fallen. It would have been folly for the men in blue to charge again, and it was the chief business of the Southern troops to hold them back. Therefore they stood in their positions and watched. Harry judged that the bulk of Fremont's army was not yet up. It was this failure to bring superior numbers to bear at the right time that was always the ruin of the Northern generals in the valley, because the genius on the other side invariably saw the mistake and profited by it.

Harry and Dalton still waited, wondering. Jackson himself sat quietly on his horse, and issued no order. The Northern troops were motionless, and Harry, who knew how precious time was, with the rest of Fremont's army coming up, wondered again. But Trimble, the commander of the Southern riflemen hidden in the wood, saw a chance. He would send his men under cover of the forest and hurl them suddenly upon the Northern flank. Ewell gave his consent, and said that he would charge, too, if the movement were successful.

Harry, watching, saw the Southern regiments in the wood steal from the forest, pass swiftly up a ravine, and then, delivering a shattering fire at short range, charge with the bayonet upon the Northern flank. The men in blue, surprised by so fierce an onset, gave way. Uttering the rebel yell, the Southerners followed and pushed them further and further. Ewell's quick eye, noting the success, sent forward his own center in a heavy charge.

Fremont, from the rear, hurried forward new troops, but they were beaten as fast as they arrived. The batteries were compelled to unlimber and take to flight, the fresh brigade dispatched by Fremont was routed, and the whole Southern line pressed forward, driving the Northern army before it.

"General Jackson was wise in trusting to General Ewell," said Dalton to Harry. "He's won a notable victory. I wonder how far he'll push it."

"Not far, I think. All Ewell's got to do is to hold Fremont, and he has surely held him. There's Shields on the other side of the river with whom we have to deal. Do you know, George, that all the time we've been sitting here, watching that battle in front of us, I've been afraid we'd hear the booming of the guns on the other side of the river, telling that Shields was up."

"We scorched their faces so badly there in Cross Keys that they must be hesitating. Lord, Harry, how old Stonewall plays with fire. To attack and defeat one army with the other only a few miles away must take nerves all of steel."

"But if Ewell keeps on following Fremont he'll be too far away when we turn to deal with Shields."

"But he won't go too far. There are the trumpets now recalling his army."

The mellow notes were calling in the eager riflemen, who wished to continue the pursuit, but the army was not to retire. It held the battlefield, and now that the twilight was coming the men began to build their fires, which blazed through the night within sight of those of the enemy. The sentinels of the two armies were within speaking distance of one another, and often in the dark, as happened after many another battle in this war, Yank and Reb passed a friendly word or two. They met, too, on the field, where they carried away their dead and wounded, but on such errands there was always peace.

Those hours of the night were precious, but Fremont did not use them. Defeated, he held back, magnifying the numbers of his enemy, fearing that Jackson was in front of him with his whole army, and once more out of touch with his ally, Shields.

But Stonewall Jackson was all activity. The great war-like intellect was working with the utmost precision and speed. Having beaten back Fremont, he was making ready for Shields. The first part of the drama, as he had planned it, had been carried through with brilliant success, and he meant that the next should be its equal.

Harry was not off his horse that night. He carried message after message to generals and colonels and captains. He saw the main portion of Ewell's army withdrawn from Fremont's front, leaving only a single brigade to hold him, in case he should advance at dawn. But he saw the fires increased, and he carried orders that the men should build them high, and see that they did not go down.

When he came back from one of these errands about midnight, just after the rise of the moon, he found General Jackson standing upon the bank of the river, giving minute directions to a swarm of officers. His mind missed nothing. He directed not only the movements of the troops, but he saw also that the trains of ammunition and food were sent to the proper points. About half way between midnight and morning he lay down and slept in a small house near the river bank. Shortly before dawn the commander of a battery, looking for one of his officers, entered the house and saw Jackson, dressed for the saddle, sword, boots, spurs and all, lying on his face upon the bed, asleep. On a small table near him stood a short piece of tallow candle, sputtering dimly. But the officer saw that it was Jackson, and he turned on tiptoe to withdraw.

The general awoke instantly, sat up and demanded who was there. When the officer explained, he said he was glad that he had been awakened, asked about the disposition of the troops, and gave further commands. He did not go to sleep again.

But Harry's orders carried him far beyond midnight, and he had no thought of sleep. Once more repressed but intense excitement had complete hold of him. He could not have slept had the chance been given to him. The bulk of the army was now in front of Shields, and the pickets were not only in touch, but were skirmishing actively. All through the late hours after midnight Harry heard the flash of their firing in front of him.

The cavalry under Sherburne and other daring leaders were exchanging shots with the equally daring cavalry of the enemy.

As the dawn approached the firing was heavier. Harry knew that the day would witness a great battle, and his heart was filled with anxiety. The army led by Shields showed signs of greater energy and tenacity than that led by Fremont. The Northern troops that had fought so fiercely at Kernstown were there, and they also had leaders who would not be daunted by doubts and numbers. Harry wondered if they had heard of the defeat of Fremont at Cross Keys.

He looked at the flashing of the rifles in the dusk, and before dawn rode back to the house where his commander slept. He was ready and waiting when Jackson came forth, and Dalton appearing from somewhere in the dusk, sat silently on his horse by his side.

The general with his staff at once rode toward the front, and the masses of the Southern army also swung forward. Harry saw that, according to Jackson's custom, they would attack, not wait for it. It was yet dusky, but the firing in their front was increasing in intensity. There was a steady crash and a blaze of light from the rifle muzzles ran through the forest.

He took an order to the Acadians to move forward behind two batteries, and as he came back he passed the Invincibles, now a mere skeleton regiment, but advancing in perfect order, the two colonels on their flanks near their head. He also saw St. Clair and Langdon, but he had time only to wave his hand to them, and then he galloped back to Jackson.

The dusk rapidly grew thinner. Then the burnished sun rose over the hills, and Harry saw the Northern army before them, spread across a level between the river and a spur of the Blue Ridge, and also on the slopes and in the woods. A heavy battery crowned one of the hills, another was posted in a forest, and there were more guns between. Harry saw that the position was strong, and he noted with amazement that the Northern forces did not seem to outnumber Jackson's. It was evident that Shields, with the majority of his force was not yet up. He glanced at Jackson. He knew that the fact could not have escaped the general, but he saw no trace of exultation on his face.

There was another fact that Harry did not then know. Nearly all the men who had fought successfully against Jackson at Kernstown were in that vanguard, and Tyler, who had deemed himself a victor there, commanded them. Everybody else had been beaten by Stonewall Jackson, but not they. Confident of victory, they asked to be led against the Southern army, and they felt only joy when the rising sunlight disclosed their foe. There were the men of Ohio and West Virginia again, staunch and sturdy.

Harry knew instinctively that the battle would be fierce, pushed to the utmost. Jackson had no other choice, and as the sunlight spread over the valley, although the mountains were yet in mist, the cannon on the flanks opened with a tremendous discharge, followed by crash after crash, North and South replying to each other. A Southern column also marched along the slope of the hills, in order to take Tyler's men in flank. Harry looked eagerly to see the Northern troops give way, but they held fast. The veterans of Ohio and West Virginia refused to give ground, and Winder, who led the Southern column, could make no progress.

Harry watched with bated breath and a feeling of alarm. Were they to lose after such splendid plans and such unparalleled exertions? The sun, rising higher, poured down a flood of golden beams, driving the mists from the mountains and disclosing the plain and slopes below wrapped in fire, shot through with the gleam of steel from the bayonets.

Tyler, who commanded the Northern vanguard, proved himself here, as at Kernstown, a brave and worthy foe. He, too, had eyes to see and a brain to think. Seeing that his Ohio and West Virginia men were standing fast against every attack made by Winder, he hurried fresh troops to their aid that they might attack in return.

The battle thickened fast. At the point of contact along the slopes and in the woods, there was a continued roar of cannon and rifles. Enemies came face to face, and the men of Jackson, victorious on so many fields, were slowly pressed back. A shout of triumph rose from the Union lines, and the eager Tyler brought yet more troops into action. Two of Ewell's battalions heard the thunder of the battle and rushed of their own accord to the relief of their commander. But they were unable to stem the fury of Ohio and West Virginia, and they were borne back with the others, hearing as it roared in their ears that cry of victory from their foe, which they had so often compelled that foe himself to hear.

But it was more bitter to none than to Harry. Sitting on his horse in the rear he saw in the blazing sunlight everything that passed. He saw for the first time in many days the men in gray yielding. The incredible was happening. After beating Fremont, after all their superb tactics, they were now losing to Shields.

He looked at Jackson, hoping to receive some order that would take him into action, but the general said nothing. He was watching the battle and his face was inscrutable. Harry wondered how he could preserve his calm, while his troops were being beaten in front, and the army of Fremont might thunder at any moment on his flank or rear. Truly the nerves that could remain steady in such moments must be made of steel triply wrought.

The Northern army, stronger and more resolute than ever, was coming on, a long blue line crested with bayonets. The Northern cannon, posted well, and served with coolness and precision, swept the Southern ranks. The men in gray retreated faster and some of their guns were taken. The Union troops charged upon them more fiercely than ever, and the regiments threatened to fall into a panic.

Then Jackson, shouting to his staff to follow, spurred forward into the mob and begged them to stand. He rode among them striking some with the flat of his sword and encouraging others. His officers showed the same energy and courage, but the columns, losing cohesion seemed on the point of dissolving, in the face of an enemy who pressed them so hard. Harry uttered a groan which nobody heard in all the crash and tumult. His heart sank like lead. Hope was gone clean away.

But at the very moment that hope departed he heard a great cheer, followed a moment later by a terrific crash of rifles and cannon. Then he saw those blessed Acadians charging in the smoke along the slope. They had come through the woods, and they rushed directly upon the great Northern battery posted there. But so well were those guns handled and so fierce was their fire that the Acadians were driven back. They returned to the charge, were driven back again, but coming on a third time took all the battery except one gun. Then with triumphant shouts they turned them on their late owners.

The whole Southern line seemed to recover itself at once. The remainder of Ewell's troops reached the field and enabled their comrades to turn and attack. The Stonewall Brigade in the center, where Jackson was, returned to the charge. In a few minutes fickle fortune had faced about completely. The Union men saw victory once more snatched from their hands. Their columns in the plain were being raked by powerful batteries on the flank, many of the guns having recently been theirs. They must retreat or be destroyed.

The brave and skillful Tyler reluctantly gave the order to retreat, and when Harry saw the blue line go back he shouted with joy. Then the rebel yell, thrilling, vast and triumphant, swelled along the whole line, which lifted up itself and rushed at the enemy, the cavalry charging fiercely on the flanks.

Shields got up fresh troops, but it was too late. The men in gray were pouring forward, victorious at every point, and sweeping everything before them, while the army of Fremont, arriving at the river at noon, saw burned bridges, the terrible battlefield on the other side strewn with the fallen, and the Southern legions thundering northward in pursuit of the second army, superior in numbers to their own, that they had defeated in two days.

Every pulse in Harry beat with excitement. His soul sprang up at once from the depths to the stars. This, when hope seemed wholly gone, was the crowning and culminating victory. The achievement of Jackson equaled anything of which he had ever heard. While the army of Fremont was held fast on the other side of the river, the second army under Shields, beaten in its turn, was retreating at a headlong rate down the valley. The veterans of Kernstown had fought magnificently, but they had been outgeneralled, and, like all others, had gone down in defeat before Jackson.

Jackson, merciless alike in battle and pursuit, pushed hard after the men in blue for nine or ten miles down the river, capturing cannon and prisoners. The Ohio and West Virginia men began at last to reform again, and night coming on, Jackson stopped the pursuit. He still could not afford to go too far down the valley, lest the remains of Fremont's army appear in his rear.

As they went back in the night, Harry and Dalton talked together in low tones. Jackson was just ahead of them, riding Little Sorrel, silent, his shoulders stooped a little, his mind apparently having passed on from the problems of the day, which were solved, to those of the morrow, which were to be solved. He replied only with a smile to the members of his staff who congratulated him now upon his extraordinary achievement, surpassing everything that he had done hitherto in the valley. For Harry and Dalton, young hero-worshippers, he had assumed a stature yet greater. In their boyish eyes he was the man who did the impossible over and over again.

The great martial brain was still at work. Having won two fresh victories in two days and having paralyzed the operations of his enemies, Jackson was preparing for other bewildering movements. Harry and Dalton and all the other members of the staff were riding forth presently in the dusk with the orders for the different brigades and regiments to concentrate at Brown's Gap in the mountains, from which point Jackson could march to the attack of McClellan before Richmond, or return to deal blows at his opponents in the valley, as he pleased. But whichever he chose, McDowell and sixty thousand men would not be present at the fight for Richmond. Jackson with his little army had hurled back the Union right, and the two Union armies could not be united in time.

The whole Southern army was gathered at midnight in Brown's Gap, and the men who had eaten but little and slept but little in forty-eight hours and who had fought two fierce and victorious battles in that time, throwing themselves upon the ground slept like dead men.

While they slept consternation was spreading in the North. Lincoln, ever hopeful and never yielding, had believed that Jackson was in disorderly flight up the valley, and so had his Secretary of War, Stanton. The fact that this fleeing force had turned suddenly and beaten both Fremont and Shields, each of whom had superior forces, was unbelievable, but it was true.

But Lincoln and the North recalled their courage and turned hopeful eyes toward McClellan.

CHAPTER XV.
THE SEVEN DAYS

Harry did not awaken until late the next morning. Jackson, for once, allowed his soldiers a long rest, and they were entitled to it. When he rose from his blankets, he found fires burning, and the pleasant odor of coffee, bacon and other food came to his nostrils. Many wounded were stretched on blankets, but, as usual, they were stoics, and made no complaint.

The army, in truth, was joyous, even more, it was exultant. Every one had the feeling that he had shared in mighty triumphs, unparalleled exploits, but they gave the chief credit to their leader, and they spoke admiringly and affectionately of Old Jack. The whole day was passed in luxury long unknown to them. They had an abundance of food, mostly captured, and their rations were not limited.

The Acadian band reappeared and played with as much spirit as ever, and once more the dark, strong men of Louisiana, clasped in one another's arms, danced on the grass. Harry sat with St. Clair, Happy Tom and Dalton and watched them.

"I was taught that dancing was wicked," said Dalton, "but it doesn't look wicked to me, and I notice that the general doesn't forbid it."

"Wicked!" said St. Clair, "why, after we take Washington, you ought to come down to Charleston and see us dance then. It's good instead of wicked. It's more than that. It's a thing of beauty, a grace, a joy, almost a rite."

"All that Arthur says is true," said Happy Tom. "I'm a Sea Islander myself, but we go over to Charleston in the winter. Still, I think you'll have to do without me at those dances, Arthur. I shall probably be kept for some time in the North, acting as proconsul for Pennsylvania or Massachusetts."

"Which way do you think we are going from here, Harry?" asked St. Clair. "I don't think it's possible for General Jackson to stay longer than twenty-four hours in one place, and I know that he always goes to you for instructions before he makes any movement."

"That's so. He spoke to me this morning asking what he ought to do, but I told him the troops needed a rest of one day, but that he mustn't make it more than one day or he'd spoil 'em."

Happy Tom, who was lying on the ground, sat up abruptly.

"If ever you hear of Old Stonewall spoiling anybody or anything," he said, "just you report it to me and I'll tell you that it's not so."

"I believe," said Dalton, "that we're going to leave the valley. Both Shields and Fremont are still retreating. Our cavalry scouts brought in that word this morning. We've heard also that Johnston and McClellan fought a big battle at a place called Seven Pines, and that after it McClellan hung back, waiting for McDowell, whom Old Jack has kept busy. General Johnston was wounded at Seven Pines and General Robert Edward Lee is now in command of our main army."

"That's news! It's more! It's history!" exclaimed St. Clair. "I think you're right, Harry. Two to one that we go to Richmond. And for one I'll be glad. Then we'll be right in the middle of the biggest doings!"

"I'm feeling that way, too," said Happy Tom. "But I know one thing."

"What's that?"

"Not a soul in all this army, except Old Jack himself, will know a thing about it, until it's done, and maybe we won't know very much then. I passed Old Jack about an hour ago and he saw me as clearly and plainly as I see you, but he did not tell me a thing about his plans. He did not even say a word. Did not speak. Just cut me dead."

Not one of the four was destined for some days to learn what Jackson intended. His highest officers even were kept in the same ignorance. While the bulk of the army did little, the cavalry under Munford, who had succeeded Ashby, were exceedingly active. The horsemen were like a swarm of hornets in front of Jackson, and so great was their activity that the Northern leaders were unable to gauge their numbers. Fremont, exposed to these raids, retreated farther down the valley, leaving two hundred of his wounded and many stores in the hands of Munford.

Then Jackson crossed South River and marched into extensive woods by the Shenandoah, where his army lay for five full days. It was almost incredible to Harry and his friends that they should have so long a rest, but they had it. They luxuriated there among the trees in the beautiful June weather, listening to the music of the Acadians, eating and drinking and sleeping as men have seldom slept before.

But while the infantry was resting the activity of the cavalry never ceased. These men, riding over the country in which most of them were born, missed no movement of the enemy, and maintained the illusion that their numbers were four or five times the fact. Harry, trying to fathom Jackson's purpose, gave it up after that comparatively long stay beside the Shenandoah. He did not know that it was a part of a complicated plan, that Lee and Jackson, although yet apart, were now beginning their celebrated work together. Near Richmond, Northern prisoners saw long lines of trains moving north and apparently crowded with soldiers. For Jackson, of course! And intended to help him in his great march on Washington! But Jackson hung a complete veil about his own movements. His highest officers told one another in confidence things that they believed to be true, but which were not. It was the general opinion among them that Jackson would soon leave in pursuit of Fremont.

The pleasant camp by the Shenandoah was broken up suddenly, and the men began to march—they knew not where. Officers rode among them with stern orders, carried out sternly. In front, and on either flank, rode lines of cavalry who allowed not a soul to pass either in or out. An equally strong line of cavalry in the rear drove in front of it every straggler or camp follower. There was not a single person inside the whole army of Jackson who could get outside it except Jackson himself.

An extraordinary ban of ignorance was also placed upon them, and it was enforced to the letter. No soldier should give the name of a village or a farm through which he passed, although the farm might be his father's, or the village might be the one in which he was born. If a man were asked a question, no matter what, he must answer, "I don't know."

The young Southern soldiers, indignant at first, enjoyed it as their natural humor rose to the surface.

"Young fellow," said Happy Tom to St. Clair, "what's your name?"

"I don't know."

"Don't know your own name. Why, you must be feeble minded! Are you?"

"I don't know."

"Well, you may not know, but you look it. Do you think Old Jack is a good general?"

"I don't know."

"Do you think he's feeble-minded like yourself?"

"I don't know."

"What! You dare to intimate that Stonewall Jackson, the greatest general the world has ever known, is feeble-minded! You have insulted him, and in his name I challenge you to fight me, sir. Do you accept?"

"I don't know."

The two looked at each other and grinned. The ignorance of the army grew dense beyond all computation. Long afterward, "I don't know," became a favorite and convenient reply, even when the knowledge was present.

It was nearly two weeks after Port Republic before the troops had any idea where they were going. They came to a little place called Hanover Junction and they thought they were going to turn there and meet McDowell, but they passed on, and one evening they encamped in a wood. As they were eating supper they heard the muttering thunder of guns toward the south, and throughout the brigades the conviction spread that they were on the way to Richmond.

The next night, Harry, who was asleep, was touched by a light hand. He awoke instantly, and when he saw General Jackson standing over him, he sprang up.

"I am going on a long ride," said the general briefly, "and I want only one man to go with me. I've chosen you. Get your horse. We start in five minutes."

Harry, a little dazed yet from sleep and the great honor that had been thrust upon him, ran, nevertheless, for his horse, and was ready with a minute to spare.

"Keep by my side," said Jackson curtly, and the two rode in silence from the camp, watched in wonder by the sentinels, who saw their general and his lone attendant disappear in the forest to the south.

It was then one o'clock in the morning of a moonlight night, and the errand of Jackson was an absolute secret. Three or four miles from the camp a sentinel slipped from the woods and stopped them. He was one of their own pickets, on a far out-lying post, but to the amazement of Harry, Jackson did not tell who he was.

"I'm an officer on Stonewall Jackson's staff, carrying dispatches," he said. "You must let me pass."

"It's not enough. Show me an order from him."

"I have no order," replied the equable voice, "but my dispatches are of the greatest importance. Kindly let me pass immediately."

The sentinel shook his head.

"Draw back your horses," he said. "Without an order from the general you don't go a step further."

Harry had not spoken a word. He had ceased to wonder why Jackson refused to reveal his identity. If he did not do so it must be for some excellent reason, and, meanwhile, the boy waited placidly.

"So you won't let us pass," said Jackson. "Is the commander of the picket near by?"

"I can whistle so he'll hear me."

"Then will you kindly whistle?"

The sentinel looked again at the quiet man on the horse, put his fingers to his lips and blew loudly. An officer emerged from the woods and said:

"What is it, Felton?"

Then he glanced at the man on the horse and started violently.

"General Jackson!" he exclaimed.

The sentinel turned pale, but said nothing.

"Yes, I'm General Jackson," said the general, "and I ride with this lieutenant of my staff on an errand. But both of you must swear to me that you have not seen me."

Then he turned to the sentinel.

"You did right to stop us," he said. "I wish that all our sentinels were as faithful as you."

Then while the man glowed with gratitude, he and Harry rode on. Jackson was in deep thought and did not speak. Harry, a little awed by this strange ride, looked up at the trees and the dusky heavens. He heard the far hoot of an owl, and he shivered a little. What if a troop of Northern cavalry should suddenly burst upon them. But no troop of the Northern horse, nor horse of any kind, appeared. Instead, Jackson's own horse began to pant and stumble. Soon he gave out entirely.

It was not yet day, but dimly to the right they saw the roof of a house among some trees. It was a poor Virginia farm that did not have horses on it, and Jackson suggested to Harry that they wake up the people and secure two fresh mounts.

The commander of an army and his young aide walked a little distance down a road, entered a lawn, drove off two barking dogs, and knocked loud on the front door of the house with the butts of their riding whips. A head was at last thrust out of an upper window, and a sleepy and indignant voice demanded what they wanted.

"We're two officers from General Jackson's army riding on important duty," replied the general, in his usual mild tones. "Our horses have broken down and we want to obtain new ones."

"What's your names? What's your rank?" demanded the gruff voice.

"We cannot give our names."

"Then clear out! You're frauds! If I find you hanging about here I'll shoot at you, and I tell you for your good that I'm no bad shot."

The shutter of the window closed with a bang, but the two dogs that had been driven off began to bark again at a safe distance. Harry glanced at his general.

"Isn't that a stable among the trees?" asked Jackson.

"Yes, sir."

"Then we'll find our horses there. Get the other two and bring them here."

Harry obeyed promptly, and they opened the stable, finding good horses, of which they selected the two best to which they changed their saddles and bridles.

"We'll leave our own horses for our inhospitable friends," said General Jackson, "and he'll not suffer by the exchange."

Mounting the fresh horses they rode rapidly, and, after the coming of the dawn, Harry saw that they were approaching Richmond, and he guessed now what was coming.

General Jackson had in his pocket a pass sent to him by General Lee, and they swiftly went through the lines of pickets, and then on through Richmond. People were astir in the streets of the Southern capital, and many of them saw the bearded man in an old uniform and a black slouch hat riding by, accompanied by only a boy, but not one of them knew that this was Stonewall Jackson, whose fame had been filling their ears for a month past. Nor, if they had known him would they have divined how much ill his passage boded to the great army of McClellan.

They went through Richmond and on,toward the front. Midday passed, and at three o'clock they reached the house in which Lee had established his headquarters.

"Who is it?" asked a sentinel at the door.

"Tell General Lee that General Jackson is waiting."

The sentinel hurried inside, General Jackson and his aide dismounted, and a moment later General Lee came out, extending his hand, which Jackson clasped. The two stood a moment looking at each other. It was the first time that they had met in the war, but Harry saw by the glance that passed that each knew the other a man, not an ordinary man, nor even a man of ten thousand, but a genius of the kind that appears but seldom. It was all the more extraordinary that the two should appear at the same time, serving together in perfect harmony, and sustaining for so long by their united power and intellect a cause that seemed lost from the first.

It was not any wonder that Harry gazed with all his eyes at the memorable meeting. He knew Jackson, and he was already learning much of Lee.

He saw in the Confederate commander-in-chief a man past fifty, ruddy of countenance, hair and beard short, gray and thick, his figure tall and powerful, and his expression at once penetrating and kind. He was dressed in a fine gray uniform, precise and neat.

Such was Robert Edward Lee, and Harry thought him the most impressive human being upon whom he had ever looked.

"General Jackson," said General Lee, "this is a fortunate meeting. You have saved the Confederacy."

General Jackson made a gesture of dissent, but General Lee took him by the arm and they went into the house. General Jackson turned a moment at the door and motioned to Harry to follow. The boy went in, and found himself in a large room. Three men had risen from cane chairs to meet the visitor. One, broad of shoulders, middle-aged and sturdy, was Longstreet. The others more slender of figure were the two Hills.

The major generals came forward eagerly to meet Jackson, and they also had friendly greetings for his young aide. Lee handed them glasses of milk which they drank thirstily.

"You'll find an aide of mine in the next room," said General Lee to Harry. "He's a little older than you are but you should get along together."

Harry bowed and withdrew, and the aide, Charlie Gordon, gave him a hearty welcome. He was three or four years Harry's senior, something of a scholar, but frank and open. When they had exchanged names, Gordon said:

"Stretch out a bit on this old sofa. You look tired. You've been riding a long distance. How many miles have you come?"

"I don't know," replied Harry, as he lay luxuriously on the sofa, "but we started at one o'clock this morning and it is now three o'clock in the afternoon."

"Fourteen hours. It's like what we've been hearing of Stonewall Jackson. I took a peep at him from the window as you rode up."

"I suppose you didn't see much but dust."

"They certainly tell extraordinary things of General Jackson. It can't be possible that all are true!"

"It is possible. They're all true—and more. I tell you, Gordon, when you hear anything wonderful about Stonewall Jackson just you believe it. Don't ask any questions, or reasons but believe it."

"I think I shall," said Gordon, convinced, "but don't forget, Kenton, that we've got a mighty man here, too. You can't be with General Lee long without feeling that you're in the presence of genius."

"And they're friends, not jealous of each other. You could see that at a glance."

"The coming of Jackson is like dawn bursting from the dark. I feel, Kenton, that McClellan's time is at hand."

Harry slept a little after a while, but when he awoke the generals were still in council in the great room.

"I let you sleep because I saw you needed it," said Gordon with a smile, "but I think they're about through in there now. I hear them moving about."

General Jackson presently called Harry and they rode away. The young aide was sent back to the valley army with a message for it to advance as fast as possible in order that it might be hurled on McClellan's flank. Others carried the same message, lest there be any default of chance.

While the army of Jackson swept down by Richmond to join Lee it was lost again to the North. At Washington they still believed it in the valley, advancing on Fremont or Shields. Banks and McDowell had the same belief. McClellan was also at a loss. Two or three scouts had brought in reports that it was marching toward Richmond, but he could not believe them.

The Secretary of War at Washington telegraphed to McClellan that the Union armies under McDowell, Banks, Fremont and Shields were to be consolidated in one great army under McDowell which would crush Jackson utterly in the valley. At the very moment McClellan was reading this telegram the army of Jackson, far to the south of McDowell, was driving in the pickets on his own flank.

Jackson's men had come into a region quite different from the valley. There they marched and fought over firm ground, and crossed rivers with hard rocky banks. Now they were in a land of many deep rivers that flowed in a slow yellow flood with vast swamps between.

Most of it was heavy with forest and bushes, and the heat was great. At night vast quantities of mosquitoes and flies and other insects fed bounteously upon them.

The Invincibles lifted up their voices and wept.

"Can't you persuade Old Jack to take us back to the valley, Harry?" said Happy Tom. "If I'm to die I'd rather be shot by an honest Yankee soldier than be stung to death by these clouds of bloodsuckers. Oh, for our happy valley, where we shot at our enemy and he shot at us, both standing on firm ground!"

"You won't be thinking much about mosquitoes and rivers soon," said Harry. "Listen to that, will you! You know the sound, don't you?"

"Know it! Well, I ought to know it. It's the booming of cannon, but it doesn't frighten these mosquitoes and flies a particle. A cannon ball whistling by my head would scare me half to death, but it wouldn't disturb them a bit. They'd look with an evil eye at that cannon ball as it flew by and say to it in threatening tones: 'What are you doing here? Let this fellow alone. He belongs to us.'"

"Which way is McClellan coming, Harry?" asked St. Clair.

"Off there to the east, where you hear the guns."

"How many men has he?"

"Anywhere from a hundred thousand to a hundred and thirty thousand. There are various reports."

Langdon, who had been listening, whistled.

"It doesn't look like a picnic for the Invincibles," he said. "When I volunteered for this war I didn't volunteer to fight a pitched battle every day. What did you volunteer for, Harry?"

"I don't know."

The three laughed. Jackson's famous order certainly fitted well there.

"And you don't know, either," said Happy Tom, "what all that thunder off there to the south and east means. It's the big guns, but who are fighting and where?"

"There's to be a general attack on McClellan along the line of the Chickahominy river," said Harry, "and our army is to be a part of the attacking force, but my knowledge goes no further."

"Then I'm reckoning that some part of our army has attacked already," said Happy Tom. "Maybe they're ahead of time, or maybe the rest are behind time. But there they go! My eyes, how they're whooping it up!"

The cannonade was growing in intensity and volume. Despite the sunset they saw an almost continuous flare of red on the horizon. The three boys felt some awe as they sat there and listened and looked. Well they might! Battle on a far greater scale than anything witnessed before in America had begun already. Two hundred thousand men were about to meet in desperate conflict in the thickets and swamps along the Chickahominy.

Richmond had already heard the crash of McClellan's guns more than once, but apprehension was passing away. Lee, whom they had learned so quickly to trust, stood with ninety thousand men between them and McClellan, and with him was the redoubtable Jackson and his veterans of the valley with their caps full of victories.

McClellan had the larger force, but Lee was on the defensive in his own country, a region which offered great difficulties to the invader.

Harry and his comrades wondered why Jackson did not move, but he remained in his place, and when Harry fell asleep he still heard the thudding of the guns across the vast reach of rivers and creeks, swamps and thickets. When he awoke in the morning they were already at work again, flaring at intervals down there on the eastern horizon. The whole wet, swampy country, so different from his own, seemed to be deserted by everything save the armies. No rabbits sprang up in the thickets and there were no birds. Everything had fled already in the presence of war.

But the army marched. After a brief breakfast the brigades moved down the road, and Harry saw clearly that these veterans of the valley were tremulous with excitement. Youthful, eager, and used to victory, they were anxious to be at the very center of affairs which were now on a gigantic scale. And the throbbing of the distant guns steadily drew them on.

"We'll get all we want before this is through," said Dalton gravely to Harry.

"I think so, too. Listen to those big guns, George! And I think I can hear the crack of rifles, too. Our pickets and those of the enemy must be in contact in the forest there on our left."

"I haven't a doubt of it, but if we rode that way like as not we'd strike first a swamp, or a creek twenty feet deep. I get all tangled up in this kind of a country."

"So do I, but it doesn't make any difference. We just stick along with Old Jack."

The army marched on a long time, always to the accompaniment of that sinister mutter in the southeast. Then they heard the note of a bugle in front of them and Jackson with his staff rode forward near a little church called Walnut Grove, where Lee and his staff sat on their horses waiting. Harry noticed with pride how all the members of Lee's staff crowded forward to see the renowned Jackson.

It was his general upon whom so many were looking, but there was curiosity among Stonewall's men, too, about Lee. As Harry drew back a little while the two generals talked, he found himself again with the officers of the Invincibles.

"He has grown gray since we were with him in Mexico, Hector," he heard Colonel Leonidas Talbot say to Lieutenant-Colonel Hector St. Hilaire.

"Yes, Leonidas, grayer but stronger. What a brow and eye!"

St. Clair and Langdon, who had never seen Lee before, were eager.

"Is he the right man for Old Jack to follow, Harry?" asked Happy Tom.

"I don't think there's any doubt of it, Happy. I saw how they agreed the first time they met, and you can see it now. You'll find them working together as smooth as silk. Ah, here we go again!"

"Then if it's as you say I suppose it's all up with McClellan, and I needn't trouble my mind about the matter any more. Hereafter I'll just go ahead and obey orders."

The words were light, but there was no frivolity in the minds of the three. Despite the many battles through which they had already gone their hearts were beating hard just then, while that roaring was going on on the horizon, and they knew that a great battle was at hand.

Lee and his staff rode toward the battle, and then, to the amazement of his men, Jackson led his army into the deep woods away from the sound of the thundering guns which had been calling to them so incessantly. Harry was mystified and the general vouchsafed no word, even to his own staff. They marched on through woods, across fields, along the edges of swamps, and that crash of battle grew fainter behind them, but never died out.

"What do you think it means?" Harry whispered to Dalton.

"Don't know. I'm not thinking. I'm not here to think at such times. All the thinking we need is going on under the old slouch hat there. Harry, didn't we go with him all through the valley? Can't we still trust him?"

"I can and will."

"Same here."

The army curved about again. Harry, wholly unfamiliar with the country, did not notice it until the roar of the battle began to rise again, showing that they were coming nearer. Then he divined the plan. Jackson was making this circuit through the woods to fall on the Northern flank. It was the first of the great turning movements which Lee and Jackson were to carry through to brilliant success so often.

"Look at the red blaze beyond those bushes," said Dalton, "and listen how rapidly the sound of the battle is growing in volume. I don't know where we are, but I do know now that Old Jack is leading us right into the thick of it."

The general rode forward and stopped his horse on the crest of a low hill. Then Harry and Dalton, looking over the bushes and swamps, saw a great blue army stationed behind a creek and some low works.

"It's McClellan!" exclaimed Dalton.

"Or a part of him," said Harry.

It was a wing of the Northern army. McClellan himself was not there, but many brave generals were, Porter, Slocum and the others. The batteries of this army were engaged in a heavy duel with the Southern batteries in front, and the sharpshooters in the woods and bushes kept up a continuous combat that crackled like the flames of a forest fire.

Harry drew a long breath.

"This is the biggest yet," he said.

Dalton nodded.

The soldiers of Jackson were already marching off through the woods, floundering through deep mud, crossing little streams swollen by heavy rains, but eager to get into action.

It was very difficult for the mounted men, and Harry and Dalton at last dismounted and led their horses. The division made slow progress and as they struggled on the battle deepened. Now and then as they toiled through the muck they saw long masses of blue infantry on a ridge, and with them the batteries of great guns which the gunners of the North knew so well how to use.

Their own proximity was discovered after a while, and shell and bullets began to fly among them, but they emerged at last on firm ground and on the Northern flank.

"It's hot and growing hotter," said Dalton.

"And we'll help increase the heat if we ever get through these morasses," said Harry.

He felt the bridle suddenly pulled out of his hand, and turned to catch his runaway horse, but the horse had been shot dead and his body had fallen into the swamp. Dalton's horse also was killed presently by a piece of shell, but the two plunged along on foot, endeavoring to keep up with the general.

The fire upon them was increasing fast. Some of the great guns on the ridge were now searching their ranks with shell and shrapnel and many a man sank down in the morass, to be lost there forever. But Jackson never ceased to urge them on. They were bringing their batteries that way, too, and men and horses alike tugged at the cannon.

"If we ever get through," said Harry, "we're bound to do big things."

"We'll get through, never fear," said Dalton. "Isn't Old Jack driving us?"

"Here we are!" Harry shouted suddenly as his feet felt firm ground.

"And here's the whole division, too!" exclaimed Dalton.

The regiments and brigades of Jackson emerged from the forest, and with them came six batteries of cannon which they had almost carried over the swamp. The whole battlefield now came into sight, but the firing and the smoke were so great that it seemed to change continuously in color and even in shape. At one moment there was a ridge where none had been before, then where Harry had seen a creek there was only dry land. But he knew that they were illusions of the eyes, due to the excited brain behind them.

Harry saw the six batteries of Jackson planted in a long row on the hard ground, and then open with a terrific crash on the defenders of the ridge. The sound was so tremendous that he was deafened for a few moments. By the time his hearing was restored fully the batteries fired again and the Northern batteries on the hill replied. Then the mass of infantry charged and Harry and Dalton on foot, waving their swords and wild with excitement, charged with them.

The plans of Lee and Jackson, working together for the first time in a great battle, went through. When Lee heard the roar of Jackson's guns on the flank he, too, sent word to his division commanders to charge with their full strength. In an instant the Northern army was assailed both in front and on the side, by a great force, rushing forward, sure of victory and sending the triumphant rebel yell echoing through the woods of the Chickahominy.

Harry felt the earth tremble beneath him as nearly a hundred thousand men closed in deadly conflict. He could hear nothing but the continued roar, and he saw only a vast, blurred mass of men and guns. But he was conscious that they were going forward, up the hill, straight toward the enemy's works, and he felt sure of victory.

He had grounds for his faith. Lee with the smaller army, had nevertheless brought superior numbers upon the field at the point of action. Porter and Slocum were staunch defenders. The Northern army, though shattered by cannon and rifle fire, stood fast on the ridge until the charging lines were within ten feet of them. Then they gave way, but carried with them most of their cannon, reformed further back, and fought again.

Harry found himself shouting triumphantly over one of the captured guns, but the Southern troops were allowed no time to exult. The sun was already sinking over the swamps and the battlefield, but Lee and Jackson lifted up their legions and hurled them anew to the attack. McClellan was not there when he was needed most, but Porter did all that a man could do. Only two of his eighty guns had been taken, and he might yet have made a stand, but the last of Jackson's force suddenly emerged from the forest and again he was struck with terrible impact on the flank.

The Northern army gave way again. The Southern brigades rushed forward in pursuit, capturing many prisoners, and giving impulse to the flight of their enemies. Their riflemen shot down the horses drawing the retreating cannon. Many of the guns were lost, twenty-two of them falling into Southern hands. Some of the newer regiments melted entirely away under an attack of such fierceness. Nothing stopped the advance of Lee and Jackson but the night, and the arrival of a heavy reinforcement sent by McClellan. The new force, six thousand strong, was stationed in a wood, the guns that had escaped were turned upon the enemy, Porter and Slocum rallied their yet numerous force, and when the dark came down the battle ceased with the Northern army in the east defeated again, but not destroyed.

As Harry rode over the scene of battle that night he shuddered. The fields, the forests and the swamps were filled with the dead and the wounded. Save Shiloh, no other such sanguinary battle had yet been fought on American soil. Nearly ten thousand of the Southern youths had fallen, killed or wounded. The North, standing on the defensive, had not lost so many, but the ghastly roll ran into many thousands.

That night, as had happened often in the valley, the hostile sentinels were within hearing of each other, but they fired no shots. Meanwhile, Lee and Jackson, after the victory, which was called Gaines' Mill, planned to strike anew.

Harry awoke in the morning to find that most of the Northern army was gone. The brigades had crossed the river in the night, breaking down the bridges behind them. He saw the officers watching great columns of dust moving away, and he knew that they marked the line of the Northern march. But the Southern scouts and skirmishers found many stragglers in the woods, most of them asleep or overpowered by weariness. Thus they found the brilliant General Reynolds, destined to a glorious death afterward at Gettysburg, sound asleep in the bushes, having been lost from his command in the darkness and confusion. The Southern army rested through the morning, but in the afternoon was on the march again. Harry found that both St. Clair and Langdon had escaped without harm this time, but Happy Tom had lost some of his happiness.

"This man Lee is worse than Jackson," he lamented. "We've just fought the biggest battle that ever was, and now we're marching hotfoot after another."

Happy Tom was right. Lee and Jackson had resolved to give McClellan no rest. They were following him closely and Stuart with the cavalry hung in a cloud on his flanks. They pressed him hard the next day at White Oak Swamp, Jackson again making the circular movement and falling on his flank, while Longstreet attacked in front. There was a terrible battle in thick forest and among deep ravines, but the darkness again saved the Northern army, which escaped, leaving cannon and men in the hands of the enemy.

Harry lay that night in a daze rather than sleep. He was feverish and exhausted, yet he gathered some strength from the stupor in which he lay. All that day they marched along the edge of a vast swamp, and they heard continually the roar of a great battle on the horizon, which they were not able to reach. It was Glendale, where Longstreet and one of the Hills fought a sanguinary draw with McClellan. But the Northern commander, knowing that a drawn battle in the enemy's country was equivalent to a defeat, continued his retreat and the Southern army followed, attacking at every step. The roar of artillery resounded continuously through the woods and the vanguard of one army and the rear guard of the other never ceased their rifle fire.

Neither Harry nor his young comrades could ever get a clear picture of the vast, confused battle amid the marshes of the Chickahominy, extending over so long a period and known as the Seven Days, but it was obvious to them now that Richmond was no longer in danger. The coming of Jackson had enabled Lee to attack McClellan with such vigor and fierceness that the young Northern general was forced not only to retreat, but to fight against destruction.

But the Union mastery of the water, always supreme, was to come once more to the relief of the Northern army. As McClellan made his retreat, sometimes losing and sometimes beating off the enemy, but always leaving Richmond further and further behind, he had in mind his fleet in the James, and then, if pushed to the last extremity, the sea by which they had come.

But there were many staunch fighters yet in his ranks, and the Southern leaders were soon to find that they could not trifle with the Northern army even in defeat. He turned at Malvern Hill, a position of great strength, posted well his numerous and powerful artillery, and beat off all the efforts of Lee and Jackson and Longstreet and the two Hills, and Armistead and the others. More than five thousand of the Southern troops fell in the fruitless charges. Then McClellan retreated to the James River and his gunboats and the forces of the North were not to come as near Richmond again for nearly three years.

The armies of Lee and Jackson marched back toward the Southern capital, for the possession of which forty thousand men had fallen in the Seven Days. Harry rode with Dalton, St. Clair and Langdon. They had come through the inferno unhurt, and while they shared in the rejoicings of the Virginia people, they had seen war, continued war, in its most terrible aspects, and they felt graver and older.

By the side of them marched the thin ranks of the Invincibles, with the two colonels, erect and warlike, leading them. Just ahead was Stonewall Jackson, stooped slightly in the saddle, the thoughtful blue eyes looking over the heads of his soldiers into the future.

"If he hadn't made that tremendous campaign in the valley," said Dalton, "McClellan allied with McDowell would have come here with two hundred thousand men and it would have been all over."

"But he made it and he saved us," said Harry, glancing at his hero.

"And I'm thinking," said Happy Tom Langdon, glancing toward the North, "that he'll have to make more like it. The Yankees will come again, stronger than ever."